Crafting Stories for Virtual Reality

We are witnessing a revolution in storytelling. Publications all over the world are increasingly using immersive storytelling—virtual reality, augmented reality and mixed reality—to tell compelling stories. The aim of this book is to distill the lessons learned thus far into a useful guide for reporters, filmmakers and writers interested in telling stories in this emerging medium. Examining ground-breaking work across industries, this text explains, in practical terms, how storytellers can create their own powerful immersive experiences as new media and platforms emerge.

Melissa Bosworth is a visual storyteller, immersive media nerd, software developer, reporter and idealist. She's passionate about using emerging technology to find a new lens on stories. In her work as a reporter, features writer, producer and filmmaker she has covered the environment, technology, immigration and the arts across the Americas and Europe. Her virtual reality work has published through KQED, the *New York Times* and Fusion Media Group. She has developed coursework and taught 360-degree video production at the Berkeley Advanced Media Institute and guest lectured on immersive storytelling at UC Berkeley. She holds a Master's degree with an emphasis on new media from the UC Berkeley Graduate School of Journalism.

Lakshmi Sarah is an educator and journalist with a focus on immigration, migration, identity and the arts. She has worked with newspapers, radio and magazines from Ahmedabad, India to Los Angeles, California. She has written and produced for Mic, Global Voices, AJ+, KQED, Fusion Media Group and the *New York Times*. She has advised journalists through Fusion Media Group's Rise Up: Be Heard fellowship and taught at the UC Berkeley Graduate School of Journalism. She has taught workshops in various parts of the world including Kerala, India and Nairobi, Kenya. She is a graduate of Pitzer College and the UC Berkeley Graduate School of Journalism and divides her time between Berkeley, Berlin and southern India.

Crafting Stories for Virtual Reality

Melissa Bosworth
Lakshmi Sarah

Routledge
Taylor & Francis Group

NEW YORK AND LONDON

First published 2019
by Routledge
711 Third Avenue, New York, NY 10017

and by Routledge
2 Park Square, Milton Park, Abingdon, Oxon, OX14 4RN

Routledge is an imprint of the Taylor & Francis Group, an informa business

Library of Congress Cataloging-in-Publication Data
A catalog record for this title has been requested

ISBN: 978-1-138-29671-8 (hbk)
ISBN: 978-1-138-29672-5 (pbk)
ISBN: 978-1-315-09986-6 (ebk)

Typeset in Times New Roman
by codeMantra

Printed in the United Kingdom
by Henry Ling Limited

For future generations who listen to Jamiroquai and wear VR pants
And to an immersive storyworld that is both democratized and accessible to all

Contents

List of Figures   x
Acknowledgments   xii

Introduction: Evolution of Media: Where Are We Now?   1

SECTION I
Context   5

  1 **Why Tell Immersive Stories?**   7

  2 **Pivot Point: A Primer on the State of Immersive Storytelling**   14

SECTION II
Immersive Media and Storytelling Styles   21

  3 **Immersive Narratives and News**   23
    Clouds Over Sidra 24
    Climbing Giants 28
    We Who Remain 33
    Limbo 40
    The Occupation of Alcatraz that Sparked
      an American Revolution 44
    Euronews 49
    VRtually There 53

  4 **Walk-Around Virtual Reality**   59
    Kiya 60
    After Solitary 64
    Suite Life 69
    Displaced Witness 72

5 Immersive Interactives 76

Discovering Gale Crater 77
Is the Nasdaq *in Another Bubble? 81*
Testimony 86
UTURN *93*
Blackout 99

6 Mixed-Media Packages 105

Stand at the Edge of Geologic Time 106
Overheard 112
The Call Center 120
Capturing Everest 124
Hell and High Water VR 130
The Wall 138

7 Augmented Reality and Mixed Reality 145

Priya's Shakti 146
Optimism 151
Outthink Hidden 154
New Dimensions in Testimony 158
Hello, We're from the Internet 164
Four of the World's Best Olympians, as You've Never
  Seen Them Before 168
Terminal 3 172

8 Immersive Audio 180

Hallelujah VR 180
Reeps One: Does Not Exist 185
Designing Audio for Games 191

SECTION III
Bringing It All Together 195

9 Storytelling without Close-Ups: The Big Picture 197

10 Viewing Mode, Form and Content: Best Practices 203

11 Additional Features and Emerging Technology 219

12 Immersive Storytelling and the News Media 225

13 The State of Platforms and Publishing 230

14 Looking Forward 237

Glossary 247
Index 253

Figures

3.1   *Climbing Giants*, courtesy of Black Dot Films VR   30
3.2   Sample footage log for *We Who Remain*. Courtesy of
      Kevin Tsukii   36
3.3   *Limbo*, Courtesy of *Guardian* VR   41
3.4   *Limbo*, Courtesy of *Guardian* VR   43
3.5   *The Occupation of Alcatraz*, Courtesy of Seeker VR   46
3.6   Svalbard Seed Vault: built to save humanity from an
      apocalypse, Euronews   50
3.7   French Election Series, Euronews   52
3.8   *VRtually There*   54
3.9   *VRtually There* on YouTube   56
4.1   *Kiya*, courtesy of Emblematic Group   62
4.2   *After Solitary*, Courtesy of PBS Frontline
      and Emblematic Group   65
4.3   *Suite Life*, courtesy of Associated Press   70
4.4   *Displaced Witness* exhibition, courtesy of ScanLAB Projects   73
4.5   *Displaced Witness*, courtesy of ScanLAB Projects   74
5.1   How to understand the Nasdaq, courtesy of
      Wall Street Journal   82
5.2   The Nasdaq as a roller coaster, courtesy of
      Wall Street Journal   83
5.3   *Testimony*, courtesy of Zohar Kfir   88
5.4   *Testimony*, courtesy of Zohar Kfir   91
5.5   *UTURN* VR, courtesy of NativeVR   94
5.6   *UTURN* VR, courtesy of NativeVR   97
6.1   *Overheard*, Luxloop   113
6.2   *Overheard*, Luxloop   115
6.3   *The Call Center*, courtesy of Aaron Ohlmann   120
6.4   *Hell and High Water*, Jovrnalism   132
6.5   *Hell and High Water*, Jovrnalism   134
6.6   *Hell and High Water*, Jovrnalism   135
7.1   *Priya's Mirror*, courtesy of Ram Devineni
      and Dan Goldman   147
7.2   *Optimism*, courtesy of *Time* magazine   152

7.3   *Optimism*, courtesy of *Time* magazine   153
7.4   *Outthink Hidden*, courtesy of Fake Love   155
7.5   *Outthink Hidden*, courtesy of Fake Love   157
7.6   *New Dimensions in Testimony*, courtesy of USC
       Shoah Foundation   160
7.7   *New Dimensions in Testimony*, courtesy of Illinois
       Holocaust Museum & Education Center   162
7.8   MoMAR, courtesy of Aaron Venn   164
7.9   MoMAR, courtesy of Aaron Venn   166
7.10 MoMAR, courtesy of Martin Strutz   167
7.11 *Terminal 3*, courtesy of Asad Malik   173
7.12 Asad Malik in the studio   175
8.1   The spatial audio mix for Hallelujah, courtesy of Ecco VR   181
8.2   The many tracks in a "massive pro tools session" for
       spatial audio, courtesy of Ecco VR   183
8.3   A large warehouse in LA was one filming location for
       the *Does Not Exist* piece, courtesy of John Hendicott   187
8.4   Many tracks went into the audio mix for *Does Not
       Exist*, courtesy of John Hendicott   188
8.5   An equirectangular still from the final Reeps One video,
       courtesy of John Hendicott   190
8.6   The art itself is a starting point in creating a musical
       score for a video game, image courtesy of Nick LaMartina   192
8.7   Binaural audio capture, courtesy of Nick LaMartina   193
14.1 A sketch of a branching narrative (for *Terminal 3*)   238

Acknowledgments

The first round of shoutouts goes to our friends, colleagues and mentors at the UC Berkeley School of Journalism. Without the open canvas from which to experiment, create and fail fast we might not have fallen in to writing this. Thanks to Bl for supporting us. Richard Koci Hernandez for telling us to write a book. Jeremy Rue for his steady advice and support. David Cohn for his unwavering support, despite skepticism for the medium. Rachel Cassandra for her keen eye. Fan Fei, Mara Van Ells, Shaina Shealy, Zainab Khan, Harriet Rowan, Sasha Lekach, Jon Brown, Terra Thomas, Jen Arter, and Kevin Rauwolf for reading various version and drafts.

The second round of shoutouts goes to the immersive storytelling community—may we continue to find ways to be more inclusive, accessible and creative.

The final round of deep gratitude goes out to each person who answered a question and allowed us to take time from your precious schedule and busy lives to chat about all things immersive. Nonny de la Peña, Thomas Seymat, Robert Hernandez, Kevin Tsukii, Eren Aksu, Barry Pousman, Nathalie Mathe, Nina Sen, Scott Mayerowitz, Cassandra Herrman, Max Salomon, Ana Asnes Becker, Roger Kenny, James George, Alexander Porter, Yasmin Elayat, Andre La Masurier, Ben Kreimer, Francesca Panetta, Shehani Fernando, Sam Wolson, Hunter Holcombe, Trevor Snapp, Cailyn Bradley, Aneeta Akhurst, Dan Archer, Matthew Shaw, Ray Soto, Alina Mikhaleva, Josh Susong, Katie Wudel, Michaela Holland, Michael Franz, Ivaylo Getov, Mandy Mandelstein, Wes Lindamood, Nick Michael, Maia Stern, Asad Malik, Zohar Kfir, Joel Douek, John Hendicott, Nick LaMartina, Sarah Hill, Marcelle Hopkins, Graham Roberts, Jeremy Gilbert, Layne Braunstein, Mia Tramz, Jenna Pirog, Zahra Rasool, Jessica Lauretti, Nigel Tierney, Laura Hertzfeld, Benjamin Roffee, David Hamlin, Ram Devineni, Dan Goldman, Alexey Furman, Louis Jebb, Susan Abrams, Heather Maio, Amanda Berrios, David Lobser, Damjanski, Sam O'Brien, Claire Cook, David Johnston and the people we spoke with and failed to mention here. We appreciate you.

The final round of shoutouts goes out to our families, both local and global for supporting us on this bizarre endeavor of writing an old-school book about a fancy new technology.

Introduction

The Evolution of Media: Where Are We Now?

Just to be contrarian, let's start this story about bleeding-edge technology and the future of immersive media in 1793—the year when painter Robert Barker and his son Henry first drew crowds to a curious rotunda in Leicester Square in London. On the walls of the rotunda were six etchings of a view from Albion Mills overlooking the city. Lit from above, and viewed from a gazebo inside the rotunda, the panorama (a term Barker coined, from Greek *pan* ("all") and *horama* ("view") was meant, as Barker wrote in his patent specification for the 360-degree format and its viewing rotunda, to make viewers "feel as if really on the spot."[1] The invention was a huge success, and panoramas created over the next century offered entertainment, spectacle and education for audiences around the world.

The 360-degree panorama painting predated and was eventually superseded by cinema and television. It stands out because, while much of the relatively short history of media beyond oral communication has seen people moving ever further from experiential modes of consumption and toward packaged bits and pieces of reality, its popularity demonstrates that the idea of approximating direct experience has long been a captivating fantasy.

Since the late twentieth century, science fiction rooted in real innovation has captured the imagination of generations of people who have gone on to become immersive media's present-day innovators. Here are just a few examples that come up again and again in our conversations with creators: *Snow Crash* by Neal Stephenson brought us the Metaverse in 1992, and Ernest Cline's *Ready Player One* (2011) offered a similarly complete vision of a virtual world with full sensory immersion. *The Lawnmower Man* (inspired in part by the work of Jaron Lanier, who coined the term "virtual reality") wowed its 1992 audience with computer graphics of a neon-colored world of avatars that are as dated and comical to us now as this generation's work will likely be to kids in 2050. In *Minority Report* (2002), Tom Cruise used hand gestures to manipulate data on holographic screens that wrapped around the room where he stood (those graphics still look pretty sleek to the modern eye—maybe because we still have so few real examples of augmented reality to catapult that imagined version into the past). And of course *The Matrix* (1999) brought us a virtual world so true to life that it probably upended the whole concept of reality for at least a few impressionable young minds.

We could also begin this story at any number of different points in the parallel evolution of audio, visual, computing and mobile technology. After all, there is no major single technological breakthrough that has brought immersive content to the fore in the last few years, but rather the decreasing cost—driven by mobile phone adoption—of the components necessary to assemble a headset with a high resolution display and enough computing power to run an immersive experience (or do the same with a smartphone in a pair of cardboard or plastic goggles). In fact, virtual reality has seemed intermittently at the edge of mass adoption for a few decades now.

And let's be honest: At the time of writing, the headset technology is still pretty unwieldy and the publishing landscape is fragmented. Virtual reality headsets are heavy and just beginning to be available without clunky cable tethers; augmented and mixed reality is just now breaking into gadget territory for well-resourced early adopters. Practical augmented- and mixed-reality headsets are mostly still vaporware.

But this is not a book about the halting advance of technology. This book is about storytelling—and what creators are doing now to create content for technology that is finally coming tumbling out of our collective imagination and into the hands of developers, documentarians, artists, filmmakers and journalists. As the pool of creators continues to grow, what are we learning about how to use these new tools to tell stories that matter—to open people's minds and hearts, to share something only this new form can offer?

We can again look to history to glean some lessons from earlier revolutions in media. It took a long time for motion picture creators to figure out how to tell stories with film. The early films from the Lumiere brothers (first screened publicly in 1895) were single shots less than a minute long. It took another decade or so for creators to break out of a live-theater way of thinking and figure out how to string together shots to focus the viewer and compress time. Arguably half a century passed before the grammar of filmmaking was fully defined.

Given that history, it's tempting to frame this moment in media history as the prelude to what some in the film industry call the "Citizen Kane" moment—when a work achieves mastery of the form, defining a language of storytelling for future creators. And it does feel that we are somewhere in that intermediate phase. The technology for creating and consuming immersive media is there, but in a fledgling state, and we're only just figuring out a rudimentary language for telling stories.

Sometimes, our existing skill sets can even slow us down. It's been known to happen that creators with strong foundations or even a mastery in older media try to impose that language on a new medium simply because they can't see past what they know. But just as the rules of live theater don't make for a great film, expertise in film or other media can be more of a hindrance than a help in designing immersive experiences.

It's also not obvious that every medium is adaptable to a "Citizen Kane" moment. We can also look to the gaming industry—which in many ways is film's co-parent in the emergence of immersive media—where some like to say that video games are still waiting for just that. But plenty of gamers are eager to assert that it's narrow-minded to liken games to film.

For some, the analogy to the film industry implies that video game creators should be wedging movie-style narratives into an interactive medium. Is it possible that what we call gaming is simply too versatile, and too user-defined, to be codified into a single set of narrative rules?

In a similar sense, the language of immersive media is fragmented— while some very general rules of thumb have emerged (e.g. giving the user time to acquaint themselves with their surroundings, or employing audio cues to let people know where the action is), in speaking with creators we've learned that this field is fantastically broad. Creators haven't even settled on whether some of the examples in this book could be described as fitting the same medium.

So, while we can assert that immersive media has not reached a "Citizen Kane" moment—and again the parallels to the early days of film, radio or television are many—we're also not ready to assume that an analogous moment is coming at all.

But we do feel a great sense of conviction in saying that what's already out there is powerful, beautiful, bold, expert, fumbling and amateurish, all at once. It's the chaotic beginning of something big, and it's a magical moment to watch.

Note

1 Barker, Robert. "Specification of Mr. Barker's patent for displaying views of nature at large," June 19, 1787. www.bl.uk/collection-items/ specification-of-mr-barkers-patent-for-displaying-views-of-nature-at-large.

Section I
Context

1 Why Tell Immersive Stories?

In the course of writing this book, we've spoken with creators with all sorts of backgrounds, from journalists and filmmakers to artists, educators, coders and activists. The one thing they all have in common is that something about the lure of immersive storytelling drew them in so powerfully that they were willing to take a risk to bring their projects into reality. They've all poured resources and energy into passion projects in a format that is still finding its place in the media landscape, and which still garners skepticism from the uninitiated.

To the skepticism point: There are some creators who, when asked why a person or organization should be working on immersive stories, answer simply that this is where media is going, whether you choose to participate at this moment or not. If that is in fact the case, asking whether a story should be told in immersive media may soon make about as much sense as asking whether a story should be told on the internet. That is, if this is how stories are published and consumed, then it's more sensible to ask how to make an important story work in immersive media than it is to ask whether a story should be told in immersive media at all.

That said, while it's exciting to see stories that don't obviously lend themselves to immersive media being told in this way—and we highlight some of those in this book—most creators are still thinking about it in terms of stories that fit a certain set of criteria in order to tap into VR and AR's particular capabilities, and to reach audiences in new ways.

In our interviews, we asked each creator how they came to be telling stories in immersive media, and why they felt that particular stories needed be told in this way. We grouped their responses into some broad categories to help us understand the strengths and potential of immersive storytelling.

This is by no means an exhaustive study of what can be done in these new formats, but rather a set of guidelines to start thinking about what's possible. Many projects we've seen meet several of these criteria. Some meet none of them.

Exclusive Access

Probably the most common thing virtual reality creators tell us about why they chose to tell their story in immersive space is in order to "take viewers somewhere they couldn't otherwise go"—that is, to use VR to give the feeling of really standing there in a way that can't be achieved with any other medium.

This motivation brings creators and viewers to a wide variety of places, from the impossible to the impractical: the surface of Mars, the top of Mount Everest, a war zone in Iraq or the tents in a refugee camp in Jordan.

Closing Distance

As shorthand to distinguish virtual reality from augmented reality, some creators say that virtual reality brings you into the story world while augmented reality brings the story into your world. But whether it's a viewer teleporting into space or a priceless artifact being transported into your living room, the storyteller is able to close the distance between the viewer and the story.

We can make places and objects feel real and tangible in a way no other medium can, potentially reducing the viewer's sense of detachment to make a story feel more immediate and relevant. We can interact with and see the scale of an ancient artifact, sit face-to-face with people who live in completely different cultural worlds, or bring the harsh reality of a distant war right into a viewer's living room.

Perspective and Building Empathy

A major motivator for many creators is to tell an important story in a way that makes people care. With immersive media, the idea is to make an experience feel real—by putting the viewer in someone else's shoes, or someone else's environment, or by tricking their brain into feeling like they really experienced something. This potential for creating empathy by simulating direct experience is therefore one of the most compelling— and most hyped—reasons for using immersive media. While claims re- lating to the power of the "empathy machine" may be a little overblown, there are plenty of examples of stories that leverage this capability in powerful ways.

Stories that aim to build empathy vary in how they position the viewer, but they tend to play with perspective. Some of them try to create a first-person experience of being in someone else's position—for exam- ple, as a refugee trying to navigate an unfamiliar city or a female coder dealing with sexism in the workplace. Others put the viewer right next to the person with whom they're trying to create empathy, positioning that person as a tour guide to help the viewer understand how they see the world. In some cases, the viewer is a fly on the wall but gets insight into what it feels like to experience something they're unlikely to have seen first-hand, like seeing someone pull a gun in a domestic violence situation, or standing in a war zone.

Creating Intimacy

While empathy through shared experience is one angle into understanding another person's story, another way to build this understanding is by fostering compassion through a feeling of intimacy. Because virtual reality and augmented reality both have the power to let the viewer feel they are in the same space with the character—to even feel as though they are communicating directly with body language and eye contact—creators are using this to try and build connection. For example, users can immerse themselves in a "virtual support group" where sexual assault survivors share stories of their road to healing in their own words. They can ask questions of a Holocaust survivor, or sit in a cell with a person as they relate their experience of solitary confinement.

Spatial Storytelling

Because immersive media has the viewer's entire environment available as a canvas, it opens up a wealth of possibilities for using the space to tell stories. Some creators have told us they only tell stories that have a spatial component—whether that be understanding the layout of a place, the scale of something, or where objects or people stand in relation to each other.

And while every immersive piece is spatial by nature, some projects leverage this feature more consciously than others. One especially interesting subcategory for spatial storytelling is data visualization, which can allow the user to understand something spatially that might be hard to conceptualize or illustrate in other media—for example, the dramatic fluctuations of the stock market during a boom-and-crash cycle, or the height of an Olympic ice skater's jump.

Presence and Embodiment

Presence and embodiment are two overlapping keywords that come up in just about every conversation we have about immersive media. Generally, presence means the sense of actually being there, and embodiment means the sense of one's own body in a place.

While they're not reasons to tell a story in their own right, they are feelings that immersive stories have a greater power to foster than any other medium. They are the engine behind what makes viewers feel they've experienced a story or really been in the room with a virtual person. Creators often choose stories that could be enhanced by creating these feelings in viewers.

Agency and Engagement

Agency refers to the ability to manipulate the environment or affect the course of an experience.

In some sense, every immersive piece offers some level of agency, even if there's no interactivity: In a 360-degree video, the viewer is always choosing which part of the scene to look at. In a walk-around piece, the viewer also chooses where they stand. And in an interactive, the creator's imagination (plus effort) is the only limit to the level of interactivity and agency the viewer experiences.

For some creators, good stories or scenes for immersive media are ones in which it's rewarding for the viewer to exercise this agency to choose what they see or influence the story. It corresponds that these creators believe every experience should be set up so that it rewards the viewer to look around or explore, rather than coerce a linear experience.

Some believe that consuming immersive media is inherently active—compared to more passive viewing of a traditional video—and that giving a viewer agency can mean greater engagement with the content, and therefore greater impact.

What the Research Says

We've tried to be careful while researching and writing this book to maintain a healthy skepticism about both the strengths and potential hazards of immersive content. We hear lots of unbridled optimism—that it hijacks our brains to create real experiences, or that it's an "empathy machine" for making people care and a miracle cure for trauma. On the negative side, we hear concerns that it's an ethical minefield, a recipe for social isolation or a harbinger of societal breakdown. It's all anecdotal.

For now, there's still not a lot of published research to corroborate or refute most of these claims. We expect a wave of research on the power of immersive content to be published over the next few years, but in the meantime, this is a survey of a few recent studies and reports we find interesting and relevant for storytellers. It's still early, and none of them should be taken as gospel.

A Case for Room-Scale VR

In a 2017 study conducted by The Associated Press participants were interviewed after they experienced stories in VR across multiple viewing devices. They recorded their brain activity, heart rate and body motions, and the individuals also answered surveys about how each story impacted them emotionally and "whether there were particular moments in each story that sparked their feelings."[1]

The findings of this study show participants had the highest levels of open-mindedness—(defined as "being attracted to a topic, but not alarmed" on the room-scale VR headset. The participants' comments suggest this could be connected to image quality in the room-scale experience and the ability to move.

Additional findings reveal the "VR headset resulted in heightened levels of stimulation and intensity," and "room-scale VR drove the highest level of engagement, allowing participants to not only pay attention to the experience, but they did so in a state of relaxation." The findings note that topics covering science, nature and exploration benefit from room-scale VR presentation.

Living the Story, or "Storyliving"

Google News Lab's 2017 study of VR in Journalism conducted 36 ethnographic interviews. They used the term storyliving to describe the idea that users are no longer just watching, but they are living through a story. The terms comes from anthropological research and cross-cultures studies (Emigh, 1996; Maschio, 1994; Gell, 1975) "Central to this process is a sense of dual unity," (Keeler, 2017; Emigh, 1996; Leenhardt, 1979) says the News Lab report on storyliving. The News Lab report also states that "research has shown that the ability to shapeshift can help users better understand issues like climate change" (Ahn et al., 2015; Wells & Lekies, 2006).[2]

The storyliving report also points to historical anthropological research showing how humans have been taking on ideas of living a story, or embodiment, for ages—across cultural and geographic boundaries. "In Australia, Aboriginal individuals go on 'walkabouts' constructed to allow them to feel as if they are the creatures and spirits referred to in sacred stories. In Hinduism, ritual specialists often enact and embody a cosmic character."

The News Lab study also points to previous studies from 2013, in which Ahn, Le and Bailenson showed that, after experiencing a virtual simulation of impaired vision, participants opinions about disabled people changed—lasting days after the study was concluded.

A Question of Perspective

In a 2017 study on sense of presence, and attitude change, Tanja Aitamurto randomly assigned 67 people to watch UTURN, which tells two first-person stories at once, allowing the viewer to turn around to change their perspective (for more details, see our case study in

Chapter 5). The participants were randomly assigned to watch as a video in the original 360 split-view in a **head-mounted display** or the same film as 180 in a **HMD**, or as a flat control version of the video on a laptop.

The findings of this study showed that

> the 360 split-view increased the viewers' feeling of personal responsibility for resolving gender inequality, desire to rewatch the video, fear of missing out, and feeling of missing the full story. The 180 video created the strongest sense of presence, embodiment, and understanding of the character.[3]

In addition, the findings suggest people with greater egocentric projection onto the male character felt "less responsible for resolving gender inequality, particularly in the 360 split-view."

In regards to perspective-taking, the findings suggest that the participants watching the film in the 180 view felt a stronger spatial and social sense of presence and embodiment than the participants watching the film as 360 split-sphere. "Taking an actor or an observer's perspective can further influence how people perceive the story events," the study shows. "Depending on whose perspective they take, audience members may form attitudes that are consistent with or against the intent of the message."

Feeling Horror

Agatha Bochenek, Head of Mobile VR/AR Ad Sales at the game engine company Unity, monitored players of a VR horror game and found that they "exhibited the same biometric responses as they would if the terrors were real."[4]

Empathy, Action and Retention

In 2018, The Tow Center for Digital Journalism created a report[5] based on 180 people viewing five minutes of either 360-degree video or text articles. They monitored user reactions and their sense of immersion on the same day, and again two and five weeks later.

They found that those who experienced the 360-degree video had a (slightly) higher empathetic response to the content, and reported a greater likelihood of taking "political or social action." Those who had a stronger empathetic response were more likely to remember what they had seen. People who reported a greater sense of immersion also said they were more likely to take action. If the viewers didn't find the story enjoyable or were overly familiar with the subject matter, it had less of an impact. The user's level of familiarity with VR also made a difference, with a stronger impact on people who were less familiar with the technology.

The report also offered some guidelines: That character-driven narratives were more enjoyable and more effective, and that narrators should be visible throughout the story.

The Real Measure

It's important to remember that, while there's plenty to learn from research and existing projects, there's also an enormous amount of room for experimentation in immersive media. And this course of discovery can only move forward if creators continue to take risks to create powerful immersive experiences.

We all know when we see something good: It moves us, makes us think, teaches us something, or helps bring us together. And someone has to try it for us to find out whether it works. We're looking forward to seeing what comes next.

Notes

1 Marconi, Francesco. "Report: How virtual reality will impact journalism." September 26, 2017. https://insights.ap.org/industry-trends/report-how-virtual-reality-will-impact-journalism.
2 Google News Lab. Storyliving: An Ethnographic Study of How Audiences Experience VR and What That Means for Journalists. July 28, 2017. https://newslab.withgoogle.com/assets/docs/storyliving-a-study-of-vr-in-journalism.pdf/.
3 Aitamurto, Tanja, Zhou, Shuo, Sakshuwong, Sukolsak, Saldivar, Jorge, Sadeghi, Yasamin and Tran, Amy. 2018. "Sense of Presence, Attitude Change, Perspective-Taking and Usability in First-Person Split-Sphere 360° Video." In *Proceedings of the 2018 CHI Conference on Human Factors in Computing Systems (CHI '18). ACM, New York, NY, USA, Paper 545, 12 pages.* DOI: https://doi.org/10.1145/3173574.3174119.
4 "How XR will shape media, entertainment and advertising: Insights from Exploring Future Reality hosted by NYC Media Lab." November 30th, 2017. http://nycmedialab.org/whitepapers/.
5 Archer, Dan and Finger, Katharina. "Walking in another's virtual shoes: Do 360-degree video news stories generate empathy in viewers?" March 15, 2018. www.cjr.org/tow_center_reports/virtual-reality-news-empathy.php/.

2 Pivot Point

A Primer on the State of Immersive Storytelling

During the last two years, experimentation in immersive content has spanned a wide array of industries. Healthcare professionals are using virtual reality to create groundbreaking mental health treatments,[1] musicians are releasing 360-degree music videos,[2] and major Hollywood production houses are adding immersive experiences to their content.[3] Educational applications abound as well, such as Google's "Expeditions" program, which allows teachers to take their students on immersive guided tours all over the world.[4]

The *New York Times*, which mailed out a million Google Cardboard headsets to their subscribers in late 2015, began regularly producing immersive content in 2016.[5] In October 2015, the *LA Times* released a virtual-reality tour of Mars' Gale Crater. A slew of other media organizations—from *The Guardian* to the *Washington Post* to *PBS Frontline*—are publishing innovative immersive stories.

In the first half of 2016, the first two high-end consumer headsets for virtual reality hit the market, media giants YouTube (Google) and then Facebook launched 360-degree video players, and content producers began widely experimenting with immersive storytelling. Some began referring to 2016 as "The Year of VR."[6] Since then, the amount of content—and the sheer range of experimentation—has exploded, as creators have continued to push the envelope, exploring a range of virtual reality projects and more recently setting foot in the worlds of augmented and

Myriad factors—technological and social—have converged to lay the groundwork for the adoption of this medium. And each time a new medium emerges—be it the radio, the smartphone, or the virtual reality headset—storytellers must adapt to new ways of practicing mixed reality. their craft.

Many of the brightest minds in media are in the process of figuring out what that looks like. Some have been experimenting with immersive storytelling since long before most of us had even heard of it.

As the available hardware and distribution channels evolve, creators are continuously adapting their stories to push the limits of what's possible. The pace of progress lately has been unrelenting: Immersive media as it exists today is only the beginning of this storytelling revolution. Practical viewing of augmented reality (AR) and mixed reality (MR)—immersive content that overlays or is embedded in a viewer's real environment—is following close on the heels of virtual reality headsets, with a steady stream of innovative AR projects coming out since late 2017.

When we use the term immersive media, we mean it in the broadest sense—any piece in which the viewer can feel as though they are looking around (or listening) inside of the story—whether they are standing in an environment or the story overlays their world.

In order to make sense of the wide variation in the kinds of projects we've seen, however, it's helpful to lay out some distinctions to understand how they vary. Within this immersive media umbrella there are many variations in form, some major and some subtle, but they tend to vary across just a few axes.

First, projects come with varying levels of freedom of movement. In many projects, viewers can look around in all directions but they are stationary and can't move within a scene at all. In others, viewers can move around in a fully three-dimensional world.

Second, there's interactivity. Some experiences are exactly the same every time, while others give viewers agency—that is, the ability to affect the scene or the way the story unfolds.

We also divide projects up by whether they bring the viewer into a fully immersive environment (virtual reality), or the story appears in the viewer's real surroundings (augmented and mixed reality).

The number of possible permutations in storytelling form based on these three axes is very broad. Each different form brings different possibilities for storytellers and viewers.

Each of the chapters in Section 2 of this book looks at a different form, zooming in on techniques creators use to best take advantage of that form's strengths. The case studies, based on interviews with the creators of each project, give an overview of the tools that were used to create them, the logic behind the design, and key takeaways that can be gleaned from the project.

How This Book Is Organized

This is an outline of the kinds of stories we've come across in our research, and a preview of the structure of this book—but it's important to note that these are loose groupings, shaped by what's currently out there and what has worked for creators, but by no means meant to circumscribe what's possible.

In many cases, the projects we're looking at fit into more than one of the categories we've set. If we've placed a project in a particular section of this book, it's because we've chosen to zoom in on an interesting aspect of that project that is best described by that form.

Immersive Narratives and News

We use the term immersive narratives to describe stationary, non-interactive immersive stories in which the viewer has the ability to look around within a scene, but not move within that scene or interact with elements in it.

This form includes what some call "Cinematic Virtual Reality" and "Immersive Cinema." Pieces in this category are usually 360-degree video, though they are in some cases animated with 3D modeling and then exported as video. In addition to fiction and documentary-style pieces, this form also includes live breaking news, and short, experiential pieces. It's arguably the easiest way to tell a linear story using immersive media.

Walk-Around

This form allows the viewer to move around within a scene, either by walking in a tracked room or using a controller or set of gestures to move. The viewer can change perspective or get close to the action as they choose.

In some walk-around pieces there is no interactivity. We sometimes refer to these pieces as "invisible visitor," because nobody responds to the viewer, and the story plays out the same way no matter what the viewer does. In some cases, a walk-around is only a scene, with no narrative action.

We also use the term walk-around to describe this kind of environment in pieces that *are* interactive, so the term also comes up in our chapters on interactives.

Immersive Interactives

In the context of immersive storytelling and virtual reality, interactivity means the ability to interact with objects or graphics within a scene or somehow otherwise change the environment or the course of the story. The other term that comes up a lot in describing these stories is agency—the idea that the viewer has the power to influence events.

This is a huge category, and projects that fit this description vary widely—from stationary to walk-around, and from almost completely linear narratives in which the viewer only controls when the story moves forward, to free-form explorations that function more like games.

Mixed-Media Packages

Mixed-media is a catch-all category that encompasses all forms of immersive media. What distinguishes projects in this category is that we see a fusion of traditional and immersive media being employed in an interesting way.

There are two major categories of mixed media package we've observed that include immersive media.

The first is a traditional web package that brings in immersive media—for example, a news article that embeds a 360-degree video or photo to give the viewer a sense of a place. These pieces tend to isolate immersive media for its strengths, offering a sense of presence but using other media to provide context and exposition.

The other treats immersive space itself as the main canvas, embedding traditional media such as photos or video into that environment. These pieces are interesting because they begin to preview where media might be going, should people one day be accessing media generally through a head-mounted display, rather than breaking away from their usual media consumption and just putting on the headset specifically to access an immersive piece.

Augmented Reality and Mixed Reality

Some—particularly marketing reps for companies that make mixed-reality headsets—draw a firm distinction between augmented reality and mixed reality. While we don't think the distinction is especially useful except for selling hardware, it's worth defining what they mean. In that framework, augmented reality overlays and enhances the real world—for example, a train schedule appearing in the corner of a person's field of view as they approach a train station. Mixed reality brings virtual objects into the real world that interact with physical objects—for example, a graphic can be placed on a tabletop, or a virtual person seated on a chair.

For the sake of this book we've used these terms more or less interchangeably, with a preference for the term augmented reality—broadly defined as anything that combines digital and physical worlds. Many of the pieces we discuss could also be described as mixed reality.

When we first began researching this book in late 2016, we weren't sure there would be enough augmented and mixed reality pieces available for us to discuss. Fortunately, quite a few groundbreaking projects have come out since late 2017.

Our case-study chapter on augmented reality has the most projects of any of the chapters. That's because these pieces are so new that they can't quite yet be separated out into different categories, so we've lumped them all together. We think we've captured a good sampling of what's currently being done.

Immersive Audio

Audio is half the story (or more, if you ask a sound designer). While we mostly look at immersive media as a combination of sound and visuals, and address sound design in each of our case studies, immersive audio is its own, rich world.

And audio also has its own spectrum as an immersive medium—from a single channel of sound piped into both ears, to stereo audio that gives a stationary sense of depth, and spatialized audio, in which the sound mixing is dynamic and the viewer can triangulate with their ears the source of a sound in immersive space.

For that reason, although "audio" wouldn't qualify as its own immersive storytelling form, we've also included case studies that delve into the production techniques and storytelling strategy of sound-centric pieces.

Note on Stereoscopic versus Monoscopic Media

Stereoscopic and **monoscopic** are another set of terms for 3D and 2D imagery. Stereoscopic immersive media provides a different view for each eye in order to provide a sense of depth. In some cases, creators have used this to distinguish whether a piece is true virtual reality.

While stereoscopic imagery can make a narrative piece feel more immersive, and is essential for depth perception when a user is moving around in a fully 3-dimensional world, we don't think this component in itself influences the way a story is told—at least, not enough for us to draw a hard line between monoscopic and stereoscopic media.

The Next Pivot

While the categories we've described above capture most of what currently exists in immersive media, we're sure to see different permutations on range of movement, interactivity and integration of experiences with real physical space. That all depends on what new forms emerging technology enables. See Chapter 14 for a look at some of the ideas that are beginning to take shape as we wrap up research on this book, and how they might influence the ways we tell and experience stories.

Notes

1 Virtual Reality: Expanding Use in Mental Health. American Psychiatric Association, February 9, 2017. www.psychiatry.org/news-room/apa-blogs/apa-blog/2017/02/virtual-reality-expanding-use-in-mental-health-treatment.
2 Tarpinian, Katherine. "A 360° Look at Björk's Two New Music Videos" *Vice Creators*. June 9, 2015. https://creators.vice.com/en_au/article/3d5p89/a-360-look-at-bjorks-two-new-music-videos
3 Mateer, John. "Hollywood 360: how virtual reality is poised to take on the traditional movie industry." February 15, 2018. https://theconversation.com/hollywood-360-how-virtual-reality-is-poised-to-take-on-the-traditional-movie-industry-91426.

4 Matney, Lucas. Google opens Expeditions VR to the Public. July 19, 2017. https://techcrunch.com/2017/07/19/google-opens-expeditions-vr-education-app-to-the-public/.
5 Robertson, Adi. "The *New York Times* is sending out a second round of Google Cardboards." April 28, 2016. www.theverge.com/2016/4/28/11504932/new-york-times-vr-google-cardboard-seeking-plutos-frigid-heart
6 Morris, Chris. "Is 2016 the Year of Virtual Reality?" December 4, 2015. http://fortune.com/2015/12/04/2016-the-year-of-virtual-reality/.

Section II

Immersive Media and Storytelling Styles

3 Immersive Narratives and News

Stories are compasses and architecture, we navigate by them, we build our sanctuaries and our prisons out of them, and to be without a story is to be lost in the vastness of a world that spreads in all directions like arctic tundra or sea ice.

(Rebecca Solnit, The Faraway Nearby)

Case Studies

Clouds Over Sidra, United Nations VR
Limbo, Guardian VR
Climbing Giants, Black Dot Films for National Geographic
The Occupation of Alcatraz that Sparked an American Revolution, Seeker VR
We Who Remain, Emblematic Group, AJ+ and NYT-VR
360 Video, Euronews (various projects)
VRtually There, YouTube and USA Today

Take an immersive journey to witness the lives of the few who remain in the war-torn Nuba Mountains of Sudan, or of the water protectors standing up against the oil industry at their camp in Standing Rock, North Dakota. Gaze over miles of forest canopy from the crown of a giant sequoia tree, or glide through a ghost-like city to catch a glimpse of life as a refugee. All of these experiences are possible in immersive narrative form.

We use the term immersive narratives to describe non-interactive 360-degree stories within which the viewer has the ability to look around in a scene, but not move within that scene or interact with elements in it. Some pieces in this category might also be referred to as "Cinematic Virtual Reality" and "Immersive Cinema." The form can also include live breaking news, and short, experiential 360-degree videos.

All these pieces can be described as having three **degrees of freedom** (DOF), because the viewer can turn their head on three axes—horizontal, vertical, and tilting left and right. That is, they have full rotational freedom to look around without translational movement, i.e. actually walking around in the scene. Standard **monoscopic** and **stereoscopic** 360-degree videos fall into this category, as do graphically rendered experiences in which the viewer has a locked position in the scene.

360-degree video has been the most readily adopted form used for journalistic storytelling and by many creators new to immersive media. In part, this has been because 360-degree videos are easily shareable on social media platforms such as Facebook and YouTube. They can be viewed on most mobile devices and monitors and do not require the use of a head-mounted display (HMD) or devices to track the viewer's movement around a space.

This format is also arguably the easiest way to tell a linear story using immersive media, and it is less likely to run up against challenging issues that arise with other forms—such as the ethics of re-creating a scene for a walk-around piece, or the labor-intensive nature of creating an interactive game-style experience or a **branching narrative**.

Media outlets have been trying everything from live coverage and extreme sports to behind-the-scenes perspectives at factories and concerts. A common principle is to take the viewer somewhere they do not have access to, but another way of thinking about the story is to provide an intimate experience by taking on another person's perspective.

The case studies in this chapter look at pieces that incorporate 3D graphics, video, animation and photos. Based on interviews with the projects' creators, we'll survey the technology used in production, including camera rigs, video stitching and editing, 3D modeling and **volumetric** capture. We'll look at storytelling techniques including pacing, sound, structure, location of characters in a scene, and tools for guiding the viewer.

Clouds Over Sidra

United Nations VR (UNVR)
January 2015

Clouds Over Sidra, the story of a young girl and her family in a refugee camp in Jordan, was the United Nations' first VR project. Produced by Within (called Vrse at the time)[1] and the United Nations VR team, the eight-minute piece first screened in January 2015 at the World Economic Forum in Davos, Switzerland. The story broke new ground as a format for documentary and journalistic work. This was about 10 months before the *New York Times* sent Google Cardboard headsets out to subscribers, and before Facebook and YouTube introduced their 360 video players.

Barry Pousman, who was working for DiscoveryVR and consulting part-time for the UN, received a call in 2014 from creative director to the United Nations, Gabo Arora, who was looking for a director of photography. Arora was helping Within founder Chris Milk (who some call the "grandfather of VR") produce a series of three films for UNVR: *Clouds Over Sidra, Waves of Grace* and *My Mother's Wing*.

Pousman has extensive experience in traditional film, but he believes VR filmmaking has an additional capacity to evoke emotional connections with subjects. "We have an opportunity, through media, to take our audiences to places we never have before," he says.

Traveling to a Refugee Camp

Clouds Over Sidra was filmed in the Za'atari refugee camp in Jordan and follows 12-year-old Sidra, originally from Syria, around her temporary home.

Based on several interviews with Sidra, the narration of a voice actor brings the story of Sidra and her family to life, offering a glimpse into daily life in a refugee camp. She describes her school, and briefly talks about the men who go to the gym, the boys who wrestle and the computer room—even though girls are not allowed to play games. She describes the bakery and says, "the smell of bread on our walk to class drives us mad sometimes."

Some of the most powerful scenes are those that break the fourth wall. In one instance, kids look at the camera on the way to school—making the viewer feel as though they are making eye contact. In another scene the creators pair a powerful visual with a compelling audio narration: Sidra says, "There are more kids in Za'atari than others right now. Sometimes I think we are the ones in charge," as children giggle and gather around the camera.

Chris Milk's 2015 TED talk[2] on empathy came out just a few months after *Clouds Over Sidra* published. In it he discusses the aim of the project, and how it allows people to see the lives of others and feel as though they have taken a trip to a refugee camp.

Early Days of 360 and VR

Prior to filming *Clouds Over Sidra*, Pousman had never seen a 360-degree video, so the first thing he did when he received a call from Milk and Arora was to fly to the Within office in Los Angeles. There, the Within team showed him a few camera prototypes for 360 video capture. (Pousman describes one as "a circle of little cameras.") They discussed microphones and **directional sound**. Milk showed an example of the rig they filmed with on-stage during his March, 2015 TED Talk. Within is protective of its camera details and avoids sharing specifics of their custom rig.

Pousman watched his first piece of 360-degree video in headset in November, 2014. The piece was a single shot of Andy Lesniak, the chief creative technologist for Within and the camera's inventor. Pousman recalls that he saw a dog and then a person who picked up the dog and held it out toward the camera. "Immediately you feel it is real, in your personal bubble ..." Pousman says, "I got goosebumps, I felt transported to that living room."

Pousman and Arora spent four days filming in the Za'atari refugee camp in Jordan. The Within team initially thought the output of this type of camera would be one continuously filmed scene. Pousman had seen demos in Los Angeles, and didn't imagine the ability to edit the content using standard video editing software such as **Adobe Premiere**.

The footage, which featured Sidra in different scenes over the course of the four-day shoot, worked to create a narrative that feels as though it occurs over the course of a single day. "I don't think they imagined the footage we came back with would be so compelling and so intimate," Pousman says.

"There is some creative freedom and poetic license," Pousman said, describing how some scenes were filmed over multiple days and how they wanted to incorporate different aspects of the camp within the narrative—including places where Sidra didn't normally go.

Within used proprietary **stitching** software to match the images from different cameras so the final 360 video looked seamless.

They decided to use a voice-over actor, narrating in English because the original interviews were conducted in Arabic. Because they were initially aiming for an English-speaking international audience, many users would have had to read the subtitles in addition to taking in the 360 experience. Subtitles can be difficult to follow in VR, and they can also, as Pousman says, pull the viewer out of the piece—"rather than seeing the film as an experience they are in." In other words, having to read subtitles can break **presence**.

Lessons on Transporting the Viewer

Despite the new format and experimental nature of the piece, Pousman says there's not much he would change about *Clouds Over Sidra* beyond the height of one particular shot; "In a very nitpicky way, I would just lower the camera four inches," he says of the third shot in the sequence (at the :51 minute mark) in which Sidra's family is introduced to the viewer. He says he always puts himself in the shoes of his audience to see how they would experience a piece, trying not to get too distracted by thinking about traditional film editing techniques, such as quick **cuts**: "directors get caught up thinking that it is a film. Actually it is much more like a play," he says.

For Pousman, the project is all about taking the viewer to a place they would not have access to. "It turns out that we were able to put them in the shoes of a girl," he says. VR added an element that made people say: "Oh my god, I feel like I went there, I have had an experience," he says. *Clouds Over Sidra* took a risk by making something longer than what was being done at the time.[3] But as Pousman says, "As long as the story is compelling enough, you will just stay in there."

Emotional Impact and Reach

The very first edition of the project was released in time for the World Economic Forum in 2015. When asked about impact, Pousman said (anecdotally), "Half the people who do it cry." Through the Within app, the UN screening at Davos, the UN General Assembly, and the World Humanitarian Summit, Pousman says at least hundreds of thousands of people have watched. Since 2015, the piece has been translated into 15 languages.

After *Clouds Over Sidra*, UNVR published *Waves of Grace*, *My Mother's Wing*, and a piece on Nepal earthquake recovery. *Waves of Grace* is the story of a young woman during the Ebola epidemic in Liberia. *My Mother's Wing* follows a mother in the Gaza strip coping with losing two of her children in a bombing and the piece on the Nepal looks at the state of Kathmandu, just three days after the 2015 earthquake.

Takeaways

Scripted voice-over:

• Subtitles can break presence, limiting the immersive effect by reminding viewers they are watching a screen. Use of an actor for voice-over is an alternative.

Against the rules of film:

• Breaking the fourth wall through brief eye contact with the camera can place the viewer in the scene.
• Long cuts take inspiration from theater, rather than traditional film.

Transporting the viewer:

• Take the viewer somewhere they wouldn't otherwise have access to.
• Sensory cues, such as the mention of the smell of baking bread, can give an additional suggestion of "being there."

About This Project

URL: https://with.in/watch/clouds-over-sidra/
Interview Date: June, 2017
Interview Subject: Barry Pousman, Director of Photography
Team: Vrse/Within
Creative Director/Executive Producer: Chris Milk
Producers: Katherine Keating, Gabo Arora, Barry Pousman, Socrates Kakoulides, Christopher Fabian

Climbing Giants

Black Dot Films for National Geographic Partners
March 2017

Climbing Giants, released in two parts in early 2017, consists of two three-minute 360 video pieces that take the viewer alongside a pair of researchers to the top of giant sequoia trees. The videos were created by Black Dot Films, a production company run by Max Salomon and Malvina Martin, for National Geographic. Salomon was director and executive producer for the piece.

Salomon and Martin are experienced television writers and producers, both having created award-winning documentary projects with National Geographic and other major outlets before turning to immersive storytelling. Salomon says a main consideration when choosing stories to tell with virtual reality is to find ways to take people where they couldn't otherwise go.

That's true of *Climbing Giants*—few people will ever have the opportunity to climb to the top of a giant sequoia. It's also true of other pieces Black Dot Films has produced—such as *Wing Walker*, which takes the viewer along with an airshow performer onto the wing of a biplane traveling at 160 miles per hour. It's a guiding principle that fits well with National Geographic's image.

The creators at Black Dot Films have experimented and tinkered their way into a certain level of storytelling sophistication that's uncommon among 360 films. Their pieces guide the viewer, but in a subtle way that doesn't interrupt the sense of presence. Salomon says he thinks about 360 storytelling as "induced editing"—nudging the viewer toward where to look to create a gaze-based "edit" of an immersive space. "You're inducing the audience in VR to do the editing for you," he says. "In television and film, you compose the world out of broken images. In VR you give them the full image, but in a well-constructed image, there are clues that guide you where to look."

National Geographic has been releasing immersive experiences since 2016, and Black Dot Films has been a production partner since the beginning.

High among the Trees

Part I of *Climbing Giants* is an awe-inspiring look into the work of two scientists whose job it is to climb and study giant sequoia trees. Part II visits those scientists again to learn more about the challenges in understanding how (or whether) these giant trees will survive a changing climate. Most of the shots in these films are from high in the forest canopy.

These pieces are visually stunning and experiential, to be sure—their slow pacing leaves space for the viewer to take in the scenery—but they're also carefully edited to deliver a simple narrative arc and make sure the audience catches the action they're meant to see.

Gear for Every Occasion

Climbing Giants was shot over two weeks while the researchers featured were on a month-long study trip in the Sequoia & Kings Canyon National Parks in California. The crew at Black Dot Films joined for the first and last weeks, so they had time in the interim to modify their equipment to access difficult shots.

They used several different camera rigs for the shoot, all designed in-house: A 4-camera GoPro rig with fisheye lenses was ideal for shots where the camera needed to be light, such as when they lifted it up in the trees. DSLR rigs—one with Canon 5Ds and another with Sony A7S's—were useful when they needed more granular control and better image quality, like when they wanted to capture high-contrast shots of bright sunlight filtering into the dark forest.

The crew on *Climbing Giants* also puts a lot of emphasis on camera placement and movement to create dynamic shots—but the shooting circumstances made that difficult: "Those pieces were a big challenge just in the logistics of filming in a national park," Salomon says. "You're not allowed to attach anything to the trees. Drones are forbidden. So how do you get the camera to move?"

They were fortunate, Salomon says, because the scientists who study these sequoias already had some attachment points set up for bringing their research gear—and themselves—up into the trees. The team, led by rigger Curt Westergard, worked with ropes, pulleys and what was already there to create a sort of ad-hoc cable cam system to move the cameras around for different shots.

Salomon says most of their shoots are like this—a combination of constraints, serendipity and creative rigging. "The first day of shooting we usually end up spending that night at the hardware store," Salomon says, "You've got to look at your situation and then adapt and re-engineer."

"Induced Editing" for VR Narratives

Camera movement turned out to be essential in *Climbing Giants*, both to convey the scale of the trees and to guide the viewer's gaze. It's one of a suite of tools Salomon says he's learned can be used to help guide the viewer. He also relies on color, motion and sound.

In the second shot of *Climbing Giants*, the viewer finds herself up high in the trees, moving slowly toward the ground. Looking downward reveals a person below, climbing a rope up the tree.

"It's a risky shot because there's so much to look at and you can end up getting attracted by the beautiful sunset and miss the man completely," Salomon says. But he says the majority of people who watch this piece do find their way to the intended view.

Salomon says the crew filmed that shot several times to get the camera movement right, and to time it with the movement of the climber. They experimented with the camera moving up or down alongside him as he climbed and descended the tree. "But what works is the counter-movement, him going up and you going down," Salomon says. "So you can start in the shot and be perceiving 'oh my God, I'm up in the trees, it's amazing,' and then because you're sinking, you look down and discover him."

Color is important too. The man's bright red shirt draws the eye among the green foliage and brown tree trunks. And finally, there's sound. The presence of the subject's voice in that scene lets the viewer know the person speaking is likely to be somewhere in the shot.

In another sequence, the character's gaze is an important guiding tool. When Wendy Baxter, one of the research scientists studying the giant sequoias, reaches the camera height midway up a tree she's climbing, she pauses, exhales and looks out over the horizon. Following her gaze reveals a stunning view over the treetops. The scene then cuts to reveal Anthony Ambrose, her research partner, sitting among huge branches.

From that scene, a gentle audio cue tells the reader where to look. Baxter, in voice-over, describes the tree branches: "It almost feels like I'm in multiple trees, because it has all of these trunks coming up, almost kind of like a hand." The viewer is thus guided to look down into the cluster of tree branches, and that's where the action is happening when the scene cuts.

Figure 3.1 Climbing Giants, screenshots courtesy of Black Dot Films VR.

"If somebody is missing the action and always looking at the wrong part of the shot," Salomon says, "then either you're not telling your story well enough yet in VR and 360 to control the way that person is looking, or you need to do something else. You need to figure out something so that the audience is looking where you want them to look."

Voice-Over vs. Disembodied Narrator

Salomon says one thing he's learned not to do in immersive storytelling is "Voice of God" narration—as one might hear in a traditional nature documentary—in which a disembodied narrator speaks over the footage. It creates a dissonant experience, he says, for the narrator's voice to be broadcast directly into the viewer's ears.

"When you're watching a TV show and you hear the voice of God coming out of the TV screen ... you accept the fact that it's the television program talking to you. It's a passive experience," Salomon says. "When you're in VR, and you're in the world ... it gets in the way."

Aside from a few candid moments, the characters in *Climbing Giants* don't speak on camera, either—but their voices are used for narration while they're visible in the shot. Salomon, whose background is in documentary, says he's come to see the off-camera interview as an ideal way to gather audio for immersive storytelling. He says putting away the camera can make it easier for the person being interviewed to open up. And the immersive medium is well suited to that kind of intimacy:

"We do these incredibly rich nuanced interviews in which we get people to tell us their story," Salomon says. "They're telling you about their world and what it's like to be them, or to walk in their shoes ... it's that same thing that keeps you in the car after an amazing (radio) interview that you're listening to."

Salomon says people often forget about this strength of the medium—creating intimacy and the feeling of a one-on-one relationship in immersive story.

Intimacy, Eye Contact and the "Phantom Effect"

Another quirk of 360 video storytelling that the team at Black Dot Films has learned to play with is something they call the "phantom effect"—that is, the characters in the scene don't respond to the viewer. "You ultimately become a ghost in perception," Salomon says. "You're in a room in another reality, and nobody's acknowledging your existence. That never happens to us in reality."

But while there's an awkwardness to the phantom effect, it's also something that sets up the viewer for a powerful experience when it's broken by a character looking directly at the camera (i.e., the viewer): "VR is really good at eye contact," Salomon says. "When a subject looks at you, it grounds you in your experience."

Salomon points to this phenomenon in another project he directed, called *The Wing Walker*, about a woman who performs on the wings of a vintage biplane doing loops in the sky. The key moment, he says, is when Carol the wing walker looks at the camera, smiles, then looks down at her shoes.

He says that moment is strategically placed, and it's particularly effective in a headset: "She looks down at her feet and you look down at her feet and you feel that movement of the plane, and you actually feel like you're 2,000 feet in the air," he says. "It's not the moment where it goes loop-di-loop in the sky around you that you freak out. It's the footsteps that put you on the airplane. You're not just watching something; you're a part of it."

Distribution

National Geographic's 360 video content is available on Facebook and YouTube—but by far the most views come from Facebook. Six months after posting, Facebook's metrics were showing 11 million views for *Climbing Giants*.

Takeaways

Exclusive access:
- Immersive media appeals when it can take viewers somewhere they couldn't otherwise go.

Guiding the viewer's path:
- Offering subtle cues to guide the viewer toward the components of the story they need to see can create a predictable, gaze-based "induced" edit.

Breaking the fourth wall:
- Intentionally breaking the fourth wall to create intimacy and encourage perspective-taking is one tool that can be used.

Tools for guiding the viewer:
- Lighting (e.g., a brightly lit section in a dark scene)
- Color / contrast (e.g., red shirt in a green and brown forest scene)
- Quality of sounds (e.g., the sound of birds or a plane indicates to look up)
- Indirect verbal cues and descriptions (e.g., a description of tree branches)

- Camera movement (viewers tend to look in the direction the camera is moving)
- The character's gaze

About This Project

URL:

Climbing Giants, Part I: www.youtube.com/watch?v=f7wTolIlK_s
Climbing Giants, Part II: www.youtube.com/watch?v=jTN5lr877Cw
360 Wingwalker, Part I: www.youtube.com/watch?v=xjJCMSSYCgQ
Producer and Director: Max Salomon
Executive Producers: Max Salomon, Malvina Martin
Associate Producer: Natalie Jaime
Director of Photography: Eric Rochner
Rigger: Curt Westergard
Production Assistant: Erika Bergman
Editors: Barbara Ballow, Max Salomon
Additional Audio Editing: Bilal Qureshi
Post-Production Supervisor: Refah Mahmoud
Mixer: Ryan White
Production Manager: Hilary Burke

We Who Remain

The Emblematic Group, AJ+ and NYT-VR
March 13, 2017

We Who Remain brings together the stories of four different people: a student, a rebel soldier, a journalist, and a mother—all working to improve their lives in the midst of war.

It is a collaborative 360-degree video project demonstrating what's possible when multiple creators and publications join efforts. The project began after Trevor Snapp, the director of a Sudan-based news non-profit called Nuba Reports, met Nonny de la Peña, founder of Emblematic Group, at the Online News Association conference in 2015. In the fall of 2016, Emblematic sent a 7-camera GoPro rig with Snapp to the Nuba mountains of Sudan. The project debuted at the annual South by Southwest conference in March, 2017.

Kevin Tsukii, who joined the project as tech lead with Emblematic Group shortly after the video rig was sent to Sudan, says the team knew Snapp as a documentarian who would be able to tell a good story, since he had been working in the region for several years.

While the project began as an Emblematic Group piece with the intention to distribute for Oculus headsets, it evolved into a partnership with AJ+ and the *New York Times*. The final piece can be viewed on the NYT-VR app, NYT desktop, on a website hosted by AJ+ as well as social platforms—specifically Facebook and YouTube. It also appeared at multiple film festivals, including South by Southwest in Austin, Texas and the American Film Institute (AFI) VR showcase in Washington, D.C.

From the beginning, the purpose of the project was to highlight the journalism coming out of the Nuba mountains of Sudan. The team aimed to center the piece around people, and not breaking news, in order to create a character-driven, longform documentary. While the content has been broken up and presented in different ways across platforms (discussed at the end of this chapter) the primary focus of this case study is the original 15-minute piece.

Dispatches from a War Zone

We Who Remain begins with a scene of a dance, followed by visuals of a foxhole in which several people are hiding, waiting for an airplane to pass overhead. Throughout the piece, the viewer meets four different characters, who address the camera directly. As they speak to the camera, a graphical display shows their name and title. For those who are not speaking in English, their words are translated in voice-over.

About two minutes into the piece, the rebel commander gives a brief historical overview that sets the context for the story. As he narrates, the viewer finds themself in an empty classroom with a dirt floor. Animated leading lines draw the viewer's attention to wall of the classroom, where maps, graphics and video overlaid onto the wall and floor help illustrate how the Nuba mountains were not included in the new country of South Sudan when it was established in 2011—and how Sudan's government blocked aid and medicine to civilians in the region. The animated explanation also has a score with energetic drum beats and strings to match the tone of what the viewer is seeing. Since 2011, thousands have been forced to flee. As the text projected on the wall reads: "This is the story of those who remain."

Co-director Sam Wolson says the piece was done in a cinéma vérité style, essentially letting the story tell itself based on the footage the team collected in the field. It provides a closer, more intimate look at some of the challenges of living amidst warfare. In one scene, the viewer sees one of the characters take his first steps after his leg is badly injured. Wolson believes *We Who Remain* was an important project to tell using this medium for several reasons. In part, the nature of the story—the Nuba mountains are isolated. "It's a war zone; journalists have been technically banned from going there," Wolson says. "There's something really important to documentary VR work where it's giving you access to a place."

Giving viewers a sense of presence within the story connects them in an "intuitive" way. Wolson notes that not everything is important to tell as a VR narrative, but he believes allowing people to "have that feeling of being inside a cave when mortars are coming over," speaks to the issues in a way that still photos or other forms of media are unable to do.

40 Hours of Footage

In September and October of 2016, Wolson and Snapp did the first round of filming, then mailed hard drives from Sudan to the Emblematic office in Los Angeles. Tsukii began stitching the first round of footage at this time.

As Tsukii says, "I started stitching, and immediately gave them feedback on how they were shooting," to improve for the next round. He emphasized the importance of file management, because, as he puts it, "it's hard to make sense of partially organized footage from seven cameras."

The team in Sudan continued shooting in October and November and went to the Emblematic office the following February to finalize the story before *We Who Remain* premiered in March 2017. During the course of filming, Tsukii says Snapp and Wolson filled 10 terabytes of hard drive space. The nearly 40 hours of footage was eventually cut down to 15 minutes.

The Emblematic team relied on Kolor software for stitching footage from the seven cameras together, creating an **equirectangular** version to be brought into video editing software. Once the project was nearing **picture-lock**, they received some pro bono assistance from visual effects company LegendVR to assist with about ten difficult shots. Tsukii says the major challenge was that people were moving across **stitch lines** while close to the camera. LegendVR went frame by frame to fix some of the key shots—sometimes painting in an arm or hand when the subject was in-between the cameras. This can be a very time consuming process, with one 10-second shot at 30 frames per second creating 300 different images to paint.

Documentary Meets VR

Snapp and Wolson both come from a background in photography. "The best photo stories are normally non-linear," Snapp says, "they create meaning by challenging the viewer" and great photography is also comfortable being close and intimate in a similar way to VR.

"Technical hurdles were just ridiculous with these cameras," Wolson says. In contrast, Wolson and Snapp found there were aspects of VR filmmaking that offered a depth and intimacy they weren't able to get in traditional filmmaking. One positive aspect of 360 filmmaking was getting people to open up and ignore the camera. Since Wolson

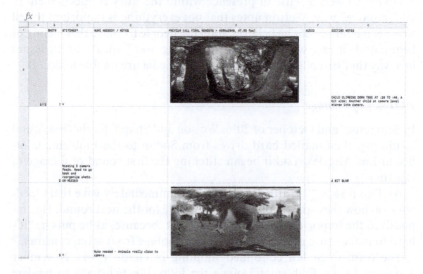

Figure 3.2 Sample footage log for *We Who Remain*. Courtesy of Kevin Tsukii.

and Snapp needed to get out of the shot, they would often leave the camera going for extended periods of time. Wolson says this provided them with an "interesting surprise" when reviewing footage. Putting together the film was in some ways just a matter of finding those "precious moments."

Overall, the shooting team in the field wasn't given a lot of guidance, which Tsukii believes helped a lot. "They had their own style in terms of being very verité, and sort of setting the camera down and not staging a lot of things," Tsukii said. This put the piece in contrast to The Displaced, one of the *New York Times*' early VR pieces, which is more produced. As Tsukii says, We Who Remain "was more raw and real."

The production was a balance between 360-video editors and more traditional documentary-style producers. Tsukii recalls how some consulting editors wanted to have shorter shots, but the fast pace didn't give viewers enough time to take in what they were seeing. After looking at the piece in the headset, the team realized it was too fast, and they needed to slow down the action. "The result is a compromise of a traditional (documentary) editor working with someone who spends a lot more time in a headset," said Tsukii.

The team considered separating each person's story, but in the end they wanted to have an "interwoven story, where the narrative of each person builds on top of each other," Tsukii said. With this in mind, one of the challenges was to tell the story in a way that wasn't confusing. After reviewing the initial footage, they noticed there weren't a lot of scenes in which the main characters were easily identifiable. In order to solve this problem, on the second round of filming the team in Sudan had each person do a **standup**—in which the person speaks directly to the camera, so they could be identified.

Explaining with Graphics

The producers and editors knew from the beginning that they wanted to have an **explainer** or animated graphic to give some context and history of the Nuba mountain region. To do so, the team spent an extended amount of time on the graphic sequence where the map is shown. They knew they would need to include background information to give the story context, but they wanted to integrate it seamlessly. As a result, they chose to use the classroom to frame the history and context lesson and then they had one of the central people within the piece—the rebel commander—framing the narrative, so it didn't come from an outside voice.

One of the major tools they used to guide the viewer's gaze was an animated red line that wraps around the video and animates mountains onto the wall and floor of the classroom. The red line catches the eye regardless of where the viewer is looking, then directs their attention to a map overlaid on the classroom wall.

The original concept was to create a roulette-type experience where a timeline moves around the viewer. Many 360 explainers try to force the viewer to turn around, but instead of directing the gaze around the scene, Tsukii and the team decided to have the story unfold primarily in one specific area—on the blackboard in a school-room scene, where the viewer is still able to see all the action in one **field of view**. When considering how to think about the explainer aspect of the story, Tsukii believes there are two things the technology can do: (1) Ask the viewer to turn around or (2) Provide the opportunity for a more intensely focused experience. After prototyping they decided to go for focus, "We wanted to use the technology so we could make people focus a bit more and get more into the story," says Tsukii.

This project also took inspiration from other 360 graphics pieces, such as the Verge's Michelle Obama 360 video[4] with animations and graphics in 360 space (released March, 2016), as well as a video from the American Museum of Natural History in New York City—about Fossil Hunting in the Gobi[5] which collages different flat videos together within the 360 experience. In contrast, both of those experiences use the entire 360 space, which requires the viewer to turn around to get all the information.

The Right Equipment

"We would basically just try to put the camera in a place and film for as long as we could," Wolson says. By leaving the camera in one place, he says eventually things happen, and putting it together is about "the dance of attention"—figuring out how to drive the story through visual and audio cues without overwhelming the viewer.

Beyond keeping the camera rolling to get the best shot, the team learned the importance of keeping track of shots, by logging the footage, making note of key points of interest as well as what shots worked and didn't work. Tsukii also says the 7-camera set-up may have made the whole process more difficult. In retrospect, Tsukii would now go with a three-camera GoPro mount with fisheye lenses, so as to be more lightweight and have fewer potential challenges. When they began in 2016, this wasn't an option.

The team in the field used a Zoom H4 audio device to capture audio from a lavalier mic as well as ambient audio. In retrospect, Tsukii says he would have given them an audio set-up that captured sounds in more than one direction, like the H2N1 for 4 channel audio. Nonetheless, they were still able to create a more immersive sound experience during the post-production process.

Getting the Most Eyeballs

The Emblematic version of *We Who Remain* was optimized for the Oculus headset and consists of one 15-minute experience. The NYT-VR experience is available on the app, as well as the homepage (as a desktop version). At the time, the piece was one of the few projects that had spent an extensive amount of time in the field filming.

The partnership with AJ+ created a unique product optimized for social platforms. Hunter Holcombe, executive producer at AJ+, says they designed pieces to appeal to a social media audience, optimizing for mobile and desktop scenarios without a headset. Overall they used larger text on screen, tighter cuts, and placed the majority of the visuals in the front 180 degrees of vision. In order to make the experience more social-media friendly, the AJ+ team divided the main feature into four shorter character profiles each less than 3 minutes long. They also added text on-screen for Facebook viewers to be able to watch without sound and created an additional fifth piece in-house, providing context about the conflict in South Sudan.

Lastly, they created a **WebVR** platform for ease in desktop viewing. According to Holcombe, as they began brainstorming various features such as interactivity and social media embedding, YouTube and other 360 players were not robust enough. "Our mantra at AJ+ has been accessibility, so we decided we wanted a WebVR version that would be globally accessible, both for desktop and mobile," Holcombe says.

Takeaways

A place where journalists are banned:
- *We Who Remain* offers access to an important story, in a place very few who aren't from there can experience.

"Eventually things happen":
- In documentary 360 video, longer takes can increase the likelihood of capturing powerful visual moments—but the trade-off is more file storage, processing and post production.

Slow down a bit:
- An initial edit was too fast-paced. Often, viewers need some time to orient themselves each time there is a cut to a new environment.

Who should I be watching?
- It can be hard to identify the main character in a 360 scene full of people. The solution in this project: Include standup scenes, in which the characters introduce themselves directly to the camera.

Narrowing focus:
- An information-dense *explainer* section of this piece takes place in a small area of a 360 scene with no action in other areas. After prototyping, the creators did this so the viewer could focus on the important information.
- One tool for narrowing focus and integrating flat videos is to project these on a wall. In this case it was done on a classroom wall.

A joint effort:
- Taking a longform project, tailoring it to different platforms and partnering with multiple outlets ensures it will be seen by the maximum number of people.

About This Project

URL:
NYTVR: www.nytimes.com/video/magazine/100000004980989/we-who-remain.html www.ajplus.net/project/sudan-vr/
Emblematic Group: http://emblematicgroup.com/experiences/we-who-remain/
AJ+: www.ajplus.net/project/sudan-vr/
Interview Date: July, 2017
Interview Subjects: Kevin Tsukii, Emblematic Group; Hunter Holcombe, AJ+; Jenna Pirog, *New York Times*; Sam Wolson, and Trevor Snapp
Directed by: Trevor Snapp & Sam Wolson

Executive Producers: Nonny de la Peña, Jenna Pirog
Immersive Video, Technical Lead: Kevin Tsukii
Produced by: Cassandra Herrman, Sam Wolson, Trevor Snapp, Nonny de la Peña
Field Producer Ryan Boyette
Edited by: Sam Wolson, Trevor Snapp, Greg Byers, Kevin Tsukii
Assistant Editor: John General Cinematography by Trevor Snapp & Sam Wolson
Post Production Stitching Services: LEGEND VR
Motion Graphics Design: Eben McCue, John
General Sound Design: Tim Gedemer
Original Soundtrack: Haim Mazar
Translator: Zach Mondesire and Anonymous for Security Reasons
Color Grading: Kaitlyn Battistelli Production Assistance
Nuba Reports Team: Anonymous for Security Reasons
Voicing: Anonymous for Security Reasons

Limbo

Guardian VR
August, 2017

Limbo examines what happens when immigrants and asylum seekers arrive in a new country. The experience begins with brief text informing the viewer of their place in the story: "You are one of the 36,846 people who applied for asylum last year." The viewer is then brought into a dream-like story, with **voice-over narration** interwoven with clips from audio interviews. Leading the viewer through the film and speaking to "you" during the story, the narrator helps guide and explain the action throughout the nearly 9-minute piece.

As the story opens, the viewer is drifting slowly through the streets of an unfamiliar city on what seems to be a bus or tram. The city is intentionally unclear. During the course of the piece, the voices of asylum seekers in the U.K. are heard throughout, such as a man saying: "I was really scared I would never return to my country." The story guides you into your shared housing with others seeking asylum, through an ethereal forest scene and then into an office in which you are being interviewed by a U.K. government bureaucrat in order to receive asylum.

The piece touches on issues of arrival, housing, work and the governmental processes that one must go through in order to be granted asylum. A narrator guides the viewer, addressing them directly: "You share this house with others who are also seeking refuge ... they, like you, are waiting. They, like you, are in limbo," the voice-over says. The use of "you" gives the viewer a feeling of personal connection.

The *Guardian* VR team worked to produce a series of seven films in 2017, with the intention for the content to be viewed in a Google Daydream

Figure 3.3 Limbo, Courtesy of *Guardian* VR.

headset in addition to social channels such as YouTube and Facebook. The team has won multiple awards, including a European Digital Media Award for best use of online video, International Digital Innovation of the Year at the news awards in 2017 and Digital Innovation at the British Journalism Awards 2016 for 6x9: a virtual reality experience of solitary confinement.

Engineering Disorientation

The *Guardian* VR team partnered with ScanLab Projects to create the visuals for *Limbo*. Matthew Shaw, ScanLab Projects co-founder, recalls they brought a clear story, a script, and an audio track—but no visuals. From there, the ScanLab Projects team worked to begin visualizing the story. While the story changed over the course of the project, Shaw says that the audio the *Guardian* team had assembled was strong from the start.

The intention and feeling throughout was to create a dream-like nightmare-style piece. Shaw says they didn't want the *Limbo* world to be too real. Initially, the *Guardian* team imagined there would be a city scene, a house scene and an interview scene. The one scene they added after doing interviews was a flashback scene to Aleppo built with photogrammetry using drone footage. ScanLab Projects went back and forth with director Shehani Fernando and the *Guardian* VR team, finalizing questions such as: Where should we be? What should the city be like?

Should it be identifiable as a particular place in the world? Does anybody need to know that it's Manchester? Once they had an idea of the concept, they began the scanning process to build the visuals for the piece. The resulting imagery is a black and white, surreal experience in which people and buildings appear as ghost-like semitransparent shapes made up of white dots and lines on a black background. The experience feels like it could be taking place in any European city.

"We talked a little about disorientation when you arrive to a new place," Shaw said. "We wanted the audience to feel this kind of rushing through the city." The story brings the viewer through some of the trials and tribulations faced by new arrivals, such as assigned accommodation.

Lidar Scans

ScanLab Projects started working with the *Guardian* in April of 2017 and from commission to launch, the project took roughly three months. They started by scanning several different homes using terrestrial **Lidar**. Lidar stands for "light detection and ranging": A scanner sends an infrared laser, waits for its reflection, then measures this distance. Each of these measurements is collected as a point to create a point cloud—a depth map of a place or object.

Shaw estimates the house they used to locate the story was scanned over a period of about five days and the city was scanned over four days on location in Manchester. The city scans used a self-developed mobile mapping technique. According to Shaw, the scale of the scanning had not been done before. In addition, one of the most difficult aspects of the project was combining static scans with moving scanned objects. This can be seen in the interview scene—when the viewer is faced with someone from the U.K. government office within a static office.

Shaw believes scanning is worth the added effort for the realism it adds within the scene—such as the moment a dog passes by on a leash, or the scene of a man hanging his clothes on the line. "You're pretty damn sure that dog is real," Shaw said. "You don't make that up. That's real."

Data management proved to be its own challenge. Shaw estimates the project file for *Limbo* was over 5TB; each 12 second clip of live action scanning is around 50GB of data. To work with the live scans, ScanLab Projects mostly uses proprietary software they have built, but they also work in **Unity**—a 3D game development engine.

A Mix of Audio Sources

ScanLab Projects and the *Guardian* VR team worked collaboratively with both audio and visuals during the production process. The teams worked together to finalize the **spatialized audio** with the audio software

Figure 3.4 Limbo, Courtesy of *Guardian* VR.

Reaper, using several individual sound sources placed in the correct location in 360 space during the post-production process.

Limbo's soundscape was made up of interviews with real asylum seekers and a narrator who leads the viewer through the experience. Overall they conducted 14 interviews—from which a handful of audio clips were included—and all the interviews helped inform the overall piece. Within the experience, the interviews serve to ground the viewer in the lived experience of those in limbo, while the narrator guides the story, moves it along and adds brief explanations which serve to bring the piece together.

Quality over Quantity

"It's not the same process as editing a film," Francesca Panetta says of the creative process, explaining how they would view the piece in a headset to see how a scene might look or feel. Fernando and Panetta see the process as continual iteration. "In terms of structure, we try to prototype things as cheaply and easily as possible," Panetta says. "We spend time making storyboards, writing scripts, cutting audio interviews. Then we make basic builds and continue to work with the storyboard and script, iterating until the end."

The *Guardian* VR team has been focused on creating high quality content specifically for the Google Daydream app—a form of future proofing. "I believe quite strongly that you have to design things quite differently if you are doing **magic window** mode or watching them on YouTube," Panetta says, "It's either immersive or it is not." She adds that there is a danger that the form won't actually take off if creators are making projects that make people feel sick or just aren't very enjoyable experiences, "I feel a responsibility towards VR journalism," Panetta says, "to be making decent content."

"The kind of VR work we do is quite embodied," Fernando says. She sees immersive journalism taking off when it is even more of a fluid part of our lives, perhaps involving more wearable technology, maps and social technology. "Even though it is definitely early, I think it is worthwhile doing," she says of experiments in VR.

Takeaways

Surreal but real:
- Scanning live action captures natural movement, which makes graphics feel more believable than in if they were animated.
- Low-resolution graphics make it difficult to identify specific locations and create a sense of disorientation for the viewer.

Addressing the viewer:
- The narrator speaks directly to the viewer in *Limbo*, narrating their experience to create a sense of personal connection.

Iterating until the end:
- The *Guardian* team see their work as continual iteration. To ease the process they spend time in pre-production: storyboarding, scripting and cutting audio scripts, and prototyping as cheaply as possible.

Multiple voices:
- By mixing narration and interview audio, *Limbo* is able to directly guide the viewer but still include first-hand accounts of interviewees.

About This Project

URL: www.theguardian.com/technology/2017/jul/05/limbo-a-virtual-experience-of-waiting-for-asylum-360-video?, available through the Daydream Guardian VR app and YouTube
Interview Date: August, 2017
Interview Subjects: Francesca Panetta, Shehani Fernando and Matthew Shaw (ScanLab Projects)
Team: Shehani Fernando, Francesca Panetta, Nicole Jackson, Pascal Wyse, Juliet Stevenson, Joe Dunthorne and ScanLAB Projects

The Occupation of Alcatraz that Sparked an American Revolution

Seeker VR
June 2017

"One of the things we really try hard to do is to contextualize the news," says Aneeta Akhurst, co-director of Seeker VR's *The Occupation of Alcatraz that Sparked an American Revolution.* "We were trying to provide this context; this is a struggle that's not just now."

The Occupation of Alcatraz is an 8-minute 360-degree video piece following the story of Dr. LaNada War Jack—a Native American activist and academic who participated in the occupation of Alcatraz Island from 1969 to 1971—as it parallels the Native American movement in the U.S. blossoming at that time. The thread leads the viewer—as it led the filmmakers—to the Dakota Access Pipeline (DAPL) protests in North Dakota, to feel the surge of energy there in late 2016 and draw a connection to its roots in the original occupation.

Akhurst and co-director Cailyn Bradley conceived of the piece during the height of the pipeline conflict, but the fully formed idea was a couple years in the making.

The team was inspired in part by The Modern Games,[6] a 2016 *New York Times* piece for which visual effects studio The Mill used archival photos to recreate past Olympic games in 360-degree video. It made their own concept seem feasible. There's of course no 360-degree footage of the Alcatraz occupation, but the history could be told with old photos and video overlaid on current footage: "It's such a cool way to look back in history as if you were there watching it unfold," Bradley says.

Archival photos and video didn't become the focal point of the story, but the piece included context that they couldn't have otherwise included in a 360 piece. Black and white photos from the occupation overlaid on current scenes of Alcatraz bring history to life, allowing viewers to stand on the island and visualize the locations where those events took place. This method allowed the creators to build a context to the activism at the heart of the anti-DAPL movement, and lent a power and historical gravity to the piece.

Walking through Memory

The Occupation of Alcatraz opens in the middle of a sunrise ceremony at a 2016 gathering of Native American tribes from all over the U.S. The piece then follows War Jack as she returns to Alcatraz for the first time since the 1969 occupation.

"We called ourselves Indians of All Tribes," War Jack says as a scene on the island opens to a wall that reads "Indian Land" in huge, scrawled red letters, "and we were there to take a stand, to demand an answer to why more than 500 treaties with the federal government promising to preserve Indian land, water and human rights had been dishonored over and over again."

To the left of the lettering—a graphical element added in **post production**—is a cut-out black and white image of the 1969 occupiers as they first set foot on the island. Overlaid on the new footage, the image has a surprising feeling of depth. Other archival images used throughout

Figure 3.5 The Occupation of Alcatraz, Courtesy of Seeker VR.

this section of the piece include an image of a teepee and photos of the occupiers during their stay. The filmmakers made their best effort to align each image with the precise location where it was originally photographed.

In other scenes, the piece uses graphics to display further historical context: A timeline of the history of Alcatraz Island wraps around the 360-space; animated maps illustrate where native land was taken or returned by the federal government; and a 1970s television set plays Nixon-era newscasts.

The piece takes the viewer to Standing Rock to witness the protest camps there. "So here I stand again, at the Oceti Sakowan camp in Standing Rock, North Dakota, fighting the same fight for our inherent rights," War Jack narrates over time-lapse footage of her standing in the camp. The narration, which Akhurst scripted based on War Jack's book manuscript and shared with her for feedback, is a mix of personal narrative and historical context.

The project's creators say they conceptualized the piece as a journey in which the narrator is a guide. Unlike a lot of Seeker's work, which includes simpler stories they call "experiences" or news videos guided by an on-camera host—with more heavy-handed narration and direction for the viewer—they sought to use subtler cues for this piece. Their aim was for the viewer to have a feeling of standing with War Jack on Alcatraz and at Standing Rock. Visiting those places in person had an impact on the filmmakers during the shoot, and the role of the physical location in the piece is to give a context to the movement that

Akhurst and Bradley believe can only be understood by having a feeling of being there.

Making Space for the Story

This project took about 6 months to complete—much longer than most Seeker pieces, which the creators say they tend to wrap up in about a month. Pre-reporting took several months, the filmmakers say, just to build rapport and trust with the people they were covering. The original occupiers were wary of the way the press would portray their story.

When Bradley and Akhurst followed the threads of their research to LaNada War Jack—who was also writing a book about the occupation— they realized the Alcatraz story they wanted to tell had to include the story of the Standing Rock movement. That also influenced the length of the piece, which, at 8 minutes, is longer than most of the pieces Seeker had previously produced. "We're in the early days, wild west of 360," Akhurst says, "and we just thought, 'let's go for it, let's try a longer piece.' The pace is a little slower."

The day after filming the sunrise ceremony in which this piece opens, Akhurst and Bradley traveled to North Dakota and met with War Jack there. They spent three days filming at Standing Rock and then, upon returning to the Bay Area, they spent one more day scouting the final shoot and one day on Alcatraz island with War Jack.

Akhurst and Bradley say they tried to film for 2–3 minutes at a time. The short duration was in part because of the limited battery life and memory card capacity of their gear—they were using a six-camera Go-Pro rig—but mostly because having to manage too much footage from six cameras quickly becomes a **post-production** headache as the files become large and difficult to work with, and every shot is made up of six different camera files. The only time they filmed for longer—about 8 minutes—was during the sunrise ceremony in the first scene of the piece, because they weren't able to retrieve the camera during the ceremony.

Post Production and the "Cone of Focus"

To complete post production, Seeker brought in the Bay Area creative agency Soap Collective to work on graphics. They produced the stand-alone graphics sequences and helped overlay the archival footage and photos. The Soap Collective had worked on immersive projects before, so they also contributed to how the filmmakers thought about directing the viewer.

"We sort of had it in our minds how you should be using the whole 360," Akhurst says, but for this piece they began to think in terms of what Logan Dwight, co-founder and creative director there, calls "the cone of focus."[7] The term refers to the idea that wherever the viewer is looking, movement within a certain range of that focal point can be used to guide the viewer from the edge of their field of view to another part of the scene.

"It's all about where is your key frame of vision and where is your periphery and what is that cut-off," Akhurst says, "and the action should be mostly in that frame of vision. And then if you want to direct the viewer, you can have things kind of leading into the periphery to make them look around."

She says they were thinking about that concept when they designed the timeline sequence, which uses leading lines to guide the viewer about three-quarters of the way around the sphere from the starting point.

Desktop or Headset?

Many of the graphics in the piece are directly behind where the viewer is oriented when the piece opens, so if they don't at some point turn fully around, they'll miss a lot of the action. In the third scene, in which the viewer finds themself inside a prison cell at Alcatraz, the loud slamming of the cell door lets them know to turn around. From there, the graphics sequence begins with a timeline that slowly wraps around most of the 360 space—ending just to the left of the **zero point** view. That's where the next **point of interest** is to be found when the scene cuts.

The filmmakers were predicting where the viewer would be looking with each of these moves. The navigation works beautifully when watching on a browser or mobile magic window—modes in which the viewer has the ability to reorient the 360 view by clicking or swiping. The point where the action ends in one scene is reliably where it begins in the next, and the action moves slowly enough that it's not hard to follow with mouse clicks or swiping.

But for headset viewing, placing a point of interest at the rear of the 360 space demands that the viewer either stand or use a swivel chair to turn fully around. The way this piece uses the entire horizontal plane for dynamic navigation makes it best suited for desktop/laptop or magic window viewing.

The Platform Informs the Story

Seeker VR, launched in late 2016, is part of Seeker—a social-media focused science publication that is itself an offshoot of the Discovery Network. The publication's focus on science is broadly defined, and they target young audiences on YouTube and Facebook.

While they have a strong viewership on YouTube, they've found their VR content is much more popular on Facebook. Bradley and Akhurst say their viewers on YouTube come in looking for specific content and are less receptive to immersive pieces. Facebook, they say, creates a much more open-ended space for audiences to discover content in their timeline.

Both filmmakers say they're excited to see what platforms such as Facebook and YouTube will do in the future with their immersive video players. Bradley says she's looking forward to seeing more stories that blend 3D-rendered graphics and video, or let users click on a point in a scene to take a different course through a branching narrative. The "point of interest" feature on Facebook, which allows creators to make videos that automatically re-orient for passive viewing, is "just the tip of the iceberg," Akhurst postulates. "We're just at the beginning of how we can use this brand new medium to tell really powerful, emotive stories."

Takeaways

Past and presence:
* Embedding archival imagery in a 360-degree space can give viewers a sense of connection to past events—or add historical context to a place.

Lead with the periphery:
* Anticipate where the viewer is likely to be looking, and use guiding action at the edges of their field of view to lead them to the next point of interest.

360 degrees of action:
* For a desktop or magic window viewer, looking at the rear of the 360 space only takes a click or a swipe—but for a person wearing a head-set it can be a challenge to turn fully around while seated.
* For viewers navigating with a mouse or trackpad (rather than in a headset), slower guiding action makes it easier to keep up.

About This Project

URL: www.youtube.com/watch?v=TBjuhFOeitE
Interview Date: July 20, 2017
Interview Subject: Cailyn Bradley, Aneeta Akhurst

Euronews

360 videos
2016–2017 (ongoing)

From June to December of 2016, Euronews produced about 60 360-degree videos. Thomas Seymat, a digital features journalist, who took on the role of immersive journalism editor, and the Euronews team

Figure 3.6 Svalbard Seed Vault: built to save humanity from an apocalypse, Euronews.

amped up their 360 production through a Google Digital News Initiative grant with the purpose of establishing the first fully-integrated 360 work-flow for an international media group. The grant-funded project aimed to establish Euronews as the first European newsroom to integrate VR journalism into their reporting, regularly publish 360 news videos, and figure out ways of monetizing the content in the process.

Euronews established a production process to integrate 360 storytell-ing as an additional newsroom tool by training journalists, producers, video editors and management. The goal was to find ways to produce more videos faster and cheaper than had been done before.

News at the Heart of Europe, for Europe

Euronews started in 1993 with the goal of covering world news with a pan-European perspective. Seymat joined the team in 2012, and began experimenting with immersive projects towards the end of 2015 and more fully in 2016. With sponsorship and cameras from Samsung, they started publishing 360 videos in June of 2016. Though the first project took a month to finish, by the end of 2016 they were turning around 360 videos in just a few days each. At the end of the year, they had produced 60 vid-eos in less than six months. "We took maybe three months to experiment to see what worked and what didn't," Seymat says.

Now, the workflow is integrated into the newsroom. Some notable cov-erage from 2016 included a nine-part series in advance of the French elec-tion and another series in advance of the German election. They decided against creating a separate and distinct VR team; instead they have incorporated 360 video into their news workflow.

Starting with Training

One of the first things Euronews did to prepare for publishing 360 video was conduct a comprehensive training with journalists, producers, editors, people in the production department and middle and upper management. The organization is housed in a six-story building and Seymat says every floor was involved: the newsroom, the digital team, IT, culture, sports, sponsored content, product team, and the legal team.

One of the most challenging aspects was helping traditional journalists cope with the feeling of losing control: "The first thing is a journalist coming to their senses in a new way," he says, and realizing, "they're not in charge anymore." 360-degree videos allow the viewer to control where they are looking, and the creator can no longer force the viewer's attention in the same way that traditional video allows. For journalists with 25–35 years' experience in flat video, this conceptual adjustment proved to be one of the most challenging hurdles. "You can still tell stories, you just have to give more power to your audience—you have to let go, a little bit."

Another part of the training was coming up with a style and format. Euronews chose to have the journalist in the shot as a host. Seymat says this adds an authenticity to the video with the journalist speaking directly to the camera, and helps the viewer navigate the space and the story by having a guide.

Reconfiguring the System

To create a new workflow, the Euronews team had to adapt and expand the current system. They bought about ten Samsung Gear 360 cameras and equipped correspondents and bureaus with the technology. Seymat basic rates for each aspect of the 360 production. He could then provide an additional budget for the creation of 360 video. If someone was going out to do a story they could add an additional number of hours for 360 video capture—all 360 videos are published on the website as part of an article.

For example, when a colleague was going to shoot a video on humanitarian efforts in Venezuela, they were able to allocate pay for an additional 5 hours and an editing shift so she could come back with enough footage for a 360 video to serve as a web bonus.

Experimenting to Get It Right

After extensive experimentation, the Euronews team settled on a solid format for what they know how to do: a 3–4 minute news video shot on the

Figure 3.7 French Election Series, Euronews.

scene. They're still experimenting on additional formats, "It works ... a lot of moving parts require oiling and making sure everything works together, but it works." Seymat says that 90% of the audience comes from Facebook, and they will occasionally boost or sponsor a post that is well performing.

One challenge was creating multi-episode series on one specific topic—like they did in advance of the French elections—but he thinks it worked for what they aimed to do: "In a post-Trump, post-Brexit world, it's really cool to take people out of their bubbles," Seymat says, and show them people they would normally never interact with.

Learning through Distribution

In the beginning of the experimentation, Seymat told most people to go ahead and try things. Now, he says, he knows what works what doesn't work for the Euronews audience. He tries to avoid stories that focus heavily on one national audience, and is also skeptical of pitches for stories when "they want to go deep into a topic, and almost use the videos as just illustration for what they want to say."

Seymat says it's been tricky to follow the metrics for their videos, which in some cases are translated into 13 languages across several platforms. "I have a headache just thinking about it," he says. But he's hoping the best-practices they've developed will carry forward into something that lasts: "Now if we can stabilize the production and keep making it a tool for journalists, for programs that are sponsored as well, that would be the real achievement—make something sustainable."

Takeaways

Hard to adjust:
* More experience working in traditional video can mean it's harder to cede control of where the viewer looks.

A trusted guide:
* Euronews concluded that for their audience, videos with a journalist speaking to the camera was most authentic, and allowed the host to guide the viewer around the scene.

Experiment for a workflow:
* Euronews found that with the right process in place, 360-degree news videos can be turned around in just a few days.
* It took concerted effort to establish a workflow and train the newsroom.

About This Project

URL: www.euronews.com/tag/360-video
Publication Date: 2016–2017 (ongoing)
Interview Date: July 2017
Interview Subject: Thomas Seymat, Immersive Journalism & VR Editor

VRtually There

USA Today, YouTube

David Hamlin, executive producer of *VRtually There*, worked on 78 VR films over a 12-month period from 2017 to 2018. Before joining the USA Today network in 2016, Hamlin went out on his first 360 video shoot as a field producer and story producer for Here Be Dragons—an immersive production studio specializing in virtual reality content, co-founded by Patrick Milling-Smith and VR director Chris Milk. At the time, the team was working on a story about giraffes in Garamba National Park, in the Democratic Republic of Congo.

Excited by the new technology, Hamlin learned by doing. "It is a whole new challenge and opportunity in storytelling and trying to capture an environment ... I loved that, because it didn't feel stale in any way," he says. He showed footage from Garamba to his wife and kids—who are normally easily bored with photos from his international work. He says it felt like a "eureka" moment: "They were there, and they were gasping too."

After spending most of his career with National Geographic as a filmmaker and executive producer, Hamlin was recruited by Gannett, the parent company of the USA TODAY Network, to work on the weekly VR show in partnership with YouTube. He took his experience as a series producer and applied it to VR. Hamlin says this project was about producing VR at scale, a different challenge than just producing a one-off high budget piece. For the first two years of *VRtually There*, the team published an episode a week for 12 weeks.

Adventures in Series Production

With an upbeat soundtrack, each episode of the first season of USA Today's *VRtually There* series includes a story "for the thrill of it," as the intro says, an "epic adventure," and a "dream destination." Using this basic formula to divide the 6–8 minute episode into 2–3 minute segments, *VRtually There*'s first season covers everything from wing-walkers, skateboarding, and surfing to Macy's Thanksgiving Day Parade prep, swimming with sharks, and visiting Hong Kong. Between each segment are 360-degree advertisements.

Season Two takes the same approach, but each segment is published as a separate video, for a total of 36 videos, two to six minutes each, uploaded in groups of three. It includes, among other things: a face-to-face experience with elephant seals, a look inside a tiger's mouth, scuba divers exploring a missile silo, kiteboarding, parkour athletes, kayaking down a waterfall, an MMA fighter training for a match and a bat colony emerging from a Texas cave.

Figure 3.8 VRtually There.

As of mid 2018, they were in the midst of planning for the next year, speaking to corporate sponsors and figuring out the best way to grow, and iterate at scale. Hamlin says Season 3 will build upon the first two seasons. Instead of the variety-pack approach, Hamlin says they'd like to have multiple shows, "and each one of those shows has its own coherence."

Hamlin says taking on a 360 series with a weekly publishing schedule was "nuts." "It called upon a lot of my muscle memory, having done a lot of series for broadcast." He also tapped into a network of VR filmmakers and journalists, and worked to develop a network of freelancers around the country.

The team didn't stick to one camera or set-up; instead they went from the high end Nokio Ozo to the lower cost Nikon KeyMission and Ricoh Theta. The show had a partnership with GoPro and used the GoPro Fusion camera in addition to the others. As Hamlin says, it was a constant process of iteration, and learning, "Frankly, we're all discovering this at the same time," he says.

Story First

Hamlin argues that ultimately the story will dictate what the best approach will be. He also says the best 360 stories are chosen by asking: "Why is this a 360 story?" and "What is it about the character, the environment, or that activity that lends itself to filming in this format? In the first season, viewers can experience an F-18 takeoff on the USS Eisenhower—something difficult to experience as a flat story. Another segment features a group of slackliners who balance hundreds of feet above the ground in Sedona, Arizona, and a third shares the experience of floating above the ground with hot air balloonists for the world's largest balloon festival in Albuquerque, New Mexico.

Hamlin says that without thinking through why it is a 360 story, the creator may be frustrating the viewer and undermining the potential of the technology, "It's a straight up rigorous question you should ask yourself," he says.

The *VRtually There* experiences are flashy and exciting, though they do occasionally lack depth to the moment or story.

Like many others in the industry, Hamlin emphasizes it is still early in the grammar of this format. "We're figuring it out together, but at the same time it's really interesting watching it evolve, even over the course of one year," he says. For example, when Hamlin started, it was taboo to cut a shot shorter than 10 or 12 seconds because the general wisdom was that it would make people throw up. But by the end he felt more confident to cut after 3–4 seconds, "It really just depends on the content and the moment and the story you're trying to tell," he says.

Hamlin sees a lot of overlap between traditional video and 360 video. "It's still ultimately the same social contract with the audience: I'm going

Figure 3.9 VRtually There on YouTube.

to give you my time, and my eyeballs and my ears in exchange for a good story, well told."

Broad Audience on a Budget

VRtually There took a broad approach to publishing content. Each show was published on YouTube as well as the USA Today app, and Google Daydream.

They didn't optimize for one specific viewing mode, but made it accessible to be viewed on a headset, laptop, or magic window in an attempt to make it platform agnostic, "Call it business reality or tactical reality … if you want to maximize the number of people who watch this and have a satisfying experience and you want to try and build for multiple platforms," says Hamlin.

Watching multiple episodes, it's clear that 360 commercials have the obvious effect of prompting the viewer to stop watching. Depending on the format, some of the experiences can feel a bit too quick for watching on a desktop (more difficult to scroll around) and others, such as the roller-coaster ride, are a bit more motion-sickness-inducing when watched in a headset. Riding along on the longest zipline in a headset is a bit too much movement, but it is fine in a magic window or desktop. Other experiences—such as seeing Brutus the grizzly bear in VR, are great in all formats, even when he's a bit too close in the headset.

Hamlin was unable to share the budget, but he says they found a way to do things cost efficiently and effectively and ended up coming in under budget.

He hopes the examples and work he's done with *VRtually There* will push the creator conversation forward and help open 360 video to more audiences, "It shows you can do it, at scale. At an economic price point in a big institution."

Takeaways

Ask the right questions:
- "Why is this a 360 story?" and "What is it about the character, the environment, or that activity that lends itself to filming in this format?" Can be useful questions when deciding what stories to tell in 360.

Creating for the right viewing mode:
- It's difficult to create a piece that will work well on magic window, headset and desktop. Publishing for all these viewing modes at once makes for difficult compromises.

Multiple cameras:
- Having multiple cameras can come in handy for varying filming conditions.

Quick cuts:
- Some say quick cuts don't work, but *VRtually There* tried it out and found there are stories or moments when they do.

Not every moment is a story:
- An exciting 360 scene isn't necessary enough to draw in viewers; strong storytelling makes even quick videos more compelling.

About This Project

Publication: YouTube, USA Today App
URL: www.youtube.com/channel/UCSIgn1BzT9oD5E3pk9ceKvg
Interview Date: February, 2018
Interview Subject: David Hamlin, Executive Producer, *VRtually There*, USA Today

Notes

1 In June 2016 Vrse changed their name to Within. Henceforth it will be referred to as Within https://medium.com/@Within/welcome-to-within-c7d3daba2b55.
2 Milk, Chris. "How virtual reality can create the ultimate empathy machine," TED Talk, March 2015 www.ted.com/talks/chris_milk_how_virtual_reality_can_create_the_ultimate_empathy_machine/up-next.

3 Since then, the question of length has been pushed even further with examples such as the 40-minute VR experience by Felix & Paul called Miyubi.
4 Michelle Obama 360, The Verge, Mar 14, 2016. www.youtube.com/watch?v=0QY72R3ZDzw.
5 "Fossil Hunting in the Gobi," American Museum of Natural History, November 1, 2016. www.youtube.com/watch?v=HDdqd8c_-hY.
6 "The Modern Games," *The New York Times*. Graham Roberts, Yuliya Parshina-Kottas, Joe Ward, Evan Grothjan, and Bedel Saget. Sep. 20, 2016. www.nytimes.com/video/sports/100000004652044/the-modern-olympic-games.html.
7 Dwight, Logan. "These VR film tips show how to direct audience attention," Upload VR, July 14, 2016: https://uploadvr.com/vr-film-tips-guiding-attention/.

4   Walk-Around Virtual Reality

Storytelling is ultimately a creative act of pattern recognition. Through characters, plot and setting, a writer creates places where previously invisible truths become visible. Or the storyteller posits a series of dots that the reader can connect.

Douglas Coupland

Case Studies

Kiya, Emblematic Group
After Solitary, Emblematic and Frontline
Suite Life, Associated Press
Displaced Witness, ScanLAB Projects

Sit with a formerly incarcerated man in his current bedroom and listen as he describes what conditions were like in prison—then be transported to a prison cell and walk around within the cramped walls. Physically stand witness as refugees step off a boat on the coast of Lesvos.

Walk-around stories allow the viewer to move around in a fully 3-dimensional world. In this way the viewer can change perspective or get close to the action as they choose. It is also known as having six degrees of freedom: The ability to look in all directions as well as move freely in the virtual space.

We also refer to this type of experience in this chapter as "invisible visitor," because the user cannot affect the story or the scenery.

Another term sometimes used to describe the 3-dimensional worlds that make up these stories is **room-scale** VR, though that term is more descriptive of the viewing mode: a **headset** with tracking so the user can navigate (at least in part) by walking around within a confined area.

Depending on what hardware is used for viewing, these experiences aren't necessarily navigated by walking, either; it's often also possible to **teleport** using a controller or gestures.

Pieces of this type use 3D modeled objects, **DepthKit**, **photogrammetry**, scans of people or rooms, and animations to create a 3D **volumetric** story. Not many of these pieces exist, but they are becoming more common as the technology to create and view them becomes more accessible.

Case studies in this chapter are based on interviews with creators, and a look at technologies used to create 3D-rendered immersive stories— including 3D modeling software, game engines, and code libraries for browser-based experiences—and explore strategies for linear storytelling when the viewer is mobile within the scene. We look at how much freedom of movement each example offers, and how its creators made this decision, given the content. And we explore the challenges—technical and ethical—that come with re-creating true stories using 3D graphics.

Kiya

Emblematic Group
2015

Kiya was originally commissioned for Al Jazeera America as a VR companion to the show Fault Lines, for an episode on gun laws and domestic homicides in South Carolina. The story of domestic homicide is based on 911 audio, and it demonstrates a powerful use case in VR storytelling—putting the viewer in the middle of the action. It premiered in 2015 and was part of the inaugural VR section of the Sundance Film Festival in 2016.

Emblematic Group often looks for stories tied to larger themes. *Kiya* evolved, in part, out of Nonny de la Peña's desire to create a piece that dealt with domestic violence and guns.

"We hear and read stories about domestic violence so often but it brings a whole new dimension to this epidemic to actually be in the story with your own body," de la Peña says. "As a friend put it to me, 'Wow, I've never been in a room with someone holding a gun before' … that kind of a visceral impact can only be communicated using this kind of technology."

Despite the fact that *Kiya* is an older example of VR, Associate Producer Eren Aksu says, "we still show *Kiya*."

Built on 911 Audio

Zakiya Lawson, who went by Kiya, was murdered in her home on June 18, 2013 by her ex-boyfriend Peter Williams, who then shot and killed himself.

Kiya came home from the night shift that morning to find Williams waiting for her. She called her sisters Toni and Niki, and they drove to her house. On the way, they called 911. That's where the virtual reality experience begins—with the viewer standing on the side of the road in Lawson's tree-lined neighborhood in North Charleston, South Carolina as the white car Kiya's sister is driving passes by. The audio opens with the sound of the 911 operator speaking to one of her sisters.

About 30 seconds into the 7-minute experience, the viewer finds themself outside Kiya's home as her sisters pull into the driveway. Audio from their 911 call continues as they exit the car and approach Kiya's door. The audio has the quality of a 911 recording—the compression is noticeable, and louder sounds are blown out.

The team was drawn to Kiya's story, in part, because it had real audio attached that could be used as the basis for a VR experience. The recordings of Kiya's sisters' 911 calls were public record, and they form the main lattice for the piece. "We put you into those perspectives to really create a narrative," Aksu says of the 911 calls. The rest of the experience is built, as he describes it, "on top of that audio." He says all the sounds were from the call, except for the cars rolling up and doors closing, but also says these are more enhanced rather than added.

Just over a minute into the experience the viewer is teleported into Kiya's living room, where her sisters have walked in and Williams is threatening Kiya with a gun. Her sisters desperately try talk him down. The life-size 3D modeled characters stand close to each other, gesturing as they speak. The graphics are blocky and cartoonish, lacking some subtlety of movement, but the way they move feels natural.

From there, the perspective jumps several more times between the inside of the house and the front yard. Each transition brings the viewer along for a change in perspective, and while the viewer is placed and treated as an invisible bystander in each scene—just a little out of the way of the action—the narrative mostly follows the perspective of Kiya's sisters. They're both outside when the gun fires. The viewer, standing on the lawn, can see a flash from the first gunshot. They can hear Kiya's sisters' cries of horror and desperation as they call out for the police to help their sister and can see them double over in grief as the police officers tentatively approach the entrance to the house.

Emblematic chose to move the viewer outside and not show the moment when Kiya is shot, not only because they did not have any visuals to know exactly how that moment looked, but also because they felt showing that moment wasn't necessary to advance the story. "We put you outside of the house and let the brain fill in the rest, while also trying to keep the journalistic integrity," says Aksu.

The team also interviewed Kiya's two sisters and used crime scene photographs as well as original photos of outside of the house to recreate the environment. Aksu says the experience is accurate to the colors of the knives inside of the house. "If we didn't know something, we didn't make it up," he says, "ever."

Figure 4.1 Kiya, courtesy of Emblematic Group

From Audio to Motion Capture

Kiya took about three months to create—mostly because of the extensive **motion capture** process to recreate the events based on the 911 audio.

At the time Emblematic Group was working on the project, companies that could be hired to capture **volumetric video** (such as **8i**) weren't yet around in their current form. The team had to rely on motion capture applied to 3D modeled characters in computer graphics. Aksu says it was an expensive and time intensive process. "We learned that people can be more forgiving if you have real audio and realistic behaviour and unrealistic characters, even though it looks very game like," Aksu says. In order to create the motion capture they had to record people acting out the actions in real-time, and then clean up the movements and bring the footage into Unity to attach the actions to the body, and develop the face features.

While live volumetric video capture might seem like the obvious alternative and technological advancement, Aksu points out a current limitation of that technology is characters recorded in that way can't be interactive. Their motions are fixed to the recording, much like a video, while 3D models can be programmed to react to inputs, like video game characters.

Because of this, Aksu says that if there is a budget to make characters look realistic—which could be anywhere from $50,000 to $150,000 dollars per character—it may make sense to do motion capture. "I think there are times when using motion-capture created characters are way more powerful," Aksu says. It all depends on the specific scenario and the budget. Aksu says the budget for *Kiya* was in the $60,000–$100,000 range and much of it went towards the motion capture.

Rendering Reality in Computer Graphics

Prior to *Kiya*, Nonny de la Peña's *Hunger in LA* was one of the first journalistic examples using CGI to tell an immersive story. Since then Emblematic has continued to push the boundaries with 360 video, volumetric capture and innovative immersive content.

Questions of ethics around recreation, accuracy and truth invariably come up in conversations about Emblematic Group's work. While there is no way to know whether the recreated scenes are precisely accurate, it seems safe to say that they are as accurate as possible, relying on police records of the scene, audio of the calls, and witness testimony.

In the Middle of the Story

Kiya brings the viewer directly into the middle of a story as it happens. It was one of the first ones to "begin in the middle of the story and have you being immersed in a way it's not really possible in any other medium," says Aksu.

Some creators are careful about what is shown in VR, precisely because it can feel so realistic. One of the lessons from *Kiya* was that it's not always necessary to put the viewer in the middle of violence or the climax of the moment, "That's not the point of the story. It's not to show you that graphic moment, it's to have your brain fill in the gaps while also feeling empathy." As Aksu says, audio can sometimes be just as powerful as visuals, if you place specific actions the right way, in the right order.

Takeaways

Empathy and experience:
- The violence in *Kiya* is out of view; there's still room in VR to let the viewer fill in the gaps with their imagination while feeling empathy.

A convincing world:
- It's not all about graphics—natural motion of the characters and compelling audio are often more important than photorealistic imagery.

Teleporting cuts:
- Moving the VR user from one scene or place in a scene to another can have the effect of a film cut in changing perspective and driving the narrative forward.

About This Project

URL: http://emblematicgroup.com/experiences/kiya/,
www.youtube.com/watch?v=qYsAIukRqog
Publication Date: TED Women, 2015
Interview Date: February, 2018
Interview Subjects: Eren Aksu, Nonny de la Peña
Team: Executive Producer: Nonny de la Peña, Emblematic Group; Pat Mitchell, Al Jazeera America/TEDWomen
Producer: Nonny de la Peña, James Pallot, Michael Licht, Cassandra Herrman
Associate Producer: Julie Young/Eren Aksu
Sound Design: Source Sound, Inc.
Creative Director: Michael Licht
Lead Programmer: Fotos Frangoudes, William Hellwarth, Michael Licht
Animation: House of Mouse, Vincent Edwards
Artist: Metal Rabbit, Heavy Iron Studios, AXYZ Design, J. Marshall Pittman
Researcher: Adrienne Haspel
Actor: Lee Sherman, Toyin Moses, Tripp Pickell, Diana Toshiko

After Solitary

PBS Frontline and Emblematic Group
March, 2017

After Solitary begins with Kenneth Moore in his bedroom, recalling his experience in solitary confinement. Moore—convicted of aggravated assault, burglary and theft—was sent to Maine State Prison at 18 years old. Though he expected to serve an 18-month sentence, after fights and behavioral problems he was sent into solitary confinement. He ended up spending over five years in solitary, and nearly 20 years in and out of prison.

The experience is a 9-minute immersive **volumetric** video produced as part of a larger project with PBS Frontline and Emblematic Group. The walk-around story can be viewed on HTC Vive and Oculus headsets, and a 360 version is available on YouTube and Facebook. The immersive story serves as one component of a broader multimedia project, including a feature-length flat film called *Last Days of Solitary* in addition to other short text pieces.

Overall, the immersive project took about 6–8 months to create (including pre-production and post-production) and was part of a $580,000 Knight Foundation grant to push the boundaries of volumetric capture and serve as a case study for other organizations aiming to do similar projects. The case study includes three immersive films: one immersive documentary on climate change called Greenland Melting, a story about DNA collection at crime scenes, and After Solitary.

Figure 4.2 After Solitary, Courtesy of PBS Frontline and Emblematic Group.

Access and Understanding

Co-director and Frontline producer Lauren Mucciolo secured access to the prison to identify potential characters through her extensive work on the topic of solitary confinement. As co-director Cassandra Herrman says, *After Solitary* had an ideal storyline for VR because it was a first-person narrative. "It lends itself to this idea that you are stepping in someone else's shoes," she says. It was also a straightforward narrative which Herrman believes made it easier to understand, rather than piecing together what happened from multiple accounts of a story in the way *Kiya* (another walk-around project) did. And it's ideal because the cell space and the bedroom space fit well in the parameters of volumetric video, Herrman says.

The team initially had some difficulty getting access with someone who could tell their story, since former prisoners on probation are unable to leave their state. They needed the person to travel so they could be recorded with volumetric video capture and they wanted to do so at 8i studio in Los Angeles. Mucciolo had been in touch with Kenneth Moore, one of the people they had been in contact with for the original Frontline video documentary—though he didn't make it into the final version of that piece. Once he was out, Moore was open and willing to be interviewed, and he was able to travel outside of Maine.

Challenges in Volumetric Capture

Volumetric capture is a much more expensive, time-consuming and post-production intensive process than recording and editing 360 video. Creating the animations in 3-D immersive space requires use of a game engine such as Unity. For *After Solitary*, the processing of the live action captures (or holograms) was done by 8i, a production-company specializing in human holograms. They took about two weeks to create the visuals of Kenneth Moore—as Herrman says, the whole post-production process with Unity was "vastly more time consuming."

While 360 videos can be as simple as a one-shot piece capturing an interesting place or moment, graphically rendered stories like this tend to require more planning, and therefore more structure. In order for volumetric video to be successfully crafted into a narrative, creating a story with a script and **blocking** cues is a helpful process. "You really have to think of the physical space and why you are there, what you are doing with it and why you are setting the story there," Herrman says. The format of the solitary experience works because it uses the confines of the space.

Throughout *After Solitary*, the viewer is in the space with Moore as he talks about his experience there. Herrman believes the viewer doesn't want to be standing there doing nothing for too long. She says the story design was more like a play about Moore and his journey. Since he's the guide, it's uncomfortable to be left without him for too long.

The Emblematic and Frontline team hired Realities.io to do the photogrammetry of the cell and his bedroom. They then worked with 8i to capture the volumetric video of Moore and place him into the scanned bedroom and prison cell.

Since Herrman knew she had limited time with Moore in the 8i studio—just 40 minutes, otherwise the file size would be too large to work with—she created a shooting script and blocked out the scenes. Blocking out scenes as would be done in a theatre production ensured she would be able to work within the area of the scanned bedroom and prison cell. Additionally, Moore's placement would help guide the viewer's focus and advance the story along.

Prior to filming in the studio, Moore's wardrobe and props had to be pre-approved by the 8i team. Some of the clothing he wore on the day of the shoot turned out difficult to scan. Despite a long hat-related conversation they had beforehand, the hat he wore still caused problems. Herrman says the hat is more noticeable in the 360 video version, but also added, "If you are staring at the hat there is something wrong with the content."

In one scene, they wanted to make it appear as though Moore is sitting on the bed in a cell. In order to make this look real, they had to find something he could sit on that was the same height, to be able to position the hologram correctly on the bed.

Ideally, Moore's dialogue in each scene would be from a continuous take. Cutting from one place in the recording to another would be disorienting, as the viewer would see Moore's hologram abruptly shift. Instead of quick cuts like one might see in traditional video, in some scenes one can see the image of Moore fade away and reappear.

An additional challenge in volumetric capture is how to move the viewer's perspective within a scene, without jolting the viewer or making them sick. They decided to move the viewer's perspective by teleporting. Overall Herrman tried not to move the viewer around too much because it would be disorienting.

Eye Line

While Moore was great about riffing about his experiences, one challenge Herrman described with the hologram as a format is that it's very disconcerting to look at someone who is not looking at you.

Since Herrman and the team had already decided that the experience would be capturing Moore's memories in a contemplative way, they instructed Moore to look around the room as opposed to staring in one spot—this served to decrease the probability that the viewer would be in his direct eyeline and avoid the possibility that it would feel as though Moore was looking through the viewer.

Guiding the Viewer with Sound

When thinking through how to guide the viewer, Herrman primarily focused on light, audio and blocking. Since the space was limited, Moore could only be in certain areas. In one scene, where he describes fishing—passing something from one cell to another—the team observed many people watching failed to turn and see the visual action happening at the door with a note sliding underneath. As a result, they decided to repeat the sound cue of a note slipping under the door. Those sounds are followed by **spatialized sound** of a guard yelling, which causes most people to turn in the intended direction.

Towards the end, Moore talks about his family and needing motivation for change. During this scene family photos appear on one of the cell walls. Herrman says when they initially premiered at SXSW she was "horrified" because half the people missed the photos. To encourage the viewer to look, they added a bird sound by the window, which she says worked for most viewers.

The only time the viewer's placement changes is when they are teleported from inside the prison cell to outside. Using light, audio and sound, Herrman and the team subtly direct the viewer's attention. The transition sound of a door slamming is used to take the reader from inside to outside. "It's sort of a way to break up the fact that you are teleporting out. There's a slam and then you are on the outside," Herrman says.

Takeaways

Challenges of volumetric video:
- Volumetric video capture often requires filming in a specialized studio, limiting who can be recorded in this format if they are not able to travel to the site.

Pulling from theater:
* When designing a story in a walk-around environment, it can be useful to think of the characters as actors in a play, and the viewers as their audience.
* Before recording volumetric capture to be placed in a virtual environment, it helps to plan, or block, the movement of the character and the placement of the viewer based on that environment.

Limiting "cuts":
* When a character appears in volumetric video in a virtual environment, it's jarring to see their image skip, so interviews can't be cut together the way they could in traditional documentary film.
* Fading a character out and back in is one way to create a smooth transition in place of a cut.

Eye contact:
* To avoid the uncanny feeling of the character looking "through" the viewer, the directors instructed their interviewee to continuously look around the room, and not rest too long on any gaze.

Sound cues:
* When possible, repeating a sound cue gives viewers a second chance to follow the action.
* Sound cues are useful to ease the transition when teleporting the viewer—in this case, a door slamming coincides with movement from one space to another.
* The kind of sound can tell a viewer where to look—for example, the sound of birds can draw viewers to look toward a window.

About This Project

Publication: PBS Frontline, Emblematic Group
Published: Premiered at SXSW March, 2017
URL: http://emblematicgroup.com/experiences/solitary-confinement/
360 version on YouTube: www.youtube.com/watch?v=G7_YvGDh9Uc
Facebook version: www.facebook.com/frontline/videos/1015408097081 6641/
Interview Date: July 2017
Interview Subjects: Cassandra Herrmann, Lauren Mucciolo
Team: Cassandra Herrman, Co-director,
Co-director and reporter: Lauren Mucciolo
Executive producer: Nonny de la Peña
Executive producer: Raney Aronson

Suite Life

Associated Press
July 23, 2015

In *Suite Life*, the Associated Press gives the viewer an experience of the "super rich" by allowing them to explore the physical space of the most extravagant suites on land, in air and on the sea through *3D* environments, **volumetrically** captured using a depth-sensing camera from a company called **Matterport**. The piece is a journalistic adaptation of a technology and platform that primarily targets the real-estate industry for creating high definition tours of homes and buildings.

The interactive, accessible from a browser or on a Samsung Gear VR headset through the proprietary Matterport platform, allows the viewer to navigate around the Four Seasons penthouse ($50,000 a night), Singapore Airlines suites ($12–14,000 for a trip), and the Queen Mary 2 Duplex Suite ($20,000 for a 7-day transatlantic journey). Unlike many **room-scale** experiences running on a game engine, this piece—and everything hosted on the Matterport platform—confines users to a set number of points in the room between which they can navigate, rather than allowing them to explore freely.

On the landing page of the browser presentation of the story, a 2D photo shows one angle of the Four Seasons penthouse—it's clear from the beginning that a flat photo can only show so much. Embedded experiences viewable through a headset or on a desktop give the viewer the ability to be an invisible visitor into the space. The user can zoom in on details, navigate onto the balcony of the suite and get close to a window overlooking a beautiful view of the city.

"We're taking you to a space that you can't otherwise get to," AP reporter Scott Mayerowitz says. He adds that the project was specific to the time—with the economy beginning to bounce back after the 2008 recession, some people were spending extravagantly. As he says, the visuals "struck a chord as the wealth gap continues to grow despite the economic recovery."

Finding a Location-Based Story

This piece emerged in part because AP's digital team was trying to figure out something they could do in New York using the Matterport technology—but that also had some news value. Scott Mayerowitz was a travel and airline reporter working closely with the digital team and together they wanted to use the opportunity to experiment and to understand the immersive media space better.

When they first got the camera, they began practicing with it and using it in different contexts to get an understanding of what it could do.

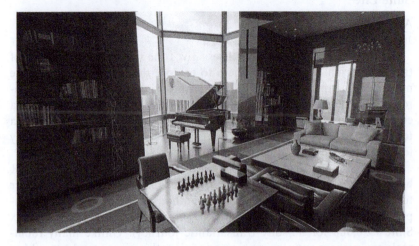

Figure 4.3 Suite Life, courtesy of Associated Press.

Some of their colleagues scanned a mock-up of the Seinfeld apartment that was part of an advertising stunt near their offices. Mayerowitz says the team came up with numerous ideas for shoots, but they had to narrow down to things that had news value. "We're a news organization—that's our primary mission. We can't just go out and shoot things because 'hey, it looks really cool.'"

At each location the team had a limited time to capture all the scans needed for the Matterport system to assemble a full 3-D image of the place. At the Four Seasons penthouse suite, the only location they were able to scout in advance, they had nearly the entire day. But they only had a few hours to shoot the Singapore Airlines and the Queen Mary suites. Mayerowitz notes that the Matterport captured incredible detail, but it was also tricky to maneuver through airport security.

The Matterport camera is remote controlled through an iPad app, which guides the user in capturing all the necessary shots to build a 3D model. For each location the team had to set-up the shot, connect to the iPad (which prompted the scanning app), hide, wait for the scan and then move the device to the next location. After capturing different locations within each space, all the scans were uploaded to Matterport's platform and stitched together. They then embedded the stitched version into an article explaining the project and rationale. Matterport shows two options for viewing—a "dollhouse" view or a "floorplan." The dollhouse shows the space, as seen from the outside or above, like a dollhouse, while the floor plan allows the viewer to jump into the space and move from one scanned point to the next.

Quick Turnaround Scanning

At the Four Seasons, the team didn't quite realize just how big a 4,300 square foot space is, and how hard it would be to capture all of the space. In the end they needed the full day. The depth-sensing Matterport camera has difficulty with reflective surfaces, and the suite was full of mirrors and other glossy, reflective decor. This meant they had to retake certain shots. "There were other instances where you might want to walk 10 feet to your next shot but the camera wouldn't let us because there was too much detail, and too much information," Mayerowitz says. For these moments they'd need to do an extra scan in certain places to make sure the software would be able to bring all the images together. The model they captured of the Four Seasons has the most vantage points because of the extra time they spent scanning different areas of the suite.

For the Singapore airlines shoot, they had barely two hours to shoot once the plane arrived, was cleaned and they were allowed on board. They wanted to show the viewer the seats upright, and be able to show the viewers upstairs in business class. "People still drool over this airplane," Mayerowitz says.

Their final shoot was the *Queen Mary 2*. And again they were challenged with a limited timeframe to get it all done. "We got in there and started shooting immediately—and raced through it," Mayerowitz says. They had some additional challenges with the lighting, curtains and figuring out where to hide while conducting the scans.

Limitations of Using 3D Models for Storytelling

Primarily used for real estate, Matterport's mission is to "establish 3D models as a primary medium for experiencing, sharing, and reimagining the world." Since 2015, news and entertainment media have been experimenting with how Matterport can be used for immersive exhibits of onsite locations. The experiments have been diverse—from The Detroit Free Press tour of an auto show under construction,[1] to The Daily Show using it to create an interactive walk through of a tongue-in-cheek temporary exhibit they called the "Donald J. Trump Presidential Twitter Library."[2]

The advantages to placing the viewer at these locations are clear: "You're able to put yourself in one of the seats, to see what it would be like ... No other 360 application brings you that same level of detail and ability to move around," Mayerowitz says of the Singapore Airlines immersive experience. Certain details would be extremely difficult to get without this format, but there are still very clear limitations for storytelling.

The immersive experience of each of the locations is fully self-guided. There's no one telling the viewer where to go, where they have been or when they have seen all of the 3D model. Thus, in the Four Seasons suite it's easy for the user to click around too quickly and get lost in the space.

The Matterport platform, rather than teleporting users from one place to another instantly, shows the scenery whooshing by as they fly from one place to another in the experience. If the points are too far away from one another it's difficult to navigate around and may cause motion sickness. Matterport isn't designed as a tool for journalists—so the integration of audio or other multimedia elements to build out context is an added challenge that many news organizations using Matterport have not delved into.

A final challenge for news creators is the size of the rig and the amount of time it takes to shoot something. Mayerowitz sees more potential use-cases for feature news situations dealing with travel, real-estate or construction, where the viewer naturally wants to have more time and a static sense of place.

Takeaways

"Cool" isn't enough:

- This piece made sense for a news organization because it creates an impressive experience but also speaks to a real issue: rising economic inequality.

VIP access:

- The *Suite Life* appeals in part because it gives users a first-person view of places only the super rich (and their staff) would otherwise have access to.

A little woozy:

- Flying through VR space to get from one place to another, rather than instantly teleporting, makes some users motion sick.

About This Project

URL: https://interactives.ap.org/2015/suite-life/
Interview Subjects: Scott Mayerowitz
Interview Date: January, 2018
Taxonomy: Invisible visitor, interactive, multimedia
Team: Darrell Allen, Nathan Griffiths, Peter Hamlin

Displaced Witness

ScanLab Projects
Exhibited at The Baltic, February, 2017

Displaced Witness is a collaborative VR installation by ScanLab Projects and Embassy for the Displaced—a design collective based in London, Athens and Lesvos—aiming to examine displacement from a new media lens. The piece was part of an exhibit at The Baltic Mill, a museum in England.[3]

Figure 4.4 Displaced Witness exhibition, courtesy of ScanLAB Projects.

Displaced Witness is a walk-around VR experience shown with the intention to "bear spatial witness to the people and landscape of Lesvos," says Matthew Shaw, director and co-founder of ScanLab Projects. It presents four different scenes created through **Lidar** scans of Lesvos, with raw wind-swept audio accompanying the piece. In the installation, the viewer stands in a room with four different squares with added sensory props on the floor—such as pebbles, rocks and life jackets—that represent the terrain in each scene.

During the course of the experience, the viewer meets three groups of people: a volunteer on the beach, a group of volunteers at a lighthouse and a pair of Iranian refugees. While there are people who have been scanned into the environment, they are completely static. "They're like these frozen casts of a moment in time," Shaw says. The viewer can take their time within the experience to go to each of the four locations, but to hear all of the stories takes about 15 minutes.

The Breaking Point of Scans

ScanLab Projects is a team of architects, artists, CG artists, software developers, photographers who are all collaboratively experimenting with new mediums. They came across Lidar scanning as a way of digitizing small objects Shaw says. The Lidar scanning process has made modeling and recreating spaces less laborious.

"We did quite a lot of work where we're explaining the relationship between spaces ... a whole series of hidden underground aqueducts underneath Rome," Shaw says. This is an example that is incredibly difficult to understand by standing on a street, without the scanned perspective.

"Our education has taught us to understand a tool to its breaking point and a breaking point is where you get creativity and unexpected things happening and all that sort of stuff," Shaw says.

Creating Immersion through Scans

Using Lidar scanners with a "few adjustments," the team scanned people (this took about 3–4 minutes) and conducted interviews for about 10 minutes in different locations. Depending on the location, they spent additional time documenting the entire surroundings.

Capturing different parts of the experience took longer than others— the scene focusing on life-vests, with terrain covered in huge piles of discarded vests, took closer to half a day. After scanning and speaking to many different groups, the final scene selection happened much later, after returning from the Lesvos trip.

They then used Unity to put all of these elements together. Though the scans are static, Shaw says: "We would argue it is as powerful, if not more powerful than a person who is actually moving there, who is actually talking to you and lip synched."

Overall Shaw says the project took about three-months of work spread out over a nine-month period. At the time, they didn't have a venue or

Figure 4.5 Displaced Witness, courtesy of ScanLAB Projects.

final product in mind for what would be done with the footage. As Shaw recalls, the opportunity to exhibit at the Baltic Mill arose, and after reflecting on the data they spent an intense two months finishing post production. An online version is not available. "For us the relationship between the tactile landscape and the virtual experience is key," Shaw says of the on-site exhibit.

Alessandro Vincentelli was Curator of the exhibition at BALTIC Centre for Contemporary Art which ran January through May 2017.[4] Vincentelli says the project was seen by 78,000 people and was a special installation to host in part because it provoked conversations with visitors.

Takeaways

Scanning for efficiency:

* ScanLab projects uses Lidar scanning to capture spaces and people in part because it is less laborious than other techniques for creating immersive spaces.

Tactile connection:

* Displaced witness was only available as a site-specific installation because the creators felt that a tactile experience of it was essential to create the experience.

About This Project

URL: http://scanlabprojects.co.uk/work/displaced-witness/
https://vimeo.com/218628035
Interview Date: July, 2017
Interview Subject: Matthew Shaw
Team: Matthew Shaw, William Trossell, Stefanos Levidis, Soma Sato, Reuben Carter
James White, Egmontas Geras

Notes

1 Detroit Free Press. "Take a virtual 3D tour of the Detroit auto show under construction," January 8, 2015. www.freep.com/story/money/cars/detroit-auto-show/2015/01/08/detroit-auto-show-3d-virtual-tour-360/21346765/.
2 The Daily Show, Comedy Central. "The Daily Show Presents: The Donald J. Trump Presidential Twitter Library," July, 2017. www.cc.com/shows/the-daily-show-with-trevor-noah/trump-twitter-library/tour.
3 "What's On. Disappearance at Sea, Mare Nostrum." Baltic Art. January 27 to May 14, 2017. www.balticmill.com/whats-on/disappearance-at-sea-mare-nostrum.
4 "What's On. Disappearance at Sea, Mare Nostrum." Baltic Art. January 27 to May 14, 2017. www.balticmill.com/whats-on/disappearance-at-sea-mare-nostrum.

5 Immersive Interactives

> *It is easy to force a reader or viewer to interact. The trick is in making them want to interact, and in letting the story unfold hand-in-hand with that.*
>
> *(Dave Morris)*

Case Studies

Discovering Gale Crater, L.A. Times
Is the *NASDAQ* in Another Bubble?, *Wall Street JournalTestimony,*
    Zohar Kfir
UTURN, NativeVR
Blackout, Scatter

Ride along a on virtual roller coaster based on the NASDAQ's steep climbs and precipitous falls, explore the surface of Mars, attend a "virtual support group" for sexual assault survivors, or cut your own script of a story told from two perspectives at once. Immersive interactives can take on a multitude of styles.

In the context of immersive storytelling, interactivity is a broad term meaning that the viewer has the ability to trigger events or make changes within an immersive environment. Because the user can influence what they see, pieces in this form tend to diverge from traditional narrative and are often non-linear. In most cases, each viewer will have a different experience from the next.

Interactives can be anything from mostly linear stories that require a defined set of user interactions to free-form pieces in which the viewer discovers the story by exploring an environment. This chapter looks at projects with varying levels of interactive freedom and very different applications of that power.

With each case study, we'll look at how creators choose interactive features based on content. We'll also explore the tension inherent in trying to convey a defined set of information while letting the user control how the story unfolds.

The people who created projects featured in this chapter each have different reasons for incorporating interactivity. One creator wanted to allow viewers to take a break from emotionally charged content; another was interested in giving viewers the freedom to make discoveries on their own. Several mentioned that interactivity promotes a kind of active viewing that increases the viewer's sense of immersion.

In general, creators of interactives choose to structure their pieces this way because they see handing over some power to the viewer as enhancing engagement. As we explore interactive pieces across the spectrum from linear narrative to free-form exploration, we'll look at the different circumstances that call for each of these styles in a virtual-reality project.

Discovering Gale Crater

L. A. Times
October 2015

As Armand Emamdjomeh, the journalist and programmer who created *Discovering Gale Crater*, describes it, the inspiration for the piece was pretty apparent: "We have these satellite photos of the surface of Mars. Wouldn't it be cool to fly around it?"

Len de Groot, director of data visualization for the Los Angeles Times and a self-described "data pack rat," had been holding on to a set of elevation data from NASA depicting the surface of Mars for about a year before he and Emamdjomeh decided they could move forward with a project. The virtual-reality tour of Gale Crater—the 96-mile diameter crater that the Curiosity Rover has been exploring since it landed there in 2012—was a proof-of-concept and a learning process in how the newsroom could create web-based VR experiences.

But this piece isn't just designed for wow factor or virtual tourism—it falls firmly into the category of data visualization, as the piece is rendered based on detailed elevation data and satellite imagery. Its creators were thinking hard about what immersive media had to add in terms of data visualization. De Groot has a litmus test rooted in thinking about infographics: "Can you help people understand in a way that would be hard to understand otherwise?"

Several years since the piece was released, it continues to be one of very few examples of **WebVR** experiences created by a journalistic organization. It is built with HTML, CSS and JavaScript. It relies on some **open-source** code as building blocks, is itself open-source, and stands out because it is an immersive interactive viewable through open web applications rather than a proprietary player or game engine.

A Guided Tour on Mars

As *Discovering Gale Crater* opens, the viewer sees the title page of the project over a reddish martian landscape with the Gale Crater at the center of the field of view. The viewer has the option to "Tour" or "Explore."

Taking the tour option triggers a guided experience that feels almost like traveling on rails, zooming across the scenery to see eight labeled locations. At each point in the tour, the voice of NASA's Fred Calef (who was also the source of the data, and is known as "Keeper of the Maps" at the Mars Science Laboratory) explains what the viewer is seeing. There is otherwise no sound in the experience.

When the viewer chooses to explore, they are given a set of keyboard controls on a desktop that allows a wide range of motion. In the mobile version, the viewer controls where they are looking by tilting or turning their phone or headset. They can control start and stop with a single button or a tap on their headset, and their location in the experience otherwise travels toward wherever they have set their gaze.

The eight points of interest that are highlighted in the roughly 3-minute tour are also available to find through free exploration. Here, a click or **gaze** triggers the audio explanation.

Technology behind the Experience

Emamdjomeh says it took some time to learn the fundamental coding skills—mainly with Javascript—that allowed him to work on this project. "I think if I tried to do this a year or two before, I would have just gotten lost," he says. He came into the project with knowledge of mapping concepts and web development, and learned along the way how to use code to manipulate graphics in 3D space.

In the "How We Did It" article[1] published shortly after the project was released, Emamdjomeh described in detail the tools he and the team used to build it. One of the big challenges he faced was keeping the frame rate of the content up. In gaming and interactive graphics, frame rate refers to how often a new image is rendered, and it's essential that it be high enough for the motion to look smooth. That's a difficult thing to achieve when trying to make a project available across devices, some of which will have limited graphics processing capability. But if the frame rate is too slow, an experience can start to feel unresponsive, and it can make the user dizzy or nauseous. Emamdjomeh says they were aiming for a 60 frames-per-second target. The final product tends to render at about 50 to 55 frames per second.

One trick they used to reduce the amount of processing required was by creating two sets of graphics to represent the ground. The first is the ground the viewer sees. The second is an invisible element, commonly used in gaming, called a "collision detector." It approximates the shape of the ground and functions like an invisible fence, making it impossible for the viewer to go through the ground in the simulation. Separating it out the meant that it could be a less detailed shape than the surface the viewer sees, and this made it much easier to use in calculations.

Another trick more commonly used by data visualization creators and web developers was to scale down the level of detail of the image based on the device that would be displaying it. On a mobile phone, the experience will have the same behavior as on a desktop, but the graphics will look blockier. The polygons that make up the shapes will be more evident.

Game or Story? Navigation Design and Cueing the Viewer

While Emamdjomeh was working on coding the project, he and de Groot were also going back and forth on the storytelling elements of the piece. They decided early on—once they had the first rendering of the 96-mile wide Gale Crater—that they would need to offer a guided tour to help viewers understand what they were seeing. But they also wanted to let the viewer navigate, because people would likely feel cheated if they didn't get to explore the 3D model on their own.

Emamdjomeh says the creative process for this project prompted him to think about the way data visualization in virtual reality can learn from video game design. "The language for navigation in 3D space already exists in games so it makes sense to adopt those concepts," he wrote in his making-of article. In fact, the controls in the desktop version are borrowed from PC-gaming standards.

He points at the way the best video games—many of which already operate in 3D space if not in virtual reality—very rarely put their audience in a situation in which they have no instructions for what to do next. But there are more and less graceful ways to orient the viewer. Careful and minimal instructions can be helpful; too much information can get in the way.

That's not a principle that's unique to gaming, though; Emamdjomeh says in creating interactive data visualizations—3D or not—choosing how to incorporate instructions takes a lot of consideration. Much like a VR environment without context can be overwhelming to a viewer, a large amount of data, even if beautifully presented, doesn't tell a story without careful thought about its presentation.

Emamdjomeh also thinks in terms of **affordances**, a term used in game-design to refer to actions the user believes are possible. It's a design layer above simply making something possible. A handle, for example, could indicate to a user that an object can be picked up. Without that, they might not try.

In the case of Gale Crater, the tour serves to orient the viewer to the environment and give a sense of the possible range of movement before they begin to roam on their own.

The Sound of Space

One piece of data that was not available for the Gale Crater project was the sound of the environment. Emamdjomeh says he went back and forth on whether to include sound in the experience, but had ethical concerns about crossing the line at which reconstructing something turns into "just making it up." In the end, he decided against including any kind of ambient sound.

Emamdjomeh says if he could do the project again, he would try it with background sound to strengthen the immersive effect. He says he would research what the surface of Mars could plausibly sound like and use that to choose the audio.

Sound isn't the only place where a the question of creative license came into play on this project, either. Natural terrain can look really flat in a graphical rendering, so it's common for developers to exaggerate heights: "That's something we did here," Emamdjomeh says, "so why would sound be any different?"

Developing for All

It was still the early days of **WebVR** in 2016 when Gale Crater came out. In addition to some helpful **libraries** for creating 3D graphics, an open source code repository called WebVR Boilerplate,[2] created by developer Boris Smus, made it possible for the piece to work across browsers—the majority of which didn't have built-in VR capability when this project was created.

Even with those tools, the project took somewhere between two and three months of solid work for Emamdjomeh to build. But then, he and de Groot didn't choose the easiest way to create this project. They could have gotten it done faster using a proprietary gaming engine and releasing for high-end headsets. But they agree it was worth the extra effort to make the project available to a general audience without the need for specialized hardware. The *L.A. Times* is a general interest publication, de Groot emphasizes, and their objective is to create projects that are accessible to the widest possible audience.

In addition, the open-source code and thorough documentation lays the groundwork for other teams—at the *L.A. Times* and beyond—to build upon this project without having to purchase expensive software or be locked into a particular platform.

Emamdjomeh thinks he could create this project or something like it much faster after having done it once—but he says he would still have to measure the amount of work against the story, and any future VR project would need to be the right content to merit the effort.

Takeaways

Accessibility takes time:

* The advantage of using WebVR is democratization of access to the project without specialized hardware or software; the disadvantage is it takes longer to develop projects that work on many browsers and devices.

Learning from games:
- In interactive experiences, it's important to clearly signal to users which interactions are possible in the virtual world.
- The best games and interactives rarely put their audience in a situation in which they have no instructions for what to do next—but giving instructions that are intuitive and unobtrusive takes a lot of thought.

Two options to explore:
- Offering a tour of an interactive space can help orient users and deliver important information, while free exploration satisfies the desire to self-direct.

Surrounded by data:
- Immersive media can offer a different lens on data visualization by adding a spatial element.

The ethics of sound:
- The makers of *Gale Crater* chose not to invent ambient sound for the surface of mars. For journalistic applications, it's an ethical decision whether to create a soundscape.

About This Project:

URL: http://graphics.latimes.com/mars-gale-crater-vr/
Interview Date: July 12, 2017
Interview Subjects: Armand Emamdjomeh, Len De Groot
Created by: Armand Emamdjomeh, Len de Groot

Is the *Nasdaq* in Another Bubble?

A Virtual Reality Guided Tour of 21 Years of the Nasdaq

Wall Street Journal
April 23, 2015

Roller coasters in virtual reality were a popular idea around the time 360 video became available on major platforms such as YouTube and Facebook. Given the ability of erratically moving immersive experiences to trigger adverse vestibular responses, they're not for the faint of stomach.

But the *Nasdaq* VR roller coaster is not your standard thrill ride—it's an interactive **WebVR** data visualization that allows the user to see and feel the dot-com bubble burst of 2000, the 2008 recession, and the eventual recovery, with all the turbulence along the way. The Nasdaq serves as the U.S.'s second-largest stock exchange and an indicator of

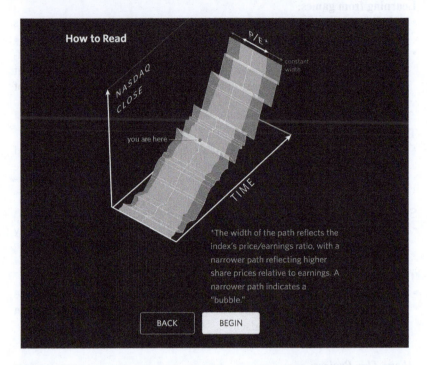

Figure 5.1 How to understand the Nasdaq, courtesy of *Wall Street Journal*.

the strength of U.S. markets—especially tech. The *Wall Street Journal* released the project to coincide with the index hitting its highest mark in more than 15 years—finally reaching full recovery after the 2000 crash.

While some who don't follow the stock market may need to watch the experience several times to understand the basics, the genius of this piece is that it makes stock market movement—an abstract and sometimes alienating topic—feel concrete, informative and fun (a roller coaster!).

The Right Time

Both creators on the *Nasdaq* VR project—Roger Kenny and Ana Asnes Becker, were fascinated by VR. Becker had tried the Oculus headset and been to a data journalism conference (NICAR) discussing graphics and immersive experiences.

Kenny had been working with *Wall Street Journal*'s interactive graphics department for four years when he began experimenting with visualizing data in an immersive environment. He was inspired in part by the release of Google cardboard in June 2014. Kenny began with experiments in combining the D3 and three.js (Javascript libraries for data visualization and 3D graphics, respectively) and put together a rough prototype to

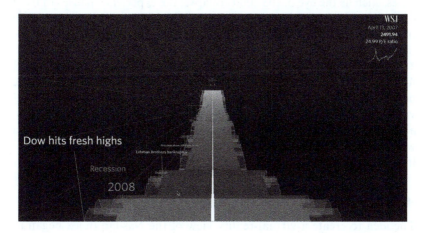

Figure 5.2 The Nasdaq as a roller coaster, courtesy of *Wall Street Journal.*

show to his editors at WSJ. "It sort of dawned on me that—I could really do something with this and it could be tangible," Kenny said. While there was some resistance, there was enthusiasm for the concept as well. As he recalls, one editor basically said: "I don't care what happens, just build this thing."

Kenny had originally envisioned creating a tour of this type based on the Dow Jones Industrial Average. But the project evolved into the *Nasdaq* VR roller coaster because right around the time he began experimenting with VR graphics it became very likely that the index would climb to a pre-2000 high. As a result, the question on many people's minds was: "Is the Nasdaq in another bubble?" In an effort to answer this question, the immersive experience allows the viewer to ride the sometimes-precipitous slopes of the stock-market line chart.

A Bumpy Ride

Prior to seeing the roller coaster, the viewer clicks through several screens of basic instructions for navigating the interactive in different viewing modes (desktop, mobile, *cardboard*) and interpreting the graphics: "The width of the path reflects the index's price/earnings ratio, with a narrower path reflecting higher share prices relative to earnings. A narrower path indicates a 'bubble.'"

Advancing through each of these brings the viewer to a starting position, where they can begin the bumpy ride along two decades of Nasdaq index values, represented by height. Along the sides of the roller coaster, callout lines mark years, and highlight notable dates in history, such as Yahoo's value rising 154% after its IPO in 1996. At several especially significant dates, such as the eve of the 2000 collapse, the experience pauses in front of text cards that provide context. The user must select an arrow on each of these text cards to continue. At the end of the ride, the user is given the option to ride the coaster again, at regular or "rocket" speed.

Kenny says the whole purpose of the project was not just using VR for the sake of it, but actually having a reason for being in VR. The hope is that by experiencing the data—and the undulations of it— viewers will understand it viscerally. It may take a few repeat rides to absorb much of the contextual information that flies by, but taken as a whole the piece provides a spatial, experiential angle into understanding a complex topic.

A Deadline Roller Coaster

The idea to create a virtual-reality view of the Nasdaq index began as more of a "floating pipe in the sky" concept, as Becker recalls. They also thought about possibly having a host explain the data. After a meeting with Kenny, Becker says the idea sprung into her head to make it more of a roller-coaster experience.

The team had an unusual publication window for the *Nasdaq* VR project: Because of the question the project asked, it would need to go out on the date or within days of the Nasdaq reaching 5048.62 (the highest level before the 2000 crash) for the *Wall Street Journal* to publish it. "It was really a mess," Kenny says of trying to finish a complicated project in time for an unknown publication date, "It was kind of like your worst nightmare because it's a wholly unproven technology."

As Kenny recalls, the publication date got pushed back a few times because the Nasdaq didn't actually hit the mark when they thought it would. Both Kenny and Becker were content with the project as it came out, but Kenny also said the original version used close to 6 gigabytes of RAM, though he has fixed that since the initial publication.

Accessible, Comprehensible, Informative

Because the goal was to reach as broad a target audience as possible, Kenny and Becker didn't want users to be forced to download an app. As a result, they chose to make it accessible in a browser on desktop, on mobile and also made it available to be viewed with a cardboard headset. After months of experimenting with concepts, it took the team an intense few weeks to put the piece together once they got the green light.

Becker says she spent a significant amount of time trying to design efficient instructions, especially since few people were familiar with watching using cardboard. Though they didn't have much time to think about the pace of the roller coaster ride, they wanted to have an experience that would not make someone sick. Kenny applied smoothing to the animation so the ups and down would not be too abrupt.

For the overall speed of the roller coaster, they wanted to make sure a user would be able to read the information as it went by. When thinking about guiding the viewer, they let the roller coaster metaphor guide how users would be looking and interacting.

Kenny believes the power of data in this medium is the ability to connect and gain a better understanding of dense or complicated data sets in a way that no other medium can. "This is the first time in history that we've actually been able to manipulate our 3-D environment in a way that actually speaks to the capacity of the human brain," Kenny says. Describing how the ability to view multiple data points in an immersive environment can give viewers and regular people "superpowers to connect with data."

The Right Data Story for VR

For Becker, one of the strongest aspects of VR is that the creator is able to garner visceral or emotional responses, such as being in an environment where you are standing on a line chart versus looking at it. Yet Becker is cautious about telling data stories in VR: "Using VR to tell a story with data isn't necessarily the best way," Becker says. It can be more difficult to read in VR thus—"it may make your graphic less legible rather than more," she says.

Her advice to others is to keep it simple: "Keep the story simple—keep the mechanics simple." She added that sometimes adding complexity can take away from the story you are trying to tell. Becker hopes creators use VR in more thoughtful ways, instead of making projects in VR because it is seen as cool. "[Working in VR] makes it harder to create stuff, but I think the product is more rewarding," she says.

Looking back at the project, the team feels the strength of the content meant it could withstand the test of time. Kenny has since moved from the interactive graphics desk to the Dow Jones innovation lab, where the mandate for the scope of his projects is to "experiment and solve problems and foster an environment of creativity and innovation." More recently the team has been tackling augmented reality. But before he moved, he was thoughtful enough to share the tools he used for the *Nasdaq* VR piece in a write-up for Storybench.[3]

The *Wall Street Journal Nasdaq* VR experience received positive reception and an award for innovation in visual digital storytelling at the 2015 Online News Association Awards. Becker says she was excited that people seemed to get the point, specifically at the peak in 2000 where there's the feeling of ascending to the top of a roller coaster and thinking: "Wow, that's a long way down."

Takeaways

A cognitive advantage:
- Visualizing data in an immersive 3D environment can give viewers a new way to connect with and comprehend it.
- The creators of the *Nasdaq* roller coaster looked for VR data use cases that can generate a "visceral" or "emotional" response.
- Looking down a steep drop from the top creates a more immediate mental/physical response than looking at that slope on a line chart.

Keep it simple:
- It can be difficult to read in VR; complex data sets that rely heavily on text can become less legible in immersive space.
- Keeping the mechanics simple helps keep an experience comprehensible.

Not too bumpy:
- The makers of the *Nasdaq* roller coaster applied some smoothing to the coaster. They wanted a visceral response, but they didn't want to make people sick.

One less hurdle:
- Creating the project with WebVR for browsers meant a wide audience of people could experience it without having to download an app.

About This Project

URL: http://graphics.wsj.com/3d-nasdaq/
Interview Date: August-September, 2017
Interview Subject: Ana Asnes Becker, Roger Kenny
Team: Roger Kenny and Ana Asnes Becker

Testimony

Zohar Kfir, Selena Pinnell, Kaleidoscope VR, Evolving Technologies Corp.
March 2017 (Tribeca), November 2017 (WebVR)

"*Testimony* is the project that I always wanted to produce," says Zohar Kfir, the artist behind the experience. The piece, which was executive produced by Kaleidoscope VR and supported by Oculus, features the stories of five sexual assault survivors, told in their own words.

Testimony is informed by Kfir's professional experience. As a gallery artist and experimental filmmaker, she has training in thinking about physical environments and storytelling that lends itself to working in immersive space. She says virtual immersive space can easily simulate a gallery: "It's just like a big white cube that you can do whatever you want to," she says. "It's like a clean slate." The project is also motivated by her personal experience. She is herself a survivor.

According to RAINN (Rape, Abuse & Incest National Network), the anti-sexual violence organization that tracks U.S. statistics, 1 in 6 American women and 1 in 33 American men have been the victim of an attempted or completed rape in their lifetime. That is to say, sexual assault survivors worldwide make up a substantial audience all on their own—and, in large part, that's who Kfir made this project for. She imagines it functioning as a virtual support group and a chance for more survivors to tell their stories as part of the healing process, despite a system that all too often silences them.

In 2016, Kfir was invited to participate in DevLab, a VR incubator program for artists put on by Kaleidoscope VR and Oculus, and she already had a pretty clear idea of the project she wanted to pitch there. She wanted to build something non-linear and interactive that would allow viewers to create their own story. She believes that viewers engage more deeply with a subject or story when they are able to exercise some control in their experience, or as she puts it, engage in "active viewing." And she wanted to use immersion to elevate the receptivity of her audience. She says she was thinking of VR less as a tool for intimacy, and more as a medium that demands a certain commitment from the viewer: "I really wanted people to confront being face-to-face with an assault survivor and listen, to really resonate with the testimony," Kfir says.

The final piece, which premiered at the 2017 Tribeca Film Festival, works on Oculus and Gear VR headsets.

In late 2017, Kfir expanded the project into a WebVR platform available in a browser and opened it up to allow survivors to share their own stories. Her goal is for the platform to function as a multimedia resource hub—an online database of survivor stories. The stories there are told in VR but also in text, for those who aren't comfortable revealing their identities. This case study focuses primarily on the original VR version released at Tribeca, though the conclusions in many cases apply to both versions.

From 2D to Immersive

As *Testimony* opens, the viewer is in a black space, surrounded by 25 black-and-white circular images of survivors looking toward them. The faces were recorded in 2D video, and within the sphere, they are angled toward the viewer. There are five people in total, and five images of each of those people. Wavy white lines connect the portrait images of each survivor. Each portrait image is one of five nodes that make up that person's story.

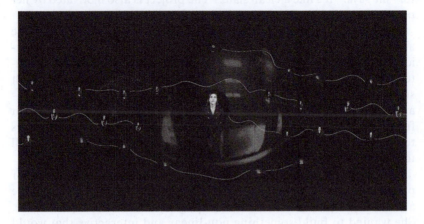

Figure 5.3 Testimony, courtesy of Zohar Kfir.

The interactivity of the piece is triggered by the viewer's **gaze**. When the viewer fixes their gaze on a portrait, that video begins, and as the person begins speaking, the video grows larger, filling the field of view. If the viewer follows one survivor's string of nodes from left to right they will hear a semi-chronological version of that person's story.

This design made for broad potential for publishing across devices, since all headsets at the time of release in April 2017 had at minimum gaze tracking, even if they didn't have any other controls. Each video is triggered organically by the user's interest. "When you're not interested to watch it anymore, or if you feel like it's too emotional, you can easily just move your head and move to either another testimony or just take a moment to breathe," she says, "empowering viewers to make their own decisions and become active participants with complete agency in the experience."

The piece doesn't impose any particular order for the videos; the viewer is free to hop around between nodes. As the viewer turns their head away from a node they were watching, that video retreats and the sound fades out.

Production Process

The final presentation for *Testimony* holds true to the original mockups that Kfir created. To realize this vision, she brought in additional collaborators.

Kaleidoscope VR offered creative support and helped her find funding. She collaborated closely with Selena Pinnell, the organization's creative director, who is also one of the survivors featured in the story.

Kfir conducted all the interviews herself, capturing them on flat video that was placed in the sphere—and from the nine original interviews she chose five stories to include in the initial project. She says all of the interviews she collected were powerful, but the five she chose were the most diverse and fit the best together for the project she was trying to create.

Kfir says she only lightly edited the survivor interviews because their stories were so personal. She would have felt uncomfortable editing with a heavy hand, but she adds that she was amazed at how the survivors all knew how to tell their stories very clearly and precisely. She believes it's because survivors carry their stories for such a long time that they have a clear sense of how they want to tell them, and how they want to be represented. When the video does cut, television-like static washes over it for the moment of transition.

Two developers—Loren Abdulezer and Christopher LoBello of Evolving Technologies Corporation—helped turn Kfir's vision of these stories into reality, using the game engine **Unity** to build a 360 interactive presentation.

The most difficult part of the production process, Kfir says, was figuring out how to arrange the nodes of the story in immersive space without having them feel crowded or overly static. She wanted to create a way for the viewer to naturally discover the story threads and move around as they took in the different testimonies—but she didn't want viewers to overlook any pieces of content. The team tried having four quadrants for the content, but that version ended up looking static and boring. Another attempt had all the nodes connected by a single line that spiraled from the bottom of the sphere to the top.

A third version, which Kfir calls a "more magnetized" look, had the nodes clustered more tightly around the forward-facing visual field, leaving the space directly behind the viewer empty. Ultimately, they chose to have the nodes wrap around the full 360 space, creating a narrative thread for each survivor. "It was the best iteration that we could fit everything together and it seemed organic and correct, and it was like a big a-ha moment," she says.

For each different possible arrangement they imagined, Abdulezer and LoBello coded an algorithm to mathematically work out the spacing. The final product is a platform that takes media—video files and sound files—plus time codes that tell it when to trigger certain actions, and arranges the content in immersive space.

A Comfortable Listening Environment

Each of the survivor's narratives is accompanied by its own score. In some, supporting imagery and sounds are triggered in the background at certain points in the story—for example, audio and video footage of a person walking over gravel. Each piece also has white smoke rising against the black background with constellation-like geometry. The animations accentuate the stories and give a dreamlike experiential quality to the narratives. Kfir describes the design of the visual environment, the interaction and the sound as "floaty." She says the design decisions she made were all intended to foster a "comfortable listening environment."

For the sound design, Kfir hired Josephine Wiggs, a musician who had scored some of her previous work, and asked that she design audio for the piece as a whole—Wiggs wrote a 6-minute track, which loops during the experience, as well as the scoring specific to each person. The music is subtle, but it creates a tone throughout the piece and amplifies the immersive effect.

From Headset to WebVR

There was also a downside for Kfir to making this project immersive, in that building it in virtual reality at the time of its initial release meant it would only reach a limited audience: the original piece was only available for those with a VR headset.

"When it came to questions around VR and access, measuring impact and dissemination, it was obvious to me that *Testimony* needed to expand beyond the headset and become platform agnostic in order to reach wider audiences," Kfir says.

The **WebVR** version of *Testimony* is viewable on a computer screen (with mouse navigation), a mobile device, and in a **cardboard** headset. It carries over much of the design from the original piece, but it's adapted for scalability. It was developed by the design firm Dpt., and is built using Wordpress for content management and **A-Frame**, a web framework for building virtual reality sites that work across devices.

Rather than being broken into multiple nodes, each of the video testimonies is presented as a single piece about 15 minutes long. The platform also supports text and audio testimonies. Audio testimonies appear as a floating sine wave animated into the 3D environment, and text testimonies are clickable quotes that open as a window with scrollable text. As of May 2018, the platform had 17 video testimonies, two expert interviews and one text testimony, with new audio testimonies soon to be added.

To help accommodate a growing database of stories, the web version gives viewers the ability to filter the stories by different tags—such as "acquaintance rape", "campus rape" and "childhood sexual abuse"— that are visible when looking directly downward in the experience.

Unlike the original **Gear VR** version the site is participatory—people can submit their own stories in text audio or video. For the time being, Kfir and Selena Pinnell have been doing the filming of the additional videos to keep them visually consistent—and because they've found that, as survivors, they're able to help the people tell their stories that way.

Kfir says they are also working to create a dynamic infographic of all the data gathered from people who submit their stories to the site—with details such as year, location and type of abuse.

Figure 5.4 Testimony, courtesy of Zohar Kfir.

Audience and Artistic Vision

While *Testimony* was released for a general audience, it's created with survivors in mind. In this way its content differs from most media; its characters are also its primary target audience. The piece is not meant to be about the details of sexual assault, but rather about the road to recovery. As a survivor, Kfir is close to the concept and also has a deep personal sense of the power of healing through storytelling. She was careful to allow the people featured in this piece to control their own stories, by giving them the freedom to tell them however they chose. She also gave each person the option to have their story removed from the project at any time, for any reason.

The project, despite its challenging content, has a gentle feel to it, and Kfir says she sees it as a virtual support group and symbolic of a wider network of survivors. After experiencing the finished project for the first time, one of the people featured in it told Kfir she was amazed at how much she felt the presence of the other survivors, none of whom she had met in person.

Testimony *as Education*

In October 2017, she launched a college campus tour and began promoting *Testimony* as an educational tool.

"The feedback and people's reactions to *Testimony* constantly surprise me," she says. "I'm amazed how watching the work really opens people up, how it creates a soft spot for discussion about sexual assault."

Kfir says a lot of students who have seen the project are amazed at its effectiveness, and for some the experience is cathartic—often leading to emotional conversations about misconceptions people have about sexual assault and PTSD recovery. "I can clearly see the power of this unique container of testimonies," she says, "which offers a space for women and men to feel a sense of restorative justice."

Takeaways

Active viewing:

* *Testimony* allows the viewer to hop around between story nodes based on their interest, simply by changing where they are looking.
* The hypothesis: Allowing the viewer to make choices and assemble their own story can help them engage with the content.

A virtual support group:

* Testimony relies on the viewers' sense of presence to give the feeling the characters are a support group, for each other and for potential survivors viewing the story.

A comfortable environment:

* The creator of *Testimony* used comforting sound and imagery to help her audience be open and receptive to the difficult subject matter.
* Testimony's gaze-based interaction gives viewers the ability to take a break from a challenging story and come back to it, without having to take off the headset.

Subtle effects:

* Testimony is scored throughout. Though it's subtle, the music supports its tone.
* Added sound effects and visuals highlight details in the spoken narratives, and heighten the experiential quality of the piece.

About This Project

URL: http://testimony.site/
Interview Date: July 12, 2017
Interview Subject: Zohar Kfir, Director & Producer
Team:
Director & Producer: Zohar Kfir
Creative Producer: Selena Pinnell
Original Music: Josephine Wiggs,
Executive Producers: Kaleidoscope VR
Evolving Technologies Corp., Unity Development (Oculus version)

Dpt., Web Development and Design (WebVR version)
Advisor & Expert: Judith Lewis Herman, MD
Project Advisor: Lisa Lynch, PhD
Funded by: Oculus VR for Good

UTURN, Episode One: The Tech Startup

NativeVR
2017 (Samsung Gear VR release)

"What if you could turn around and see your blind spot?" asks Nathalie Mathe, creative director and visionary behind *UTURN*, a fictional immersive series (of which this is the first episode) following the story of a young female coder and her male boss during a critical moment at a tech startup. The piece has a twist: The two perspectives unfold simultaneously with the use of some clever interactive audio playback and two 180-degree videos placed back-to-back.

Mathe says the driving goal behind *UTURN* is to serve as a vehicle for dialogue about gender dynamics in the workplace, by letting viewers step into the experience of a set of events from two perspectives. The hope is that by using virtual reality to put the viewer into the shoes of a woman working in tech it can heighten their awareness of gender bias, and do so with what Mathe describes as an inclusive approach—by including the first-person perspectives of both a male and female character.

A convergence of factors led to the unique design for this piece. An experienced 360-degree video creator, Mathe had been contemplating how to make immersive video pieces more engaging, more interactive and give the audience a greater sense of embodiment. She knew she wanted to create something with live actors, so that participants could look down and see a body, and she had been considering the way that immersive media allows viewers to step into different perspectives. "So everything came together," Mathe says, "and I just thought 'oh, let's split the screen in two and have them turn around.'"

As the stories run in parallel, the audience chooses which part of the piece to watch at any moment by turning to the side that draws their interest. Each viewer may come out with a different take on events based on whose perspective they were watching and hearing. "Everyone makes up their own version, in some sense," Mathe says.

Cutting Your Own Script

Due to the way that *UTURN* works—with two perspectives running in parallel—the viewer could in theory spend the entire time with one character and never see the other side of the story. Generally, viewers see some of both sides. The interactivity is somewhat invisible to the audience, but turning one's head triggers dynamic mixing of separate audio tracks with divergent scripts.

If viewers follow the woman's side of the story, they'll see her working to fix the start-up's broken database, spending a late night at the office to debug code so her boss can pitch to investors the next morning. They'll see her frustration as her coworkers take credit for her work. If they follow the man's side of the story, they'll see him schmoozing with potential investors, video-chatting with his wife from a hotel room, and nervously pitching the product.

The two sides of the story are synchronized, too, so that they're perceived to be happening at roughly the same time. At some points, when the main characters interact, they intersect. A Skype call between the boss and the female coder early on serves to establish their connection—and show their faces to the viewer.

Scripting Two Stories in Parallel

Screenwriter Ryan Lynch was responsible for working out most of the details of scripting the two stories in parallel. It took careful thought to make sure the viewer could understand the major points of the storyline without seeing the entirety of both sides. While the team didn't try to predict the exact path a viewer was likely to take between the two sides, they did pay attention to when the two stories were competing with each other to avoid major plot developments being lost.

The two sides are also timed to cut at different moments. The woman's side of the story has seven scenes, whereas the man's side of the story has five. That way, Mathe says, if a viewer waits for a cut to look around and see what's happening on the other side, they're unlikely to miss entire scenes on either side. The moments in which the two main characters interact are also designed to remind the viewer of the other side of the story, and motivate them to turn to see what's happening.

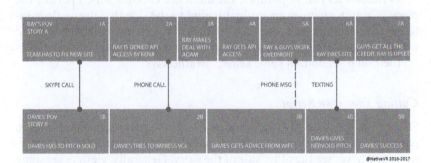

Figure 5.5 UTURN VR, courtesy of NativeVR.

First-Person Perspective and Embodiment

Role-reversal videos show up from time to time as a way to illustrate inconsistencies in the way people are treated based on their gender—like the 2016 Buzzfeed video, "Being A Man in the Workplace," in which a man passes out and wakes up in a workplace run by women who constantly undermine him. Videos like this poke at the issues with humor by highlighting the absurdity of a flipped power structure.

But the goal of *UTURN* is to go beyond pointing out the discrepancy. This piece is an experiment in whether the power of immersive media can actually put the viewer inside another person's role. Can a man watching *UTURN* embody how it feels to be a woman in the workplace? Can a woman watching get insight into why her male boss behaves the way he does?

Mathe says the pressure *UTURN*'s structure creates for viewers to try to follow both stories at once is meant to help communicate the stress of being a woman in the workplace. She was also adamant that in order for the viewer to have a chance at feeling embodiment, they had to be able to look down and see the body of a live actor, their view had to be at a convincing height from the body, and the first-person voice had to sound like it was coming from the right place.

Getting all these details right took a great deal of testing and experimentation. A head-mounted camera rig wouldn't work, because the viewer would look down and see the top of the actor's head. Justin Chin, the director of photography on the project, designed a rig using Go-Pros modified with fisheye lenses that would sit right at the eye level of the actor. That meant the actors had to tilt their heads out of the way while they were filming their scenes in order for the camera to be in the right position.

The filmmakers also intuited that in order to feel embodiment, viewers needed to be able to see the faces of the actors whose perspectives they were seeing. This couldn't be done simply, given that the camera rigs covered their faces as they were filming in each scene and the point of view looks out from their eyes. A video call between the two main characters early on in the story serves to show what they both look like.

The team put effort into making sure the actors would make and break eye contact with the camera in a way that felt natural, rather than having them staring into the camera (which can feel to the viewer as if the actor is staring directly at them). Mathe says that was easier to achieve in 3-person scenes than 2-person scenes. That way the actors could more actively make and break eye contact throughout the scene and take some of the pressure off the connection between the visible actors and the head-mounted camera.

One camera trick was borrowed from improvisational theater, Mathe says—playing with the relative heights of the characters by having them sit or stand in each scene according to their power status. The woman's eye level is almost always lower than the other characters in the scene, except at the triumphant moment when she fixes the big code bug and saves the day after an all-nighter (while her coworkers are napping in the office lounge area across the room). Her boss, on the other hand, is positioned at the same level or higher than other characters in every one of his scenes.

Bringing 2D Scenes to Life

Mathe, who has extensive experience working with **stereoscopic** 360-degree video, says the decision to make *UTURN* **monoscopic** had its roots in a few considerations: Budget was the main factor, but it was also because the first-person camera rig needed to be small, and because she wanted the scenes to feel intimate, which required the actors to be close to the camera. Stereoscopic video, she says, would have been too challenging at the time of production to achieve those goals. Stereoscopic rigs require twice as many cameras, and working with a different file for each eye compounds post-production difficulties arising from **parallax** errors. The production cost would have tripled or quadrupled.

The team was also limited in how much they could move the camera. They quickly determined that if they wanted to have a first-person perspective and the project was meant to be experienced in a headset, they should keep movement to a minimum to protect viewers from motion sickness. As a result, there is no camera movement in the final version.

The question, then, was how to create dynamic scenes and a sense of depth while filming with a stationary, monoscopic camera.

A big part of what gives *UTURN* a strong sense of depth is the spatial sound. Rich layers of foreground and background sound give shape to each scene.

The team also sought to achieve depth through creative set design and **blocking**. Actors and objects at varying distances from the camera signal depth and perspective to the viewer, and movement of actors across the scene—like a person on a scooter in the office, or a waiter moving through a restaurant—brings it to life. The actor's hands moving in the near foreground give a sense of depth up close. Mathe believes these efforts were successful, as many of the people who have watched *UTURN* think it was filmed with a 3D camera rig.

Two Stories, Separated with Sound Design

The sound design in this piece is a key component to its interactive quality. As the viewer moves their head, they control which side of the story they hear, creating a personalized edit with two separate but intersecting scripts.

Figure 5.6 UTURN VR, courtesy of NativeVR.

While many immersive pieces use **ambisonic** or **spatialized audio**, in which the sound behaves as a 360-degree field and the user hears stereo sound based on their viewing angle, *UTURN* relies on **quad binaural** sound to tell two sides of one story at once. The quad binaural format uses four stereo files—one for each quadrant of the sphere—that the video player blends together to create a different sound mix depending on where the viewer is looking. The format was Samsung VR's answer to spatial audio at the time the project was created. The sound for *UTURN* is an off-label use that takes advantage of the fact that, by allowing four independent audio tracks, the Samsung VR player gives creators more granular control of what viewers hear at different viewing angles.

The team needed this level of control to manage how much sound from one side of the story would filter in when a viewer is watching the other side.

If the viewer is looking directly at the line between the two story hemispheres, they will hear one script in one ear and one in the other. As they turn toward one hemisphere or another, the sound of one story fades out until it is inaudible. Hearing both stories at once the entire time, which would potentially be the case with an ambisonic track, would create a dissonant and distracting viewing experience.

Sound designer Shaun Farley created the spatialized soundscape using audio from a combination of sources—a boom mic and lavalier mics on the actors—plus sound effects and ambient audio added in **post production**. The voice recordings of the main actors created their own challenge because they needed to sound like they were coming from inside the viewer's head—a much different audio quality than the sound of an actor across the room. Mathe says she learned after filming just how important sound is, and she intends to focus much more closely integrating sound design from the start in future projects. She sees it as a powerful and often undervalued route to creating depth and immersion in a 360-degree piece.

Reaching an Audience

Because UTURN relies on quad binaural sound, at the time of completion it was only viewable in the Samsung VR player. The other players available at the time used different formats for spatial audio.

Mathe says this was a creative choice the team had to make. If they wanted to tell the story they were imagining, they would have to live with limiting their distribution channels. The alternative would have been to create their own app or to persuade other companies to add a quad binaural option to their players. Mathe and the *UTURN* team are actively pursuing both these routes.

Since finishing the project in early 2017 Mathe has showcased it at festivals in North America and Europe. In September 2017, it took home the grand prize at the first annual Jump Into VR Festival in New York City and has been nominated as Best Narrative VR Experience at FIVARS in Toronto and Raindance in London. It is also being used in diversity and inclusion workshops for tech companies and at universities. It was released on the Gear VR platform in March 2018.

The episode was also part of a Stanford user study that sought to measure how viewers interacted with it—and how it affected them. The study compared viewer responses to seeing the 360 version of the story, versus watching one perspective after another. It found that users felt more empathy after watching the two sides separately, but had a higher sense of personal responsibility for improving gender equality if they watched the 360 version.

Mathe's hope is to produce more episodes of *UTURN* that dive deeper into its themes, further develop the characters, and explore possibilities for episodic VR storytelling.

Takeaways

Illustrating depth in monoscopic shots:

- Place characters and objects at varying distances from the camera to create multiple layers of depth in a scene. Bring it to life with movement.
- Choose settings with leading lines that help create a sense of perspective.

Creating a first-person viewer experience:

- Consider the viewer's eye level.
- Be intentional about the relative heights of the characters in each scene.

- If a character is looking at the camera, the feeling of unbroken eye contact can be unsettling. Three-person scenes offer a way for eye contact to break and connect more naturally.
- Think about ways to let the viewer know what their character looks like (e.g., a video call).

Sound:
- Ambisonic sound isn't always the best solution for spatial sound. Quad binaural sound—which allows four separate mixes—can offer more granularity of control.

About This Project

URL: www.uturnvr.com/
Interview Date: July 13, 2017
Interview Subject: Nathalie Mathe, Creative Director
Team:
Creative Director/Producer: Nathalie Mathe
Co-Creator/DP/Editor: Justin Chin
Writer/Director: Ryan Lynch
Sound Designer: Shaun Farley
Produced by: NativeVR

Blackout

Scatter, March 2017 (Tribeca)

Scatter, a production company based in NYC, designed *Blackout* to simulate what happens when people "step toward" one another. This virtual, interactive **walk-around** experience, based on interviews with real people, is a surreal subway ride zooming in on the stories, experiences and emotions that lie beneath every passing interaction. Scatter has two main goals: To democratize the tools of creation and to create original content.

The first version of *Blackout* premiered at the Tribeca film festival in March 2017—showcasing **DepthKit**, the product used to create it, as well as the process the team went through to capture each person's story. Blackout was Scatter's first project with multiple cameras to create a **volumetric** experience.

A Train Ride Unlike Any Other

Blackout opens to volumetric video of passengers standing and sitting in a virtual subway car. The passengers ignore the viewer and each other as one normally does on the subway.

The train feels as though it leaves the station and about 30 seconds later—train sounds fade away and a cacophonous murmur can be heard.

Moving through the space, the viewer discovers snippets of stories, framed as the internal monologues of each person they approach. One person is worried about being late, another is speaking in Mandarin, and a woman wearing a hijab is reading. Once a few minutes have passed and the viewer has had time to get oriented, the lights gradually dim and there's a surreal illumination around each person. Here the nature of their thoughts change into more personal stories. After another few minutes, there's a shift in the mood. Colors are changing, and the experience starts to feel more dramatic. The people on the train begin to talk more in-depth about personal experiences they have had—experiences around universal themes such as being part of a community, feelings of belonging on a national and personal level.

Each person's experience of *Blackout* is different—not only because of the viewer choosing what to see, but because the virtual people sharing the train are placed by an algorithm designed by technical director James George. Behind the scenes, all the content is meta-tagged, and the algorithm selects a general theme randomly, then assembles the virtual passengers around that theme to create a coherence among the personal narratives the viewer will hear.

After a few minutes, a subway entertainer performs a brief dance or plays a song. The music interrupts the "blackout," the lights come up, and everyone goes back to ignoring one another.

As of May 2018, each experience is 10 minutes long, but co-director Yasmin Elayat says this is more of a sketch to showcase the work-in-progress prototype.

The project is in part a response to the political climate in the Trump era—speaking about otherness, identity and what it means to be living in America, as a sort of "This American life for VR," Elayat says.

In the Tribeca version of the experience, before putting on the headset, viewers entered a room designed to look like a subway train car, complete with seats and subway poles. Throughout the experience, the viewers could choose to walk around, sit, stand or hold onto the subway pole.

Radically Close to Home

The team at Scatter is conscious of finding a balance between new technology and experimental story forms. "You can get away with esoteric techniques and stories but you can't do both," director Alexander Porter says. Instead of taking the viewer to a faraway place—such as skydiving, beneath the ocean or to Mars—Porter wanted to use VR to transport the viewer radically close to home. He asks, "How can we actually use this to engage with our own lives and context?" The train came to mind: an approachable and familiar place for many, "a wonderful space of radical difference where everyone is sharing inconvenience at the same time," Porter says.

He wanted to illustrate how people exist with one another on a daily basis, despite complex differences. With division, bigotry and hate on a national level, *Blackout* shows what happens when you make space for a moment of shared humanity.

Mechanics for a Complex Story

As the team began working on *Blackout*, they were also developing a tool for others to use called DepthKit, which is open source software to enable the capture volumetric video (see the DepthKit section below). They had to adapt their system to the use of multiple cameras in order to create a full 3D image of each person. Multiple cameras added to the production time, but it also meant that the people within the scene felt more real and present.

Once they figured out the technology and prototype, Porter says it took the team 2–3 very intense months of work to finish the first iteration.

To film the passengers for *Blackout*, who are all real people relaying their own thoughts and experiences, the team used five DepthKits in a diamond shape around the person and one above them. These captures were brought together to form a unified character. Extensive audio interviews that make up the internal monologues were captured separately. It took anywhere from half an hour to three hours to capture the audio portion, and then another couple of hours for the depth capture.

The experience was then built with **Unity** game development software. There were three sources of assets: (1) the volumetric capture, (2) the static environment capture, and (3) 3D modeling. The subway platform uses a 3D scan; the train car itself was a recreated 3D model.

Using Unity, they combined the audio with the DepthKit video capture as well as light and visual effects, and were able to track the viewer's **gaze** and movement. Porter says one of the biggest challenges in design and implementation was making the viewer's body part of the experience and getting the gaze-based activation to work. The viewer must be close enough to a person and looking at them for the audio to play. This audio continues to play until the viewer steps away.

Creating the Passengers

"There's a reason why we picked everyone we picked," Elayat says of the passengers in the experience.

They approached the casting process with the desire to find people with a wide variety of backgrounds, and complicated perspectives on different things, Elayat says. For example, one of the people featured is an African-American veteran who served in Afghanistan. "He tells stories about racial discrimination and in the same breath he supports Trump, and has complicated views of Arabs and Muslims," Elayat says.

Exploring through Interaction

In *Blackout*, the viewer is able to hear others' thoughts as a disembodied observer, and "fulfill the ultimate people-watching fantasy," George says.

As George explains, the way each iteration of the experience is assembled borrows from a concept in gaming called "procedural generation," which refers to content that is constructed according to a set of rules at runtime rather than being stored. In this case, it means every time you go into *Blackout* it will be inhabited by different people in different places. As of March 2018 they had interviewed 40 people, and about 15 of them appear in each instance.

As a creator, George says there is a freedom in allowing the program to decide—"there's no perfect story or a perfect configuration; it's new every time." Still, there's structures to the overall piece, guiding the viewer through three acts for every person. "Just as if you spend more time with someone in real life, you might actually get deeper into their life experience, but you have to kind of get through the small talk to get there," George says.

George says the main lesson is to experiment with what works and "don't try to put too much in there." Sometimes the role of the director is much more like a guide—"you have to put your audience member somewhere and almost guide them; it's almost more shamanistic than it is editorial," he says, "you're overseeing their journey and making sure that you're leaving clues along the way."

Storytelling through Sound

Antfood, an audio studio in Brooklyn, designed the sound for the piece. George says they wanted it to feel like a spatialized podcast, where the user can create their own story.

There are two audio sources—the background of the train and the voices of the people on the train. The team took a set of **binaural** audio recorders onto the New York subway around 4 a.m. to catch the specific ambient noises of the train stopping and accelerating. With a shotgun mic they also captured the sound of the doors closing. If they were to do it again, the team would opt for an **ambisonic** array instead of multiple binaural set-ups.

Perhaps what is more important from an auditory perspective is when the interview audio plays. George designed a system of logic for this, so the user could listen to a story, but there was also a "sort of a stickiness to it"—the more attention a viewer pays to one person, the more that person's audio will stay with them as they begin to look around or move away.

A Shared Tool and Production Process

Open-source access to tools is part of the Scatter team's philosophy. Porter says it is "immensely personally gratifying" to share tools such as DepthKit with creators. He believes creators should be free to spend their time grappling with the meaning of a story, not how to build it. "Our lives would be so much more interesting if we released our tools and our approaches to the commons," he says.

"This idea of representation is tied to the tool and the approach," says Elayat. In immersive media, it's often scripted and Blackout is literally their voice, and them being represented as themselves. I think you don't see that very often. The cast themselves are co-creators and collaborators, taking risks to tell their stories.

Reach and Impact

The team doesn't yet know where this project will live in the world— potentially on one of the immersive platforms, but perhaps also accessible to schools, museums and cultural spaces.

Though the team would like to see their content have the greatest reach possible across multiple platforms, for now the experience is limited to a headset. Without a headset, the full interactivity and intimacy of the project is lost. In the future, Porter hopes to distribute it on the HTC Vive, and build an adaptation that works on mobile devices.

For Porter, the overall experience is meant to be empathic. "One of the main things for us, is the ability to use your body as a narrative device," he says. Emphasizing the active experience of the viewer, Porter describes how the viewer is only rewarded if they commit to a story by stepping towards a character.

Porter says the most moving example of watching a person experience *Blackout* was when a young undocumented man who is featured in the piece presented it to his mother. One of the things he said in his interview for *Blackout* was that his family doesn't talk much. During the experience, his mom sat next to the virtual version of him as he talked about what it means for him to be undocumented. When she took the headset off, she was crying. "It was incredibly moving," Porter says. Porter says seeing someone use the project for dialogue they aren't otherwise able to have within their family feels like a kind of "pseudo wizardry." As George says, "the really core deep reason which is propelling us is—we have a desire for art to reflect life." They want to be as close in proximity to the lived reality, to represent and understand the world through these kinds of experiences.

Towards a More Diverse and Inclusive Future

"There's what can you make today, and then there is what is possible in a five-year time horizon," George says. As evidenced by his previous projects, George is interested in the idea of database driven cinema where a viewer has a copious number of interviews and captures of people.

"This idea of allowing a viewer's curiosity to traverse some idea spaces is something many people are exploring especially in the direction of choose-your-own adventure stories." George also adds that he'd like to see a larger diversity of people involved in the creative process.

Takeaways

Depth provides a visceral sense of story:
- The visual language communicated through body language and physical depth adds to the auditory story being told.

Guiding the viewer:
- Triggering audio based on gaze and proximity makes for a natural-feeling interactive story driven by the user's interest.

Radically close to home:
- VR can take viewers somewhere they could never otherwise go, but it can also take them somewhere familiar with a fresh perspective.

About This Project

URL: Full experience not available online
Team: James George, Alexander Porter, Yasmin Elayat, Mei-Ling Wong and Hannah Jayanti

Notes

1 *L.A. Times.* "Discovering Gale Crater: How we did it," October 26, 2015. http://graphics.latimes.com/mars-gale-crater-how-we-did-it/.
2 Smus, Boris. WebVR Boilerplate, https://github.com/borismus/webvr-boilerplate.
3 Kenny, Roger. "Storybench, How to make a simple virtual reality data visualization." May 20, 2015. www.storybench.org/how-to-make-a-simple-virtual-reality-data-visualization/.

6 Mixed-Media Packages

Two things make a story. The net and the air that falls through the net.
(Pablo Neruda)

Case Studies

Stand at the Edge of Geologic Time, NPR
Overheard, Minneapolis Institute of Art & Luxloop
The Call Center, Good Magazine
Capturing Everest, Sports Illustrated
Hell and High Water, Jovrnalism
The Wall, USA Today and *Arizona Republic*

This category incorporates elements from all of the immersive forms already discussed in this book—mixing and matching immersive video, photo, audio and even AR—in innovative ways.

What these pieces have in common is the importance of story, whether or not it is a fictional narrative encouraging a physical exploration of space (like *Overheard*) or multiple stories about the border (in *The Wall*). These mixed-media pieces aren't relying solely on any one format and the stories themselves bring the viewer to a variety of different places, adding a sense of presence and wonder as the viewer ponders geologic time or climbs to the top of Mount Everest.

These pieces are web packages—or comparable: Some of them give the viewer interactive control—whether it be moving forward in a linear story, exploring a variety of multimedia elements, or triggering a set of predetermined events. Elements of *The Wall* could easily have gone in the walk-around or interactive VR sections of this book. The audio strategy in these pieces varies widely too, supporting navigational cues, creating atmosphere and providing context.

This variety in presentation among these pieces is something we expect to see more of as immersive media technology becomes better integrated in publishing platforms—whether it be traditional film or photo components embedded in a piece viewed on a headset, or browser-based pieces incorporating immersive content alongside other multimedia elements.

What prompts the choice to combine immersive and other media? In this chapter we explore some of the choices made along the way, and what might be lost in asking viewers to transition between viewing modes (e.g., browser to headset). These case studies explore structure, transitions, and the technology used to create these pieces.

Stand at the Edge of Geologic Time

NPR, July 20, 2016

Stand at the Edge of Geologic Time, released in July 2016, was part of a wider NPR editorial initiative to mark the 100th anniversary of the U.S. National Park Service, with broad coverage touching on a range of topics surrounding the national parks.

The project, which incorporates narration, **binaural** soundscapes, 360-degree photography and text, is all built into a browser-based experience that uses WebVR to immerse its audience in scenes of the Rocky Mountains. It was an experiment for NPR and the people who worked on it. While the group came to it with substantial experience in audio and visual storytelling, they previously had very little exposure to immersive media.

Stand at the Edge is a sound-first project. Not only was the sound the guiding focus in bringing the project together, but the creators imagined the visuals as a backdrop to the sound. It's meant to create a meditative, atmospheric immersive experience that would allow viewers to focus intently on the narration and the binaural soundscapes that accompany each scene. All the sounds heard in the project were recorded on location in Rocky Mountain National Park.

Wesley Lindamood, who envisioned and designed the project, says a lot of other news organizations seemed to be focusing on the visuals in their VR projects, and he thought NPR might be able to create better sound for a VR piece—in particular in terms of enticing the audience to listen more intently to the sound.

A Sound Journey and Photo Collage

Eleven 360-degree photos and accompanying soundscapes make up the immersive content in *Stand at the Edge of Geologic Time*, but their presentation varies throughout the project and depending on the viewing mode.

The experience begins at a landing page with the project title, at which point the viewer can click to watch the story in "360" mode or on **cardboard**. If they're coming to it on a mobile device, each of these options leads to the same content, adapted to the viewing mode. The 360 version is a **magic window** view, and the cardboard mode divides the view for watching with a **headset**.

This first portion of the project is a 5-minute narrative story with audio over 360 scenes.

As the piece opens, the viewer finds themself in a snow-blanketed valley, a frozen lake below them and high peaks all around. The sound of flowing water and chirping birds fades in. About 15 seconds in the voice of geologist Eric Kirby comes in.

While the binaural audio in the piece makes it feel as if it's video, this guided tour can best be described as a 360 photo slideshow accompanying an audio track. Each of the nine scenes is a photograph with a soundscape created from on-site recordings by Bill McQuay, who was formerly an audio engineer at NPR and is now at the Cornell Lab of Ornithology.

As the scenes progress, Eric Kirby describes how glaciers carve out the landscape, and talks about the age of the earth and thinking in geological time: "It is a massive and almost unknowable depth of time," he says as the viewer looks down from the peak of a mountain over a vast snowy landscape.

The piece introduces the viewer to some basic concepts of geology in an environment that encourages them to understand the grandeur of the rockies from a geologist's perspective—as evidence of the constant reshaping of the Earth's terrain, on a time scale we can hardly fathom. In the final scene, Kirby describes the dramatic effect humans are having on the Earth. "The changes that we as a society and we as all societies are making now are changing the direction at which the planet is heading," he says. "And 10,000 years out what that looks like is very uncertain, but I'm certain it looks very different than it does today."

Once the guided experience ends (or if the user chooses to leave early), the viewer drops out of the 360 space and is given the choice between six immersive scenes—each with a soundscape but none with narration.

Different Experiences for Different Viewing Modes

The desktop version of the guided tour of this project plays like a traditional video; all the panning and movement is programmatically done, and the user does not have the ability to click and drag to look around. Through ad hoc usability testing, Lindamood says, they discovered that users were not interacting with the screen in desktop mode during this narrative. Instead viewers were more inclined to treat it as a "lean-back experience," and they were missing the 360 image before cutting to the next scene. As a result, the team decided to choreograph the movement through each 360 image on desktop for the guided tour.

"The soundscapes were a different story," Lindamood says. "Because the soundscapes were designed as an environment to explore and not a narrative journey, we found that folks were more inclined to click and drag to move around a scene in that context."

The Right Story

This project and its content came together for a few reasons. First, the National Park Service centennial had NPR journalists brainstorming stories related to the parks. Second, Christopher Joyce had been looking for an opportunity to do an audio project featuring geologist Eric Kirby (who narrates the piece). Third, the team was interested in experimenting with telling immersive stories with a focus on sound.

David Al-Ibrahim, who was working as an intern at NPR, had done some work with 360 video as a student. Other than that, the team was new to immersive storytelling.

Bill McQuay, Wes Lindamood and Christopher Joyce had teamed up on other explorations in audio storytelling for the web. For example, Bat Sounds[1] is a 2014 project that features binaural audio of endangered bats on the backdrop of a looping (flat) video of the inside of a cave. The sound brings the scene to life. McQuay and Joyce also worked on another feature on the sounds of national parks as part of the centennial project.

They chose Rocky Mountain National Park in part because Joyce and McQuay had already been doing work in Colorado, and were able to do some location scouting. They were looking for places that would look good in 360 and provide inspiration toward exploring topics in geology. They interviewed Kirby in a handful of locations and in May 2016 Bill McQuay, Wes Lindamood and David Al-Ibrahim went out to shoot.

Binaural Audio

The team initially considered using **spatial audio**, but Lindamood says creating spatial audio for WebVR wasn't feasible at the time they created this project.

McQuay made the recordings using a Jecklin Disc, which is a binaural recording device that uses two microphones at a precise angle and distance, separated from each other with a padded disc. The disc serves as sound baffling between the two microphones to create a recording that mimics the way human ears hear sound (the disk basically stands in for a head).

They hypothesized the binaural recording would be a big improvement, producing a more natural sound than the stereo audio they'd been hearing in a lot of VR experiences. When listened to on headphones, the binaural sound does add a feeling of depth to the scenes, despite the fact that it doesn't adapt as the user turns their head. Lindamood says he's still interested in trying spatial audio in future projects.

Styling the Piece

The team decided on a series of photos instead of video in part so they could have an easier time producing clean visuals. They were focused on making clean stitches of just a few images, but Lindamood says it was mostly because they were focusing on sound. "We wanted the image to be there as a backdrop for the sound, but we really were focused on the sound itself," Lindamood says. If they had been doing the project with video, there would have been additional challenges in terms of the sound design, because all of the sound would have to be synced to motion.

While the piece is educational, the team didn't want it to be an **explainer**. "We wanted it to, as much as possible, be a narrative journey," Lindamood says. He says he's learned that in science reporting it helps the audience emotionally connect to a story if there's something in it that communicates why the scientist cares about the material being presented.

Lindamood says the decision to aim for a "feeling of contemplation" was in part inspired by the state of the medium—whereas many VR stories aim to wow their audiences, Lindamood believes VR experiences with lots of action or drama for novelty effect can create dissonance for a viewer who is unable to interact or move around in the experience. "We thought that it would feel more comfortable to a user to be put in a situation where they could just look and not feel the need to move," he says. In shooting, they took some inspiration from the cinematic style of filmmaker Yasujirō Ozu, who often used low angle shots to give the feeling that the viewer is seated on the floor.

Tyler Fisher, Wes Lindamood and Brittany Mayes built the project using WebVR—which means they were able to use the same code base with customizations to work on desktop, mobile (magic window) and in a cardboard-style headset. It also means it's available on the open web, and not tied to a proprietary platform.

Sound-Centric: The Visuals Support the Sound

"One of the challenges that I think we always face when telling an audio driven story is getting the user to focus on the sound," Lindamood says, "to not just passively listen, but listen in a deep way, listen intently."

The theory in creating a VR story, he says, was that because it asks the user to fully immerse, a virtual reality project is less likely to have viewers watching half-distracted, scanning content or flipping between multiple browser windows. "To experience a VR story in its truest sense," Lindamood says, "you are fully committed to the story."

Ironically, this project ended up getting a lot more desktop views than mobile or headset views, so it is possible the viewers were distracted after all. In terms of the immersive experience, however, even for the undistracted there is still a level of tension present. After all, immersive media with sound and visuals can in itself be an overwhelming sensory experience.

The team talked—especially when they were considering using spatial audio—about using sound to indicate to the viewer to look one way or another, for example by using the sound of water placed directionally. In the final product, Lindamood says, they didn't offer any deliberate sound cues. The narration, however, does let the viewer know what to look for in some parts, when Kirby describes a particular geological feature.

In other parts, the narration is thematically connected to the visuals without direct reference to any particular element. In that sense the piece takes a contemplative tone, but the only uninterrupted moments of soundscape in the guided tour are about 15 seconds at the beginning, the end, and for a few seconds during some of the visual transitions between scenes. Since a viewer presented with new scenery in VR is likely, at each juncture, to need a few moments to adjust to their surroundings, that means there's not a lot of time to relax into the sounds and scenery. To get an uninterrupted experience of any of the soundscapes designed for this project—that is, to really have a moment to meditate on the surroundings—a viewer will need to try the six soundscapes available after the tour.

A Mixed-Media Experience

Accompanying each soundscape in the desktop and magic window views is a click-to-reveal text section that describes the scene and some of its geology, and also identifies the birds in each soundscape. From there, the user can also click on the names of the birds heard in each scene to be linked out to the Cornell Lab of Ornithology's page about that bird.

Since the content is not embedded in immersive space, and can't be accessed from the cardboard view, a viewer using cardboard has to take off their headset to jump between the immersive scene and the additional context.

Lindamood says that was a technical limitation. He says that early in the project they prototyped **gaze** detection experiments that would allow for navigation in headset mode, but the prototypes were too buggy for production. While the additional information adds rich and interesting context to the project, it feels somewhat like a missed opportunity that in order to see it the user must break out of immersion—or repeatedly jump in and out of immersive space.

But the NPR team was balancing accessibility as well, having the project work in a headset wasn't the top priority. "First of all, we didn't have easy access to the hardware, so we had no way to test it," Lindamood says. "Second, our priority for this project was to experiment with WebVR in hopes that the story would be available to a wider audience by making it available in web browser." They also considered building for the Samsung **GearVR** headset, but after quick testing, they determined it would be too much work to troubleshoot their code for that platform, and had to abandon the idea.

There's a boldness to the decision to include several layers of content in different media in this project, but the unwieldiness of this feature highlights the difficulty of merging immersive content with other media elements. It's already a lot to ask of a viewer to commit to an immersive story; asking them to jump out and then come back to immersive space doubles down on that ask.

Creating a Sense of Awe

Lindamood says the majority of people who saw the project watched it in desktop mode. Viewership numbers tend to be reflective of what's driving traffic, he says: If people are finding a project via the NPR homepage, it will get more desktop viewers, whereas if a story is popular on Facebook a larger audience will be coming to it on mobile devices.

That also means a large number of viewers may have experienced the story without ever seeing a 360 scene, since the guided tour on desktop doesn't have click and drag functionality. And the binaural audio wouldn't be useful without headphones. This speaks to the challenges inherent in trying to design VR projects accessible to a wide range of audiences—this piece meets audiences where they're at, but that happened to be the form in which it is least immersive.

Lindamood says that since the project was published, he's seen examples of it being used in classrooms to help children understand concepts of geology and deep time. To him, that's a sign of success: "It was really just to create a sense of awe and wonder for a general audience."

More experiments at NPR

After *Stand at the Edge of Geologic Time* was published, an NPR team led by Nick Michael received a $15,000 reporting grant through the Journalism 360 challenge to develop best practices for immersive audio. They set up a low-cost rig for capturing 360-degree video with ambisonic sound, and wrote up a beginner's guide to spatial audio in 360-degree video[2] that was published on NPR's training blog.

In May 2018, they published a story and video titled Restoring Power To Puerto Rico's Last 2 Percent, which documents in 360-degree video—with spatial sound—efforts to bring electricity back to people who were still without power 6 months or more after Hurricane Maria devastated the island. The powerful piece is another step toward bringing more immersive audio into NPR's workflow, though Michael points out that the technology is still changing quickly enough that it's hard to create technical guidelines that don't go out of date almost immediately. He says a measure of the success of that project would be if binaural audio were to be used in an NPR podcast as a result of his work.

Takeaways

Encouraging listening:

- VR can easily overwhelm with overlapping sensory inputs; steady scenery can leave more space for contemplating sound.
- Immersive media is an opportunity to feature sound, because it demands attentiveness in a way that audio-only storytelling doesn't.

Sound with depth:

- Binaural audio adds a feeling of depth and can be easier to create than spatialized audio.
- Rich, layered audio can give a sense of movement to a still image.

Mixed-media challenges:

- When incorporating various media, be conscious of how often a user is being asked to jump in and out of a headset.

About This Project

URL: https://apps.npr.org/rockymountain-vr/
Interview Date: December 21, 2017
Interview Subjects: Wesley Lindamood
Produced by: Wesley Lindamood
Edited by: Christopher Joyce
Field recordings and audio production: Bill McQuay
360 images: David Al-Ibrahim
Expertise and narration: Eric Kirby
Design and development: Tyler Fisher, Wesley Lindamood and Brittany Mayes
Field recordings and audio production: Bill McQuay, Cornell Lab of Ornithology
Additional photos: William l/360cities.net and pix/360cities.net via Getty Images

Overheard

Luxloop and Minneapolis Institute of Art, Minnesota
2016

The *Overheard* app allows visitors to the Minneapolis Institute of Art to "overhear" different fictional narratives as they walk through the museum. With headphones on and the app open, users can choose to follow the path of these audio stories through the art museum. After opening the app, a brief instructional audio clip plays, telling the user: "As you explore, the app will recognize your location, allowing you to overhear characters as if they are right next to you." As the user wanders around the museum a sound and notification lets them know they have discovered a story to be followed. On the app interface, users can see which characters they're following and track their journey through the content. If they get lost or can't find a story, there are hints referencing landmarks within the museum to help them rejoin a character or group.

At the very basic level, *Overheard* could be understood as something akin to an audio tour available at a museum. However, this experience goes a step further by using beacons throughout the museum to prompt the next part of the audio story. And it is not a tour, but a series of fictional stories, each about 15–20 minutes. The separate stories speak to generic profiles of potential museum-goers—there's a story with two guys who are musicians, a couple on a first date, a few female friends walking around the museum, a story about parents, and another with two children who walk around the museum with their grandfather.[3]

As a location-based audio guide, *Overheard* stands out as a unique combination of story and location. Some of the stories may seem to have a cheesy quality to them, emulating what might be said in a museum, but they mimic the ways different people talk—using colloquial ways of speaking and humor not heard in many museum tours. As two of the characters talk about the name of one artist—Junius Brutus Stearns, they say "That name sounds completely made up, it's like the name you would use when you are wearing fake Groucho Marx glasses as a disguise." As the audio stories progress, the characters comment on some of

Figure 6.1 Overheard, Luxloop.

the art, and occasionally the stories briefly intersect, like when the musicians run into the kids. At this point, the listener can choose to follow the kids' story (by tapping the app) or continue following the musicians.

Each story adds a subtle element to a discussion of the art, but the audio stories feel much more like moments, literally overheard, than a tour or explanation. This is intentional. Each story is meant to feel as though the user is eavesdropping or overhearing the action. "Instead of living in this known medium of the rectangle or the screen it's been pulled into a space," says Ivaylo Getov, the technology director of the project. Getov and Mandy Mandelstein—the creative director settled on calling it "a work of **immersive theater**" as the easiest way for people to gain an understanding of the format.

Developing the Concept

Getov and Mandelstein developed an experience design studio called Luxloop based on their backgrounds in film as well as a strong desire to use technology for storytelling. The concept for this project began as a proposal to the global company 3M. Luxloop won a $50,000 grant from 3M to explore art and technology for *Overheard* with the Minneapolis Institute of Art.[4] After receiving funding, Getov and Mandelstein got to work scripting the five different stories. Part of their mission was to represent the different kinds of people at museums and another goal of both the museum and the creators was to have something that allows the listener to see the art with new eyes. Even though it's an app, it's a "heads up" experience, says Meaghan Tongen, the digital program manager at the Minneapolis Institute of Art. She says the immersive performative quality set it apart from other projects pitched during the 3M competition.

The idea for the project came from the team's own practice of going to museums for inspiration. They'd see people in museums and make up stories about them. As Getov says, soon they realized this idea of overhearing stories within a space was fertile ground for playing with the idea of story within a specific location.

The team worked with a screenwriter to create the stories. Mandelstein says during development they talked a lot about *Sleep No More*, a site-specific theater piece created by British theater company Punchdrunk. It is an adaptation of Macbeth without spoken dialogue, and is considered immersive theater or promenade theater because the audience walks through theatrically designed rooms. This was the first immersive theater experience they'd seen successfully operate on a large scale. "We wanted to see if we could use a location aware app to give a similar experience in a museum," says Mandelstein, without overhead of running a live theater production. "We were drawn to the idea of having multiple stories unfolding in real time, giving the user the option to wander between stories as they unfolded." At the end they had the stories start and stop based on the user finding or leaving a character's path.

Inspiration and Concept

For a greater understanding of museums as a whole as well as museum culture, the team dove into academic and observational research. They thought about who visits museums and why, had discussions with the Minnesota Art Institute staff and aimed to construct stories that would be inclusive for art connoisseurs and casual visitors alike. "This particular museum has a really strong initiative to get people to take ownership of the museum and to get people to feel like the art was theirs, and that they belong," says Getov.

They discussed some of the reasons that people are embarrassed to talk about art, decided that for the audio stories they wanted the characters to have opinions about at least one specific artwork over the course of the story—showing the listener that it's ok to have an opinion on the art, even without a professional art education. In one overheard moment

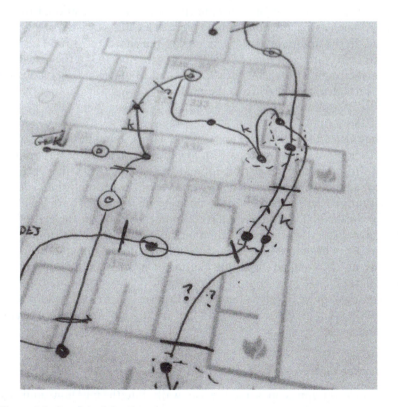

Figure 6.2 Overheard, Luxloop.

the listener hears the musicians talking about a painting saying: "You know what my favorite thing is—how exasperated these two ladies on the side are."

Luxloop also designed the stories in a way that would bring people into parts of the museum that they might not know about, or may not have planned to go into. With a range of collections from Japanese armor to impressionist paintings, Getov and Mandelstein intentionally mapped out stories to lead people through at least two of the broad areas of the museum.

Timeline and Recording Audio

Beginning in January 2016, Getov and Mandelstein aimed for a projected release date in mid-June. They spent time researching, conducting a test trip to the MIA, planning routes within the museum, and scripting each story.

They practiced on-site and then had some voice actors at the museum and others record in studios. They wanted to avoid dialogue such as "Hey let's go to gallery 452" or "Let's go north." Instead, to transition between places within the museum, they rely on "navigational touchstones" such as a giant stone door, a piece of a Chinese castle, or a Greek statue. In the first-date experience, one of the characters says: "Let's go to this courtyard style house." Each scene attempts to put the listener in a specific room with visual cues. Getov and Mandelstein accomplished this through research trips to the museum, taking flat photographs as well as 360 photographs to geographically orient themselves as they wrote the scripts.

They also edited the audio and worked with a sound designer to make soundscapes of certain rooms with low murmurs, and cinematic sound design for some of the period rooms. In the story with the kids and grandpa, the Connecticut Room comes to life with nighttime sounds as Grandpa tries to get the kids to imagine what it might have been like to live in the historic house. Another moment occurs at the end of the First Date story, when they begin dancing in the French Ballroom. For these scenes Mandelstein designed the audio with the intent to bring the rooms to life, complete with the chatter of people and clinking plates and glasses.

Aiming to move beyond a temporary experience, they wanted to create something that people would want to return to—giving visitors a reason to come back.

Navigating through Technological Limitations

As soon as the app is open and the user walks into the museum, audio dialogue begins. The characters are the entry point to each story, and they lead the listener through additional scenes and locations. If somebody walks away from the conversation that's happening then that story fades away as they leave the room.

At a couple of points throughout the process they conducted formal testing at the museum. They had tables for people to check out the device, and then answer a list of questions on both form and content. "It challenged some of our assumptions about how people would use the app," Mandelstein says, "People gamified it a lot more than we thought they would." She describes how some listeners wanted to find everything in the museum and didn't want to stop until it was done.

Throughout the process they were constantly iterating, trying one story, and then testing to see how it would go. "It was a huge learning process," says Mandelstein. They also did test recordings in the museum. "You don't really realize until you are there, how long you are standing in a room," she says. Some of the audio (especially ambient audio of the rooms) was recorded on-site at the museum; other aspects of the audio stories were recorded with voice actors during a few sessions in New York, Los Angeles and Minnesota.

Initially they didn't allow for the listener to replay the audio. They wanted to lean into the idea that as a listener you are overhearing people's conversations. But, after testing they realized users wanted to be able to re-play when they missed a detail. This was one of the biggest changes they made after user testing.

Mandelstein says the biggest unforeseen challenge was that the art in the museum moves. The team needed to work with the curatorial staff to understand what does and doesn't move. They worked to write around the movement of certain objects and they also redesigned the app to allow for certain art to move. "Each story has a few key pieces that we know are important to the dialogue," Mandelstein says. When a user starts the app, the app tracks the digital database and sees whether that piece is still on view. If it's not, that story won't be an option for the user.

Social Listening and Reacting to Art and Design

After listening, watching and experimenting the team came away with a few key observations. "The thing we found about this experience was how easy it was to add this layer of narrative experience," Mandelstein says. "It wasn't just this thing that you would have to go out of your way to specifically go to—you overheard it fade very organically into a museum visit."

They also noticed a social experience with the app. Mandelstein says there'd be someone in the room listening and someone else with headphones would walk in and they would have a shared moment of listening to the same story, "that was really cool to see," she says. In a similar way, they began to realize how visual the experience was. Even though it was conceived of as audio experience, the scenes guide people where to stand. Occasionally other museum-goers become part of the narrative—like when the listener hears the family talking and sees a family walking through the gallery. "You kind of begin to imagine the family … you begin to make that connection to use your imagination to flesh out these characters," says Mandelstein.

Anecdotally, feedback to the museum on the project has been mixed, Meaghan Tongen says, noting how "questioning what a standard audio tour is was somewhat divisive." She says some people loved it, and some struggled with the concept. A Girl Scout troop that wanted to be able to wander and discover asked for the piece to have a map.

Initially the app was intended to be available for the latter half of 2016. As of January 2018, it's still being used, though some of the stories are not available since the art has changed location.

The Importance of Timing and Location

Ensuring story flow for a location-based physical experience requires a slightly different sense of time and space. Mandelstein says "relying on the listener to imagine the characters around them … you can certainly feel the weight of certain scenes lasting longer or shorter than you naturally want to stay in a certain room." In part this has to do with the medium and the tools of audio storytelling. Compared to a movie where creators can use angles and editing to keep a viewer's attention during a long scene, "when they are in real space, you only have real-time dialogue to move their eyes around the room as a scene plays out," Mandelstein says. Rehearsing the scenes in the galleries of the museum helped make the script and determine when scenes felt too short or too long, Mandelstein says.

Upon reflection, another surprise was how the architectural elements of a space might change the way one would naturally talk and move within a space, "which is important to keep in mind when designing audio to layer into the real world," says Mandelstein. During the scripting process, they worked to include as many as possible of the navigational cues as "diegetic conversational moments, rather than explicit instructions," Mandelstein says this was helpful for keeping the experience feeling fluid. "Location aware storytelling is a powerful tool that is only beginning to be explored, and leaves a lot of room for experimentation and learning in the future."

Continued iteration

Mandelstein and Getov say there's nothing to prohibit another iteration, or even another series of episodes with the same characters at a different location. The museum's digital media department will soon need to decide whether to pull and replace the beacons (they have an 18–24 month battery life). The museum sunset the project in the spring of 2018.

Mandelstein and Getov have begun to experiment with more visually based augmented reality for site specific projects. "We'd like to see if there's a place where we can fit a more visual experience organically into something like a museum visit," says Mandelstein.

Takeaways

Working with what's there:
- Using what viewers and visitors already have in their hands (mobile phones) can be a simple way to engage with content that already exists (such as a museum).
- An audio-only project can use the real surroundings as immersive visuals.
- A rich audio soundscape can change the feel of a room.

User testing:
- Initially they didn't allow for the listener to replay the audio. But, after testing they realized users wanted to be able to re-play, when they missed a detail.
- User testing also helped with timing to anticipate how long or short it felt comfortable to be in each room or location.
- With a variety of things to discover, users tended to "gamify" the experience—trying to see it all.

A divergence from immersive theater:
- While the piece took inspiration from a theater piece with stories unfolding simultaneously in different rooms, *Overheard* stops and starts stories when the user jumps between them.

Subtle navigation:
- To get users following the path of the characters, Overheard uses cues that are built into the story, rather than explicit instructions

Adapting to changes:
- When a user starts the app, the app tracks the digital database and sees whether the pieces discussed are still on view. If not, that story won't be an option for the user.

About This Project:

URL: https://itunes.apple.com/us/app/overheard-mia/id1116319582?mt=8
Interview Date: December, 2017
Interview Subjects:

Ivaylo Getov, technology director
Mandy Mandelstein, creative director of Technology
Meaghan Tongen, digital program manager, Minneapolis Institute of Art

The Call Center

Lives on the Line in Iraq, in the Line of Fire

GOOD Magazine
November 2017

The Call Center 360-degree video opens on an empty dirt road in Qayyarah, in Northern Iraq, in a desert landscape dotted with low gray buildings, many of which are badly damaged. Beyond the two buildings in the center of the scene, a huge plume of black smoke rises from an oil fire. There is only ambient audio, which sounds like wind blowing across sand. About 10 seconds in, the sound of a phone ringing cuts in and an operator answers in Arabic.

The man on the line has panic in his voice. Between phrases, he coughs. "The smoke here is killing us," the subtitles read, "I have sick children because of the burning oil wells."

A slow, heartbeat-like melody fades in as the call continues. This music runs through the rest of the film, subtly heightening the sense of tension.

"Every day in Iraq, this UN Call Center fields hundreds of calls from people fleeing sectarian violence," the text reads as the scene cuts to a sterile-looking office where ten employees sit at their workstations, fielding calls. From inside the call center, it looks like it could be anywhere.

In just under three minutes, this straightforward 360-degree film takes the viewer to five different sites in Iraq to glimpse the hardships facing

Figure 6.3 The Call Center, courtesy of Aaron Ohlmann.

Internally Displaced Persons (IDPs)—the UN's term for refugees who have fled violence within their own countries. Each scene is accompanied by audio from a different call, with the scenes serving as illustration rather than showing visuals specific to that call. Callers complain of dangerous oil fires, refugee camps lacking basic necessities, destroyed homes and missing family members. At the end of the film, the operator asks a caller to write down the phone number for a service that can help.

The film is a central piece of a multimedia web package. In its original presentation on the *Good Magazine* website, it is embedded a few paragraphs down in a written narrative titled, "In The Line Of Fire: An American therapist heads to Iraq and finds remarkable strategies for survival." Also embedded within the story are 12 photographs and an Instagram post. The story links out to a photo essay containing additional images by filmmaker Aaron Ohlmann and by Al Kamalizad, another journalist and filmmaker who contributed to the project.

Separately, each component of this multimedia package stands on its own. Together, they tell a much more complete story—with each medium employed for its strengths.

Replicating a Feeling

This 360 film emerged out of another project on the same subject: Aaron Ohlmann had been working with the UN to create a piece on the call center, and wanted to do something that could more accurately capture what he had seen. "Standing in the middle of the room you just got this incredible sense of existential dread," Ohlmann says of being in the call center, hearing the phones ringing and the operators speaking to war victims in crisis. "It's just a really disturbing and memorable experience."

For that original assignment, Ohlmann created a flat mini-documentary in which he added **voice-over** narration to give context. But he came out feeling that traditional video storytelling wasn't enough to convey what he was trying to share with viewers: "It was kind of a frustrating experience in some ways, because I never was able to really effectively replicate that feeling of standing in the middle of the room," he says.

A few months after finishing that initial project, Ohlmann tried out a 6-camera 360 video rig in Los Angeles and realized 360 video was within reach for him as an independent filmmaker. From there, he began planning his return to the call center.

Ohlmann recruited his friend Adam Kaplan, a counselor and writer, to come along and help. The two spent about a week there, fitting in a few days of filming between logistics and travel.

The experience in the call center made a strong impression on Kaplan, too, and though he wasn't initially intending on writing a piece, he took thorough notes that eventually became the written story.

The 360 scenes, several of which are absent of people—like the front steps of the burned out public library in Mosul, where the lawn still has some color; or the ruins of a home filmed from inside a burned-out kitchen—give a sense of the magnitude of loss and destruction these people experience.

The Call Center is atmospheric, establishing in broad strokes what the center does, and offering a 360-degree view of what war looks like for the internally displaced in Iraq. It is designed to be minimally distracting. Embedded text is kept to a minimum, allowing the users to take in the scenes without feeling overwhelmed. The audio carries the main storyline, and the **head-locked** subtitles allow viewers to look around the scene without missing information.

The film is not exclusively experiential. It carries a simple narrative, from the moment the phone rings to the point at which an operator at the call center is able to connect a caller with the service they need. And while the meaning-making in the accompanying written piece is largely managed by the strong perspective of its author, the film is much more an open canvas for the viewer to experience. It gives the viewer greater autonomy to compose their own interpretation of the story.

The film works as both a standalone piece and as a component of a wider multimedia package—and *Good Magazine* did publish the film directly to Facebook. Viewed without the added context of the written piece or the photographs, it channels the terror of war.

Complementary Components

"In a lot of ways, one needs the other," Ohlmann says of the film and the narrative story.

In creating the film, Ohlmann says, he was concerned that he wouldn't be able to sustain a viewer's attention for more than a few minutes. He saw 360 video as a great tool for creating a sense of place, but not for providing the necessary context that would allow a viewer to connect to the material. "I just don't want people to be bored," Ohlmann says. "It's too serious and important and good a topic to make something boring."

When they were pitching to Good, it occurred to the team that they could build a multimedia package with the material they had. Ohlmann says he realized then that, "you could create a whole world around it with photos and storytelling."

Katie Wudel, the editor at Good who helped put all the pieces together, says she came to this story as an editor who mostly focused on words and not video, and it was interesting to see the components of the story in different combinations. "It's almost like we wanted to explore how all the media played with and against each other," she says.

Many of the photos that accompany the story were taken during that first assignment by Al Kamalizad, a photographer and documentary filmmaker who was there with Ohlmann. (Kamalizad also edited the initial short documentary for the UN.) Those photos and others were highlighted in photo essay format in another post on the *Good* website.

Empathy from Multiple Angles

The various media through which this project approaches its topic overlap in content, but vary in angle. Kaplan's written piece enters the story with the perspective of a trained counselor—narrating the journey to film alongside Ohlmann, and inserting his own observations about the psychological states of the people they encountered. He is attuned to signs of trauma, and his insights give readers something a casual observer might not otherwise perceive.

Looking at the two formats side by side calls into question the notion of VR as the ultimate "empathy machine." In the written piece, the interweaving of multiple storylines—the writer's own internal monologue along with the context of the war, the character development of the people featured, and the perspective of humanitarian aid workers—is far beyond the scope of the 360 film. It's also a more emotionally resonant angle into the story.

What the 360-degree film provides, on the other hand, is a sense of place in a way that other media couldn't offer. The ability to look around the war-torn landscape from a point where a displaced person might stand gives a perspective that could only otherwise be achieved by visiting in person.

Editor Katie Wudel points out that the different media can help a viewer feel different kinds of empathy. She says 360 video portion of the project feels "darker" than the written story because there isn't space within its format to step away and reflect, and care has been taken to give it the appropriate emotional weight.

"With a [written] story, because you are doing a little bit of reflection after the fact and you can provide so many additional links and details, you can kind of step outside of it a little bit in a way that you can't when it's video," she says.

Wudel does think that, had the videographers followed the characters for a longer documentary-style video, they could also have captured a level of depth and nuance beyond what they delivered in The Call Center. But she's not convinced a 360 video could carry the amount of context necessary to tell the whole story.

The video stands on its own, Wudel adds, but "having the whole context around it just makes it so much more powerful."

"I think about those folks in the tents," she says in reference to the shots in the refugee camp, "in a way that I never would have before. I think it does help me build empathy, it's just a different kind."

Takeaways

Splitting out the context:
- Using other media to establish the context for an immersive experience can leave more space for experiential storytelling.
- Different media can offer different access points for creating empathy for a single story—for example character-based or experiential storytelling.
- In a multimedia project, immersive media can be employed as a component to add a sense of place.

Leaving room for the experience:
- It doesn't take much to overwhelm a viewer of immersive media—keeping embedded text to a minimum can free up mental space to take in the experience.

About This Project

URL: www.good.is/features/trauma-in-an-iraqi-war-zone
Interview Subjects: Katie Wudel, Aaron Ohlmann
Film:
Producer: Aaron Ohlmann
Co-producers: Adam Kaplan, Hannah Bombelles, Maad Mohaamed
Executive Producer: David Clair
Edited by: Cory Fogel & Aaron Ohlmann
Written Narrative: Adam Kaplan
Photos: Al Kamalizad and Aaron Ohlmann
Fixer: Maad Mohaamed
Editor: Katie Wudel

Capturing Everest

Sports Illustrated
May, 2017

Capturing Everest is *Sports Illustrated*'s first serialized VR piece in which viewers follow along as three climbers make the journey to the top of the world's tallest mountain. The suspense of the story builds as the team climbs—will they make it to the top? Each of the four 8-minute episodes is complete with a recap of the previous episode and previews of what will come next, enticing the audience to continue watching. The series is a joint production between *Sports Illustrated* and digital video studio Endemol Shine Beyond USA and serves as a model for capturing action as it unfolds.

The 360 series is the anchoring point for the story, and main discussion for this case study, but it is a companion to a May 2017 *Sports Illustrated* cover story featuring Jeff Glassbrenner—the first American amputee to climb Mount Everest. As part of the "first virtual reality bottom to top Everest climb," a dedicated *Capturing Everest* website serves as the online home for the content.

Following a Journey

The four-part series begins with shots of climbers slowly trudging up a snowy mountain. With dramatic background music, the text on-screen reads: "Every year hundreds of people attempt to Summit Everest," followed by a timelapse of brightly colored tents with people moving in and out amidst a background of wind and snowy weather. The first few seconds set up the journey and episodes to come: "Many will fail to scale all 29,035 feet due to health or weather," the text reads. "This is the story of three climbers and their attempt."

Interwoven into the journey are the individual stories of each of the three climbers: Brent Bishop, Lisa Thompson and Jeff Glassbrenner. Bishop is the son of the late climber Barry Bishop—a member of the first American team to summit Mount Everest in 1963. Thompson had battled cancer and had a new outlook on life, and Glassbrenner is a Paralympian and inspirational speaker. The first episode finds Bishop counting backpacks and preparing for the climb two weeks before leaving home. This episode also includes footage from the airplane journey to Nepal and brief introductions to Bishop's fellow climbers. The passage of time and ascent into the mountains is marked at different times throughout the piece with an animated ticker showing the day as well as the elevation.

Bringing together a team

In 2016, Mia Tramz was approached to lead Life VR for Time Inc. The concept for the Life VR app is to extend the original *Life* magazine brand into VR and use the app as an umbrella brand to house content from all of the Time Inc. brands, such as *Time, Sports Illustrated, Travel and Leisure, Food and Wine*, and *In Style*, instead of building standalone VR for each brand. As the managing editor, Tramz built an editorial vision and a launch slate for the Life VR app.

Tramz says she was looking for projects speaking to the legacy and the history of older brands and magazines—a level of ambition warranting putting the *Sports Illustrated* name on them. At the same time, Michael Franz, the cofounder of Panogs, a production house based in Portland, was in discussion with production company 8ninths. As Franz recalls, the team said, "hey we have this project … on Mount Everest." Panogs had done VR work for Seattle's Space needle, but at the time had not delved into documentary work. Both teams met a week later with Madison Mountaineering—the guiding company that would be on the mountain. 8ninths had just sold the rights for the project to a company called

Endomol Shine Beyond, and Life VR was able to come on as a distribution partner.

They aimed to partner with the print and digital side of *Sports Illustrated* in addition to the VR distribution, so the project would reach a wide audience. The intention from the beginning was to use all of the *Sports Illustrated* platforms to support the launch of the project. To do so, they had support from the editorial team and editor-in-chief Chris Stone—who was excited about the project.

The post-production began with Endomol Shine Beyond and then continued with the Life VR team in-house. At Sundance 2016, the Life VR team showed a sneak peek and started conversations with Coors. This eventually led to sponsorship. After finding the right sponsor, they were able to settle on a May 2017 launch date, allowing the team to hit the news peg of the climbing season, and coordinate across the *Sports Illustrated* team to have a cover story as well as an augmented reality component.

Learning on the Fly

The field team consisted of four climbers who rotated their camera duties. The Panogs team was able to teach the climbers the basic workflow: They explained how to operate each camera rig, and walked through their processes for sound syncing, and offloading files. They only had about two days to cover all of the different camera setups and settings.

The piece was shot using multiple rig set-ups of GoPro cameras—a two-camera, three-camera, four-camera and six-camera set-up organized by Franz. In addition to camera rigs, the Panogs team sent the climbers with a zip line system to get dynamic moving shots, a Nikon KeyMission and H6N microphone as well as a body harness with a pole on the back (for above-the-head shots).

Timing was a challenge throughout the project. On the shooting side, after receiving funding, Franz says they had about two months to plan and gather all equipment together. He recalls some issues with file management, and mismatched camera settings on multi-camera rigs. Luckily, some of the initial mistakes were from shots at low altitude before basecamp, and the trial and error gave the team a chance to get used to the equipment.

The Right Structure for the Story

With four 8-minute segments for a total of about 32 minutes, Everest VR was one of the longer VR narratives at the time of its publication—even the individual segments were longer than most 360 videos. Tramz believes there is no optimal length for a VR experience, and the story should dictate the length. "It should be as long as the story itself merits," she says.

For *Capturing Everest*, with powerful visual content and a rich story arc to work with, Tramz says that it felt like it merited several episodes. And as the climb itself goes through several phases or stages it made sense to do a series of episodes. "It's just like film, or television ... you really have to tell the story in the way it's meant to be told," says Tramz. The technique of including "previously on" and "coming up" is lifted directly from television style, but also works well for this particular series. It allows the viewer to take a break, and then continue on or come back at another time without losing the storyline.

Multimedia and Augmented Reality

Although the project began as a 360 video series, it includes a written component and augmented reality elements. The final packaging doesn't depend on the video to tell a complete backstory of all the people featured in the video. Both text and video serve as complementary aspects to the broader story of the climb. Between the cover story on Jeff Glassbrenner, the 360 video experience and the shorter teasers on Facebook and the *Sports Illustrated*'s website, each version serves as an entry-point for a viewer.

The Coors sponsorship allowed the team to do an augmented reality element for the magazine cover. In collaboration with RYOT, they created an image-based trigger for the cover. With the LifeVR app open, holding the camera up to the cover of *Sports Illustrated* prompts an audiovisual roll of a Coors light can, with snowy mountains in the background and the option to click to reach the 360 videos directly. "It all just sort of came together in a very serendipitous way," Tramz said. For the rest of the May edition of *Sports Illustrated* they had some additional AR activations throughout the issue—some Everest-related, some not—so users could access additional AR content.

They also used their own player since they anticipated that most of their audience would be coming from the web via mobile phone. When the viewer opens the website, they can watch the video without downloading any apps. If they had embedded a YouTube video viewers arriving to the site on a mobile phone would need to open the link from the YouTube app to be able to see the mobile version, "No one's going to open another app to watch a 360 video," Tramz says.

To release all the various components, they did specific cuts, or "mini-trailers." The 2D trailers give the audience a sense of the longer video, "We call them 'look-arounds'" says Tramz. These trailers serve to entice the viewer to take time to investigate the full series. "We really leveraged the full power of the brand, to not only publish the story itself but to get readers excited for what it was," says Tramz.

The Right Shots for VR

The storyline and visuals work in VR in part because the team was able to get footage of all the important aspects of the story. For the final summit shot, Tramz says they got lucky—it was a clear day. The triumphant moment at the top serves as the backdrop for internal dialogue from Glassbrenner and Thompson, giving context about what reaching the top meant for them. "It's such a great metaphor for the journeys that they both are going on in their lives," Tramz says.

There are several shots inside tents that are particularly interesting in VR. These include the shots of basecamp in the kitchen tent, the mess hall, and then with individuals in their tents. Tramz points to these because of the way proximity is experienced in VR. "We've read a bunch of studies and done a bunch of our own studies internally to see what people do when put in proximity with a virtual person," Tramz says. "What's interesting is, even if it's a virtual person in 360, or a game-engine run experience, the viewer will tend to try to respect physical boundaries." Playing with closeness and intimacy and being inside the tents is something they wouldn't be able to do with traditional video. Some of the shots that answer the question "why VR?" are the ones in these smaller enclosed spaces.

The landscape and environment also works particularly well for this type of 360 video. Climbing up snow-packed mountains, the viewer may not be able to see all of the sweeping vistas, yet hearing the wind, the crunch of the ice and seeing the snow provides an immersive scene-setting. "We were lucky with this project that everything that the camera is capturing is interesting," says Tramz. Since they weren't staging scenes, they were at the mercy of their environment. They had compelling characters as well. Still, the team made an effort to anticipate the starting point and the opening of each shot. They did testing to guide the viewer from one shot to the next, starting a shot so that the key action would be in range of the viewers gaze at each cut.

They went through some of these transitions by viewing the project in a headset and showing it to lots of people to see whether they followed the action as intended.

There are many documentaries about Everest, but, as associate producer Michaela Holland says, *Capturing Everest* is a different experience: "I've never seen anyone else watch Everest and say, 'I don't get it, what's going on.'" This may be because the story of the climb is a universal storyline. Holland also says she believes *Capturing Everest* is one of the first 360 documentaries in which the viewer sees the action unfold over time in addition to having the more traditional sit-down interviews with characters. Unfolding action is a cornerstone of documentary filmmaking and a challenge to quick-turnaround news productions of 360 video.

A Process of Discovery

With regard to filming, Franz says in retrospect he would have done a more in-depth training with the shooters. He also believes they would have had more footage, had someone from his team been up on the mountain. If he were to do it again, Franz says, he would be on-site, perhaps climbing with the team, to be able to troubleshoot technical issues and handle file management. He also says he might opt for an easier-to-use camera rig, and consider hiring a drone pilot and perhaps even take **stereoscopic** images to be able to have additional assets to work with.

There are still a lot of rules to be broken, Tramz says. "There is a process of discovery that you sort of have to commit to going through," she says, noting there are many shots the filmmaker will end up with that someone may not have ever conceived of in advance. She says creators should be open to the process of letting the story "take you where it needs to go," knowing that there's room for innovation, and "letting these magical surprises take on a life of their own."

Takeaways

Style to match the storyline:
- Episodic storytelling works well for a narrative arc with clear stages, and gives viewers a chance to take a break.
- "Previously" and "Coming up" sections hold the story thread for viewers to leave the series and come back.

Why VR:
- Enclosed spaces, such as being inside a tent with someone, play with closeness and intimacy in a way that can't be achieved in flat video.

A process of discovery:
- Many shots in *Capturing Everest* the creators say they couldn't have been imagined before they happened; it pays to stay open to discovery.

Using the existing infrastructure:
- The augmented reality is integrated into the existing app, making it easier to use, and avoiding the hassle of downloading an additional app.

About This Project

URL: www.si.com/specials/everest-climb-virtual-reality/index.html
Interview Date: December, 2017; January, 2018

Interview Subjects: Mia Tramz, Managing Editor, LIFE VR; Michael Franz, Co-founder, Panogs; Michaela Holland, Associate Producer, LIFE VR
Team:
Editorial Director, SI Group: Chris Stone
Digital Editor, SI Group: Mark McClusky
Managing Editor, SI.com: Ryan Hunt
Managing Editor, LIFE VR: Mia Tramz
Executive Producer, Time Inc.: Josh Oshinsky
Director of Digital Projects, SI.com: Ben Eagle
Associate Producer, LIFE VR: Michaela Holland
Interactive Web Director, The Foundry: Louis Gubitosi
Front-End Web Developer, SI.com: Allen Kim

Hell and High Water VR

Jovrnalism
Fall 2016

Hell and High Water VR is a six-part immersive project that explores the potential impact of a major hurricane striking Houston, Texas. As the fourth-largest city in the U.S. and vital shipping nexus, Houston has eerie similarities to New Orleans before Katrina in terms of known vulnerabilities to disaster. The project spins off from a major investigation into these vulnerabilities published in May 2016 by ProPublica and the Texas Tribune. The series was, indeed, timely. In late summer 2017, Hurricane Harvey struck Houston.

The National Oceanic and Atmospheric Administration estimated Harvey caused $125 billion in damage (compared to Katrina's $161.3 billion), bringing flooding that displaced more than 30,000 people and damaged or destroyed more than 200,000 homes and businesses. And Harvey was not the worst case scenario as presented in *Hell and High Water*. Houston continues to be a "sitting duck," and the question posed in the run-up to this project—when a disaster looms, can VR help make people care, or act?—still stands.

While its primary medium is 360 video, the project brings a variety of multimedia elements into the 360 space to supplement its storytelling and provide additional context. It is, in many respects, a multimedia news package built into 360 space. In some ways it's conceptually similar to *USA Today*'s *The Wall* (see the case study in this chapter), in that it is a sweeping exploration of a subject rooted in geography. However, while *The Wall* targets early adopters with high end **headsets**, *Hell and High Water* VR is available on mobile, and therefore accessible for a broader audience. In exchange for **walk-around** 3D spaces and interactivity in navigation, *Hell and High Water* VR aims for accessibility. It is available in its original design on a proprietary mobile app from the USC VR program, called Jovrnalism, but it can also be found on YouTube.

The project is divided into a series of "vignettes," 2–3 minute chapters that are thematically connected but designed to stand alone. A voice-over narrator is present in each—introducing the scene, providing context, and at times directing the viewer. At the end of each vignette, the narrator suggests which experience should be seen next.

The vignettes each center around a theme. Introduction: A Sitting Duck gives an overview of the risk of a major hurricane striking Houston, and orients the viewer with a virtual flyover of the city. Storm Surge: What It Means mixes 3D graphics and 360 video to illustrate the height of a storm surge relative to that of a house. Industry: The Toxic Neighbors orients viewers to the petrochemical industry associated with the Houston ship channel, and Tanks: Surrounded By Risk delves deeper into the potential for environmental destruction should one—or many— of those petrochemical tanks rupture. The final two vignettes look at the destruction Hurricane Ike caused, with the tour of a damaged home in People: Meet The Survivors, and overlaid images of a debris-covered city in Before And After Ike.

While the pieces can be watched in any order, their presentation in the app and the narrator's **call to action** create a strong nudge to watch them sequentially, such that the project as a whole is fundamentally linear, though not requiring linear consumption.

The series is the first major project to come out of Robert Hernandez's virtual reality course at the University of Southern California. Hernandez, a new media professor who runs the course as an experimental workshop, led creation during the semester-long course that took the project from brainstorming to near completion in spring 2016. The team worked on finishing touches over the summer and published that November.

Supplementing a Big Story

Hell and High Water VR exists both as a supplement to the ProPublica/ Texas Tribune investigation that prompted it and as a standalone project. Scott Klein, Deputy Managing Editor at ProPublica, reached out to Robert Hernandez at USC while the ProPublica story was still in development. He had an interest in finding out whether VR could be a tool to help people understand the threat a major storm posed to Houston. After all, researchers had predicted and multiple publications had reported on New Orleans' vulnerabilities years before Katrina caused devastation in 2005, but the reporting hadn't helped avert disaster.

Hernandez agreed to take on the project with his students, and as the semester began they were given an early draft of the story. They brainstormed for elements that could be told or enhanced with VR. While they wanted the VR to tell a complete story, they were expecting to produce

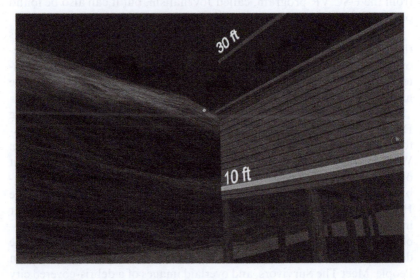

Figure 6.4 Hell and High Water, Jovrnalism.

around 15 minutes of content and didn't expect viewers to last that long watching a single piece.

Each student pitched an idea for how to approach some element of the story with VR, and the group built a rough outline that ordered those components into a narrative arc.

Once they had an outline in mind, the team met with ProPublica editor Scott Klein and reporter Al Shaw to verify that their proposal felt complete and appropriate with the content of the main investigation.

The graphical elements—3D models and overlays—were developed primarily by students, with the support of some friends in the industry. The team filmed the 360 video components over three days in Houston during USC's spring break in 2016, and used that video in five of the six chapters (the intro chapter relies on graphics and archival footage).

The "Overload" Effect

Once an early draft was ready, the group did usability testing. One of the biggest challenges, Hernandez says, was avoiding "overload" for viewers. Because there is so much information and context being presented in each chapter, they had to put a lot of work into ensuring that the voice over narration, graphics, images and text didn't compete.

Each one of the six pieces integrates multiple media elements to illustrate its message. There's the basic immersive space that makes up the background—graphical in the intro chapter and 360-degree video in the remaining five. Then there's the ambient and on-camera audio, as well as voice-over narration. Added graphical elements include text overlays with information about a place, maps to orient the viewer, 3D models, data visualizations and photo galleries. Together, these components make up a multimedia news package built entirely into the immersive space. But because the medium is video and non-interactive, timing and other strategies to prevent viewer overload were critical.

They came up with a few tricks to help with the overload problem:

First, they favored the forward-facing 180-degree field for their graphics. While captions or essential information might appear in the front and back to ensure that viewers don't miss it, they hoped that by keeping most of the graphics in the same general area they could subtly "encourage and train" viewers to always come back to the front.

Second, they tried to avoid having graphics on screen when the narrator was speaking. In the third chapter, for example, the voice-over narration pauses several times as text information appears on screen.

Finally, they came up with a prioritization system for information. If they wanted to make sure nobody would miss a key piece of information, they used multiple media to get the message across. This happens early on in the first chapter: An embedded video shows a newscaster reading an urgent evacuation warning from the national weather service in the run-up to Hurricane Ike, which grazed Houston in 2008: "... persons not heeding evacuation warnings in single family one or two story homes will face certain death." The text is also embedded, so viewers can read along with the announcement. And just to drive it home, the words "will face certain death," are bright yellow on the screen. In other parts of the project, where they deemed information non-essential, text may appear on screen without audio to reinforce it, and the voice-over audio for the most part complements the visuals, but is not redundant.

Hernandez says as viewers get more accustomed to consuming immersive media they may be able to take in more information at once. But for the time being, "less is more," he says. "We need the stuff to sink in."

A Linear Narrative, Served up in Pieces

Hernandez says it felt like too much to ask for a viewer to watch a 13 or 15 minute immersive piece. At the same time, the team wanted the piece to tell a coherent narrative and cover a lot of ground. They settled on a technique Hernandez calls the "relay race": At the end of each of the two-to-three minute pieces, the narrator suggests which experience to watch next—i.e., they pass the baton.

With this, the user gets to choose at each juncture whether to push the story forward, quit watching or jump around arbitrarily. But unlike some stylistically similar **branching narrative** style pieces in which the user's experience is likely to vary, this project continuously channels the viewer toward one specific path.

Figure 6.5 Hell and High Water, Jovrnalism.

There's a natural feel to this particular format with 360 video—especially in that it is displayed within an app in which the components are laid out in order. It strikes a balance between giving the user the freedom to make decisions and ensuring that they get the essential information. Perhaps just as importantly, since there is a single narrative the user is unlikely to walk away with the feeling they might have missed something important—a common problem that arises with true branching narratives.

Hernandez says he sees this style as in some ways analogous to video games such as *Grand Theft Auto*: There's a linear storyline to be revealed, and while the user can have a rewarding experience by exploring the game world and ignoring the story, "most people still want a linear experience." In this case, he says the tendency toward a linear experience seems especially strong because the format is still video, and not fully interactive. But he also points at the work that goes into scripting and structure in order to create momentum toward the storyline. With each chapter, the team would ask, "What is the point of this experience, and what is it doing to set up the next experience?" That thought process looks a lot like traditional narrative story development, just cut up into more discrete pieces.

The Explanatory Power of VR

Hell and High Water VR is rooted in an investigation that explores a complex subject, and in the development of this project the creators began with a brainstorm of the issues they felt were essential to address—with a particular focus on what would benefit from being explained in VR. The resulting set of topics tended toward explanatory journalism, and meant

Figure 6.6 Hell and High Water, Jovrnalism.

that the project would be information-dense in a way that pushed the limits of what had been done with the 360 video at the time.

Hernandez, who has also explored augmented reality as a format and hopes to return to it once the technology becomes more accessible, says he realized after finishing *Hell and High Water* VR that what they were doing with text and graphical overlays was essentially "AR in VR." "We immersed you into this other reality," he says, "and we augmented it with digital overlays or graphics to enhance that reality so you can understand the context of the location." That way of conceptualizing embedded multimedia has since become a standard in work his students produce.

What stands out about this context-heavy explanatory style within 360 video is its divergence from the presence-first mindset of many VR creators. While the voice-over narration and near-constant use of multimedia overlays may interfere with the user's ability to feel as though they are truly "experiencing" the story, *Hell and High Water* VR carves out a different use case for immersive media.

Rather than tugging at heartstrings, it seeks to convey information in a way that enhances understanding through a kind of spatial storytelling that is not possible using traditional media. While many projects lean heavily on the emotional power of VR's immersive effect to make people care, this project has a much more pragmatic approach toward the same end.

Audio, News, Context

The audio strategy in *Hell and High Water* VR is straightforward and has a newsy feel. There is no music in any of the chapters. Ambient scene audio is present in many of the 360 video shots, and a water sound effect supplements visualizations of flooding, but the voice-over narration is by far the most prominent audio element. In the People experience, the owners of two homes damaged during Hurricane Ike stand in briefly for the voice-over narration, describing their own experiences or showing the viewer around a scene.

The voice-over script has a documentary tone to it, but it hints at a sense of presence in a way that diverges from traditional documentary and approaches tour-guide or newscaster territory. The narrator addresses the viewer with statements such as "let's get a closer look," and suggests where to look in certain scenes by saying "look around to see," or "this picture shows ..." The method is not especially subtle, but it's thoughtful, and Hernandez believes it makes the most sense for producing an immersive news feature, given that turnaround times in the news industry often require a compromise between production level and timeliness of release. Scripted narration is an efficient way to convey a lot of information.

At times, the voice-over pace can feel quick—such as when the narrator suggests that the viewer look at a photo gallery, but resumes talking only a few seconds later. Despite the usability testing the team did to make sure they weren't overloading the viewer, providing this much information in a 360 video still poses a challenge. There may not be a clean solution to the tension between boring and overloading viewers until creators have more variable options for interactivity and responsive story design.

Hernandez says another element he would have liked to include in this project but elected not to is **spatialized audio**. He thinks audio placed within the scene could have offered an additional tool for cueing the viewer where to look, but at the time this project was created the options—both for creation and publication of spatial audio in 360 video—were still too much work relative to their return.

Distribution

"It's still a challenge to kind of figure out how to distribute these experiences," says Hernandez, who was able to secure grant funding early on for the USC program to have its own 360 video app (Jovrnalism). But he also acknowledges that, while the app gives them the ability to host their own content, it's a lot to ask for viewers to download an app to see a piece.

Hernandez says his group designs all of their projects with mobile headset (e.g., **cardboard**) in mind, though he expects that, for the time being, the majority of viewers will watch it on a desktop. Beyond that, he says even the decision to root the experiences in 360 video rather than interactive VR is a compromise for accessibility.

"I'm a journalist so I want my content to be consumed by everybody, not just with people who ... are early adopters," Hernandez says, but the distribution side "is just not there yet."

Takeaways

Hearts and minds:
- This project relies less on the viewer's sense of presence to make them care, but rather appeals to logic, taking advantage of the whole immersive canvas to explain concepts.

Training the viewer:
- Train viewers to always look in the same area to find key information by consistently putting graphics there.

Clear presentation:
- Avoid including audio and visuals that compete for attention; if there's an informative graphic in the scene, a break in the narration can help viewers focus.
- To highlight especially important information, communicate it with multiple media—for example, in audio narration, a graphic and text.

Bite-sized pieces:
- Breaking up an immersive story into smaller pieces that stand on their own can help give viewers a sense of agency by letting them choose their own path through the content.

AR in VR:
- Graphical overlays can augment a 360-degree scene with context and additional details.

Narration for news:
- Voice-over narration delivers information efficiently in a quick-turnaround project.

About This project

URL: www.youtube.com/watch?v=D0rASFoaoog
Interview Date: November 2017, January 2018
Interview Subjects: Robert Hernandez
Created by:
VR Experience: Ariba Alvi, Jason Cheng, Crystal Goss, Cristian Guzman, Melody Jiang, David Merrell, Kaitlyn Mullin, Jason Suh, Kevin Tsukii, Serhan Ulkumen
VR Advisor: Robert Hernandez
Investigation: Neena Satija, Kiah Collier, Al Shaw, Jeff Larson

The Wall

Unknown Stories, Unintended Consequences

USA Today
September, 2017

The Wall is an ambitious, content-rich **walk-around** VR experience built to supplement an even broader project of the same name, created during nine months in 2017 by a team of more than 30 reporters and photographers, plus data journalists, videographers, developers, designers and editors working at the *Arizona Republic* and the wider *USA Today* Network. Led by *Arizona Republic* VP of News and Executive Editor Nicole Carroll, the *USA Today* Network special report looks at the entire 2,000 miles of the U.S.–Mexico border through a variety of lenses, using a wide range of media.

The Wall project began, in part, as a result of The *Arizona Republic*'s coverage of the Trump campaign, with its xenophobic rhetoric and the rallying cry: "Build the wall!" *Arizona Republic* News Director Josh Susong says Carroll asked the team to think about how they could examine the subject of a wall "in as many ways as possible." Susong led the development of the VR project alongside Ray Soto, Director of Emerging Technology at Gannett (which owns *USA Today*).

The Wall may have been inspired by Donald Trump's simplistic presidential campaign promise, but the project branches beyond that concept, using it as a guiding theme into a breadth of complex issues. By way of an overview of the feasibility and potential impact of a border wall, it explores immigration policy, cross-border communities, international trade, migration, land rights, and even the notion of borders themselves. "We were trying to push the envelope for ourselves," Susong says.

The completed project, which is assembled in a multimedia presentation online, weaves together 13 mini-documentaries, text stories, footage and narration from a 10-day helicopter journey that spanned the length of the border, investigative reporting on property records, a series of podcasts and the HTC Vive VR experience.

And the creators were rewarded for their innovative work. The larger project was awarded a Pulitzer Prize for explanatory reporting in April 2018, with the judges specifically citing the VR in saying the award was given: "For vivid and timely reporting that masterfully combined text, video, podcasts and virtual reality to examine, from multiple perspectives, the difficulties and unintended consequences of fulfilling President Trump's pledge to construct a wall along the U.S. border with Mexico."

The VR experience serves to take the viewer directly to the border— something that no other medium has the capacity to do. Susong describes it as a curated version of the larger project, "incorporating elements across the spectrum."

The Wall *as an Immersive Experience*

The Wall VR, designed for use on a Vive headset, incorporates traditional video, drone footage, photos, ambient audio and voice-over narration, music, **photogrammetry**, 3D modeling and animation, all built into a 3-dimensional walk-around environment. It illustrates what can be done with savvy use of multimedia elements, and shows how news organizations can integrate already-existing media into VR spaces to great effect. The 3D-modeled experiences are unique to VR. Longer video stories from the main project are presented in 60–90 second "micro-versions." The project offers a glimpse of VR crossing over from novelty to news platform.

As the piece opens, the viewer finds herself in darkness, with only the large title in the center of the forward **field of view**. A voice-over intro begins, and as it speaks a bright yellow line appears below the title and grows outward to the left and right across the black background. "Now both countries face a new idea, a wall end to end on the southern border," the voice-over says as the yellow line extrudes upward to make the shape of a wall. A moment later, a map appears underneath the viewer's feet, showing where the border lies along the portion of North America where the U.S. and Mexico meet. The bright yellow wall now runs across that border, from Tijuana and San Diego at the Pacific Ocean to the Gulf of Mexico.

"Explore that journey yourself by starting here," the voice-over says as the Vive controller begins to vibrate and a label pops up that reads "Press the thumbpad to teleport." The user is then prompted to press the menu button on the controller and to select the first of four border-related chapters: 1. Crossing, 2. Stopping, 3. Caught in Between and 4. What's at the Border? After visiting the first chapter, the user has the freedom to hop around to any portion of any chapter. While the content isn't inherently ordered, the chapter numbers give a strong nudge toward following the roadmap those chapters provide.

When the user selects a chapter, the wall recedes and white labels rise out of several locations along the border. Another short voice-over introduces the user to the concept behind each chapter. As the viewer approaches a labeled location (by walking or **teleporting** with the Vive controller), more information and the ability to trigger media comes into view. The viewer can watch short videos (teasers for longer content that appeared on the *USA today* network) and click-through photo slideshows. The team chose not to use the full versions of the videos, because they felt it didn't use the immersive medium to the fullest extent.

In addition to the 3D map upon which the viewer stands for most of the experience, walk-around "on the ground" environments of specific locations are available within the chapters. The viewer can step into the middle of a canyon in Big Bend National Park to see the way the towering natural canyon walls would thwart any effort to build a man-made wall, or stand at the base of Mount Cristo Rey near El Paso, which is a destination for pilgrims from both sides of the border. The peak of Mount Cristo Rey is in New Mexico, but its base runs down to El Paso to the north of the border, and Ciudad Juarez to the south; geology defies borders, and the community here is intensely international.

In one of the most powerful moments of the experience, the user is able to walk around a 3D model of a fence that cuts across the border near Tecate, Mexico. Looking up at that fence, the viewer can feel its imposing nature, its incongruousness along the otherwise natural landscape. Audio recorded on scene of wind rustling in the grass supports a sense of immersion that adds to the power of standing that close to the fence—a place most people will never see at that distance, and which is probably the closest existing approximation (as of 2017) to what Trump's border wall might look like—though the proposed wall would likely dwarf it in size.

Delving into Production

The project is curated around three ideas: crossing, stopping and stopping in between. The initial brainstorming began in May, and Soto's team was able to rough out the first immersive model in August. The project launched in September.

The team collected **Lidar** data at eight hotspots along the border. The team at Gannet used photogrammetry to turn three of these scans into 3D virtual representations of the environment for users to explore—these are the on-the-ground experiences.

After conversations with Susong and others at the *Arizona Republic*, Ray Soto began working to develop ideas for what the user experience would look like with his team in DC.

Soto's team wanted to allow the user the ability to explore and discover different stories along the border, while also giving a more high-level overview. After coming up with a loose framework, they began building prototypes. After 2–3 weeks experimenting on prototypes, they began developing the user experience and the user interface elements.

Soto's team worked closely with a student group through the game studies program at the University of Advanced Technology in Arizona to work out user interaction and create some of the virtual spaces. At the same time, Soto and Susong worked with the editorial team to figure out how to create a narrative arc to put the story into context.

"What we had noticed is VR required us to build a structure that would allow users to explore the story as they wanted, but we needed to provide a narrative structure that supported the story we were looking to tell," Soto says. After iterating on prototypes, they decided to treat the experience "as a book in chapters," he says. "A user can skip ahead and go back, but there is a defined arc with a beginning, middle, and end." For additional context, they included audio narration.

Finding the Right Structure

It took several pivots to work out an appropriate level of interactivity and story arc.

At one point in development, Soto says, the team realized the structure of an initial concept was "too gamified." That concept had users picking up objects to move the story forward—for example, picking up a water bottle at the border fence would trigger narration about the dangers of crossing the border. They changed this structure because neither the editorial team nor the development team had the time to build out this level of interactivity.

Soto says the team initially modeled out a structure in which users could jump freely in and out of different parts of the experience without a lot of guidance—as they had done for an earlier project called Eisenhower VR.[5] In another test, there wasn't enough structure to the story when the user put the headset on, and users didn't know what they were supposed to do. "Folks felt as if they were lost," he says.

User Interaction for Multimedia VR

During development, the team asked: How do we make this a more compelling experience, and how do we encourage users to go and start experiencing the rest?

Soto says the most difficult thing about user interaction design was figuring out how best to display the different assets in a way that made sense for the viewer. "We couldn't simply throw everything up in the scene expecting users to understand what they were seeing and where to start," he says. "We slowly introduced the visuals to allow the user an opportunity to understand what they are seeing to develop their orientation within the virtual environment," Soto says. "The home screen (map overview) does not change throughout the experience, giving users the ability to quickly identify where they are and where to focus." They introduce additional elements gradually, with interactive **points of interest** animating into the scene as viewers approach them.

The final experience relies heavily on the user's **field of view** to direct attention. In the on-the-ground experiences, the user's initial position in the scene was an intentional design decision. "We used the layout and perspective to define the path we wanted them to take," Soto says.

Different Audio Serving Different Purposes

The Wall VR uses different types of audio to score and shape the experience. They used **head-locked** audio for narrative components—music, narration, and navigation-triggered sounds, and **spatialized** audio for environmental sounds in the on-the ground experiences.

Soto says distinguishing these two types of audio helps the user immediately recognize whether a sound is a narrative element or an environmental one.

The background music runs through the entire experience whenever the user is in the main map area, subtly reminding the viewer where they are in the experience and helping to shape the mood. "The background music was vital to create the tone of the project," Soto says. They weren't able to choose this music until the narrative components of the project were complete. They added it in once Susong had delivered the introductory narration—Soto says the tone of Susong's script inspired the music choice.

Spatial sounds in the walk-around environments were placed near the visuals they represented, where possible. These sounds were pulled from the actual locations: The team used the sound of wind rustling through the grass (Tecate), running water (Big Bend), and crowds (Mount Cristo Rey). "We wanted to ensure we captured not just the visual component but the tone of each location that supported the narrative and completed the sense of total immersion," Soto says.

An Experience Worth Revisiting

What stands out about *The Wall* VR as compared to many other immersive experiences is the sheer amount and variety of multimedia content it incorporates. It's a curated experience, as its creators put it, and more than any other news project created to date, the immersive space functions as a platform for other media. Its content mirrors what's shown in the main project's multimedia web presentation, but it's adapted to use immersive space to its strengths. The navigation is spatial, and non-immersive media is strategically embedded to integrate into this environment.

As a whole, the experience pushes the limits of content length many creators of immersive media abide—but the way it's structured and broken up means users are given an easy way to hop out and come back in. In this way, it feels like a preview of what immersive experiences might look like when users access them while browsing in a headset, versus breaking away from their typical media consumption to put on a headset.

But there are limitations too: Much like it's hard to jump from a flat media consumption experience into immersive space, it correlates that it's challenging to stand in immersive space and passively consume flat media. Notably, the experience doesn't include any 360-degree video— all the video experiences in it are flat. They have been shortened, but standing in a Vive headset even to watch a 90-second video takes a lot of energy for its level of interactivity.

The narration may also work against repeat visitors—hearing it autoplay upon each visit to the piece quickly gets tiresome. It points again to the tension between guiding the viewer to see certain parts of the story and not get lost, while still giving them the interactive freedom the medium promises.

An Award-Winning Audience Experience

The HTC Vive component of *The Wall* is targeted towards news consumers who are early adopters of VR technology, but it has been shown and demo-ed for a range of audiences. Susong says there's a balance to strike in how to guide users through the experience, depending on their level of VR knowledge.

"In our experience, we probably over explain for a pro-user and for a first-time user, we definitely under-explained," Susong says. In spite of the explanations, Susong says people tended to be impressed, even when they weren't quite sure what to do once they had the headset on. "The technology itself is so overwhelming that universally people say 'wow,' even if they have no idea if they are doing what they are supposed to be doing," Susong says.

Susong admits Vive ownership is small compared to the *USA Today* audience on the web, but he says there is value in the audience knowing that the *Arizona Republic* (and *USA Today*) is continuing to experiment at the cutting edge of technology.

Looking at the project from an audience engagement perspective, Soto says the team noticed that on average users spend about 15 minutes with this experience, but to explore in full would take closer to 30 minutes.

After demoing at an event in Arizona, Susong was surprised that several people reacted by saying the experience made them want to visit the places they had seen. "That just warmed my heart in such a pure journalism way ... We created this experience that was all about trying to give people objective ideas and more to think about than political rhetoric around an idea," he says. Susong describes the difficulty in creating the experience to allow people to be transported to the bottom of a holy mountain, and say "OK, now I want to take a road trip and go there in real life. It's like how can you even encapsulate the power of that idea from a journalistic standpoint?"

Soto and the *USA Today* Emerging Technology team use projects like these as opportunities to learn. He says he is continuously asking: "How can we expand our offerings to different audiences but create something that still tells a very powerful story?" With this project, the team was able to show a unique perspective on an ongoing story.

Takeaways

Know why you are using the immersive element:
• The sense of scale and perspective on the border takes the viewer both to a physical place and allows them to gain a perspective they may not normally be able to.

Massive scale and multiple reporters:
- The sheer breadth and depth of this project allowed for bringing together multiple perspectives on one issue. Not only the topic, but the local expertise helped to bring the whole thing together.

Exploring in an immersive experience:
- Breaking an immersive experience into chapters allows viewers to leave and come back.
- Finding a balance between a linear narrative arc and free exploration can give users agency but keep them from getting lost.

The best of sound:
- Using spatialized sound in addition to head-locked audio for narrative elements can help to create an overall sense of immersion.

About This Project

URL: www.usatoday.com/border-wall/, https://www.viveport.com/apps/3f16c881-0be2-475b-be59-7da4b1d0093f

www.usatoday.com/border-wall/usa-today-network-border-project-about-vr-podcasts-map/

www.azcentral.com/story/news/politics/border-issues/2017/09/22/trump-border-wall-project-9-months-on-us-mexico-border/691732001/

Interview Date: November, 2017

Interview Subjects: Josh Susong, news director, *The Arizona Republic*, Ray Soto, Director of Emerging Tech, Gannett

Team: Gannet with the support of UAT Game Studies

Notes

1 Bat Sounds, NPR, 2014: http://apps.npr.org/bats/.
2 A beginner's guide to spatial audio in 360-degree video, Nick Michael, NPR http://training.npr.org/visual/a-beginners-guide-to-spatial-audio-in-360-degree-video/.
3 Due to the geographical nature of this piece, the authors were not able to experience the piece first-hand. However, we were given access to listen to the full audio versions and spoke with Minneapolis Institute of Art as well as the creators.
4 Casement, Sue. "Did you hear that? An interactive art experience helps draw new fans." Accessed December 2017. www.3m.com/3M/en_US/particles/all-articles/article-detail/?storyid=a38c9241-42d9-4608-9de4-e50d0db70480
5 Eisenhower VR, *USA Today* Network, www.viveport.com/apps/ec3f2e37-799f-4629-8d1e-842ea1200563.

7 Augmented Reality and Mixed Reality

People try to treat technology as an object, and it can't be. It can only be a channel.

(Jaron Lanier)

Case Studies

Priya Shakti, Ram Devineni, Lina Srivastava, and Dan Goldman
Optimism, *Time* magazine and RYOT
Outthink Hidden, Fake Love for NYT Brand Studio
New Dimensions in Testimony, USC Shoah Foundation, Illinois Holocaust
   Museum
MoMAR, various artists
Olympians in AR, *The New York Times*
Terminal 3, Asad Malik

Luckily, we've evolved past the AR farting app of late 2017 and AR is beginning to be used in more complex ways beyond altering faces and catching Pokémon.[1] Headlines abound proclaiming 2018 as the year of AR, but how to tell a story with this format is still an elusive challenge. Over the course of the next few years, both the quantity and quality of AR apps is expected to increase dramatically.[2]

Often AR adds digital elements to a live view, through a smartphone, tablet, or headset. In the current media landscape, the most common and most referenced examples of AR in daily life are Snapchat filters and the Pokémon Go craze of 2016. AR can consist of both two- and three-dimensional digital visualizations and in this chapter we've also included a location-based audio example and a holographic theater that requires no headset.

Apple's release of ARKit in mid-2017 and Google's upgraded version of ARCore in Feb 2018 have provided developers and creators a foundation to build from. Businesses and developers from a wide variety of industries are exploring the AR landscape for training, education, and tourism in addition to other fields. Pearson is experimenting with immersive learning for history and geometry and a company called ARt Glass is creating AR experiences for cultural sites.

The vice president of Blippar has said that "AR campaigns have an average dwell time of 75 seconds—this is 2.5 times the average of radio or TV ads," according to the RYOT white paper on AR. The Kaleidoscope report on the VR & AR Industry recommends artists and studios "embrace short, iterative projects in AR until they develop a clear thesis for what makes a compelling AR experience."

In this chapter we've included some groundbreaking projects that have experimented in some way, offering lessons to be learned in order to take AR to the next level.

Priya's Shakti

Priya's Shakti *(Chapter 1),* **Priya's Mirror** *(Chapter 2)*

2014, 2015

When the creators of *Priya's Shakti* launched their interactive booth at Mumbai's Comicon in December 2014, Ram Devineni says it was "mind boggling ... it was kind of like magic." The team had charmed many writers with something new and different and it was written up hundreds of times. At that time it was indeed groundbreaking—two years before Pokémon Go wowed the world with its AR capabilities.

Priya's Shakti is the first comic in the series, and brings readers from all backgrounds into the life of Priya, who survives a rape and fights back. At first glance it may not appear to be anything extraordinary, but the pages reflect a powerful story of women's empowerment and resilience in the face of challenges, with an added augmented reality component. Part of Devineni's rationale for creating the comic was that no teenager would want to watch a documentary on rape, but many would be excited to read a comic book. To get the comic into more people's hands, they partnered with an Indian NGO called Apne Aap which focuses on ending sex-trafficking by preventing inter-generational prostitution.

The AR components on each of the comics are visible through the BlippAR app. BlippAR is a technology company specializing in augmented reality and its app serves as an AR browser. By opening the app and holding it up to the comic, it's brought to life, giving an added layer of movement and providing a deeper context with audio, video and occasionally an extra layer of visuals that seem to turn the comic into a pop-up book.

The creators teamed up for a second edition, *Priya's Mirror*, which premiered in 2016. It is based on acid-attack survivors and co-written by Indian feminist Parmita Vohra. They hope to do a third as well. There are about 20 AR components in *Priya's Shakti* (the first comic) and about 25 in *Priya's Mirror*, each edition also has 6–8 videos scattered throughout the AR layer.

Figure 7.1 Priya's Mirror, courtesy of Ram Devineni and Dan Goldman.

Centering the Stories of Women Fighting Back

In the first comic, *Priya's Shakti*, the Hindu Goddess Parvati is horrified to learn about the sexual violence women on Earth face—this prompts Priya to break her silence. Throughout the comic book are added videos, audio and layered images coming to life by viewing with the BlippAR app. But the comic does not rely on the augmented reality; it uses it as a tool to add further context on the real stories behind the comic, and to entice younger viewers to the content.

In the second edition of the comic, Priya joins a group of acid attack survivors, helping them to fight against a demon-king. Funded by The World Bank, *Priya's Mirror* features survivors from New York City, Bogota and New Delhi.

Chance Meeting to Partnership

In 2012, after a brutal gang-rape in India, U.S. Filmmaker Ram Devineni recorded interviews with rape survivors for what he thought might turn into a documentary film. He met U.S.-based comic artist and illustrator Dan Goldman in late 2012 at a tech meetup, and they decided to create a comic book instead of a film. The book is a modern mix on the traditional Indian comic style.

When they began the project, in early 2013, there were very few examples of AR projects. They were inspired by the way digital media and online viewing of comics was changing the way comics were being read, and they wanted to create something that would have an impact and change the way young people think about rape. During the creative development process, they were certain the story should be a physical comic book and the AR should add to it, and that the comic should not rely on the AR for the story to be understood. "Everybody needed to be able to get the story, not just the rich kids with smartphones," Goldman says.

Devineni says they wanted to use AR to turn the comic book into a "pop-up" book—and embed social activism into the augmented reality. For Priya's Mirror, one of the AR activations allows the viewer to take a selfie with a mask on—like the mask one of the women who was the victim of an acid attack had to wear. The Last Mask Campaign allows users to show their solidarity with acid attack survivors. Goldman added that the project goals were to reach young boys and girls with two sets of messages: First, they wanted to create a story in which readers would empathize with the main character and see that sexual violence is wrong. They also wanted to raise awareness and show that, if something does happen, there is solidarity and assistance for survivors.

Adding to Reality

Prior to jumping into the project, Devineni had no experience with AR. He'd seen the 1992 science-fiction horror film *Lawnmower Man* in all its

1980s VR glory, and he'd seen *Minority Report*'s gesture-based interface, but not much beyond that.

Devineni says part of his inspiration was the Sistine Chapel. When he visited, he thought, "wow this is the greatest comic book ever drawn in the world." Devineni appreciated how the panels serve to tell a series of stories, each of which connects to the larger story of humanity, yet it was also incredibly difficult to see close up because all the drawings are far away on the walls and ceilings. The natural thing for him to do was to get his smartphone out and use the camera to zoom in, "I saw the images close up and then I said 'okay if I could do that with this phone, it must be a way of life.'"

When he got home he searched for examples of AR projects, found half a dozen companies and emailed them all. BlippAR responded and eventually agreed to work with him.

For the production of the AR elements for the BlippAR app, Goldman used a series of layers in photoshop files to create basic animations adding color or basic movement to a page. Devineni also created some flat video elements "to give people a sense of what was going on—on the ground in real life," says Goldman.

Devineni says the comic, which avoids overt messaging, is not a typical social activist or NGO comic book, "which is incredibly boring and far too direct."

Balancing Story, Audience and Experience

There are many challenges with augmented reality—especially when creating for an audience that may not be familiar with the medium. Thinking through how one might experience the story, what kind of phone and internet connection would be necessary to experience it was also necessary to reach a broader audience. AR easily drains a phone battery and it can be slow to transition from one piece of AR content to the next. Some of the videos seem long for the AR format as well. "With AR, make sure it fits the medium or artwork you are creating," says Devineni. "AR works beautiful for comics and exhibition ... almost as if it was designed for it," he says. He adds that the AR should enhance and add a new dimension to the medium. When it fails to do this, it will appear "gimmicky," he says.

One useful feature of having an app that contains the AR is that it can be updated at any time. When they launched they had content for nearly all the pages, but after launch they added more images, interviews and audio. "The good thing about AR is you just update on the spot, and even though that person has the same comic book, when they go back and scan the same page they might get different content six months later," Devineni says.

Devineni says one of the most difficult aspects was downgrading the augmented reality content for it to play over a 3G mobile connection in order to reach their Indian target audience. To do so, Devineni aimed for each piece of video content to not exceed 20 megabytes. BlippAR has app limits for the video size, but they are also able to link the video to YouTube so the videos can be watched there.

Launching Priya *into the world*

Sharing the comic series with the world has been a continual process—translating, partnering with different organizations and showcasing both the comic and the AR functions. For the first comic, Devineni says they had about 50,000 views (or instances of activity on the app). From watching many people read and interact with the app, Devineni noticed that in most cases people just read the comic book straight through. At the end of the comic are instructions for the AR, and at that point, they'd download the app and go back and randomly pick pages.

There were minor speed bumps, Goldman says, such as getting the comic translated and then getting it into the hands of their target audience—young boys and girls. "I see the limitations in the way that it's distributed and that frustrates me a lot ... I wanted to reach the audience that it's designed to impact more than I want it to be global."

Despite the challenges, Goldman believes doing it in a comic book form was an effective method to reach people. They are still in the process of getting it translated into more languages for India's multilingual audience. As of April 2018 it was available in Hindi, English, Spanish, Chinese, Portuguese, and Italian.

Going beyond Comics

The team would like to create more comics, and it's become increasingly more cost-efficient now that they know the process, and have done it before. The first comic book cost roughly a quarter of a million dollars to make, Devineni says, while the second one was closer to 70 thousand dollars. The cost differential is mostly due to paying for art, promotions, exhibitions as well as printing 12–15,000 comics to be given for free to NGOs. Initially they received funding from Tribeca as well as the Ford Foundation, and for *Priya's Mirror* they received funding from The World Bank. Devineni and Goldman are both pursuing other projects, but continue to promote *Priya's Shakti* and *Priya's Mirror* and consider what Priya might do in future comic editions.

Takeaways

Awareness of audience:

*   Creating for an audience with limited internet means ensuring the main product (in this case the comic book) could stand alone without the AR element.

- The additional layers of information are not necessary to the story, yet they provide context for those interested in learning more.

A living medium:
- AR elements can be added and updated over time.
- Using the BlippAR app has allowed for the team to change and update what happens when a trigger is identified—this could also mean they could update it again in the future.

Make sure it fits the medium:
- AR works well for comics, but it can also be seen as a gimmick if it doesn't serve to add anything.

About This Project

URL: www.priyashakti.com/
Interview Date: December 2017
Interview Subjects: Ram Devineni, Dan Goldman
Team: Ram Devineni, Dan Goldman, Paromita Vohra, Shubhra Prakash, and Lina Srivastava

Optimism

Time magazine
January, 2018

The January 4, 2018 edition of *Time* magazine was unique: It was the first time the magazine had a guest editor in its nearly 100 year history and it was the first edition to have multiple augmented reality features. Bill Gates served as guest-editor for the *Optimism* issue, assisted by friends such as Bono—lead singer of U2 and philanthropist.

The **trigger**-based AR in this issue brings behind-the-scenes videos, infographics and original animations narrated by Gates and Bono to the reader's phone. After clicking on the AR camera icon inside the Life VR app and holding it up to the *Time* magazine cover, the viewer sees a 1-minute animated **explainer** voiced by Gates. Inside the issue, *Time* magazine teamed up with RYOT to create an animation based on Bono's doodles. "Since you're using your phone for the activation, it's almost like having Bono and Bill Gates in your hand," Mia Tramz of LifeVR told Adweek.[3] On another page, a teaser for an interview with guest editor Bill Gates plays. The final AR feature is a teaser for a behind the scenes video on how the issue was made.[4]

Nigel Tierney directed and produced the AR elements for the RYOT team. Tierney has a background in computer science and animation. Tierney came to the Life VR *Optimism* project with a background in animation—working for Dreamworks on animated films. He says when he first saw AR he was blown away, and he wanted to figure out how to do more.

Figure 7.2 Optimism, courtesy of *Time* magazine.

Bono Wants to Do AR: Deadlines and Trigger Images

After RYOT collaborated with Life VR on a few AR projects—specifically a *Sports Illustrated* cover (discussed in *Capturing Everest*, Chapter 6) and an *Entertainment Week*ly project, the *Optimism* cover was a slightly more extensive project with two AR-specific activations and the additional behind-the-scenes content.

When the user holds the app up to the page, a 2-minute animated explainer on gender equity plays. It's based on a doodle Bono created. The team originally had about a month to complete the project, and animator Steve Gordon completed the piece in about two weeks. Mia Tramz took the lead on crafting the script for both the Bono and Gates AR.

The process of making the animated explainer with Bono was similar to a flat video, with the additional element of making sure it comes to life with the correct trigger. They scripted the audio, animated the doodle, recorded Bono and then matched Bono's audio to the animation.

The cover prompts a different style of animation—a more colorful infographic style rather than the hand-drawn sketch from Bono.

Figure 7.3 Optimism, courtesy of *Time* magazine.

Working with the print deadline, the team had to make sure the animations were not only ready to go, but also that they were using the correct trigger image to play in the app. Tierney says the final image didn't come until the day before they were supposed to release.

Serving an Impatient Audience

The AR adds value by bringing to life brief micro-documentary pieces, but the experience isn't seamless. Users have no way to pause the video as it plays, and accidentally turning one's phone so the camera is not directly on the trigger will stop the video.

Tierney notes that triggered AR is an older technology, and cautions that it would perhaps be more accepted if it were viewed through glasses. In retrospect, he also says two minutes is "pushing it" from a user's perspective, saying he thinks the average AR user is going to have a "wow" moment at about 15 seconds, "unless the content is super captivating. They'll be like, oh, that's amazing. That's really cool. But why do I want to hold up a phone?"

Takeaways

Adding video to text:
* Trigger-based AR can add an additional layer of content to a magazine format.

Keep AR short:
* For phone-based AR the current wisdom suggests keeping AR to no more than 2 minutes so viewers don't get tired of holding up their phones.

About This Project

Publication: RYOT for *Time* magazine, Life VR
URL: http://time.com/5084021/optimism-ar/
Publication Date: January, 2018
Interview Date: April, 2018
Interview Subjects: Nigel Tierney
Team:
Narrated by Bill Gates
Directed & Produced by Nigel W. Tierney
Co-Produced by Zeda Stone
Art Direction by Alexandra Boden
Written by Mia Tramz
Sound Design by Erik Lohr & Joel Valder
Special Thanks to Travis Cook & Matt Valerio
Bono Animation:
Narrated by Bono
Directed & Produced by Nigel W. Tierney
Co-Produced by Zeda Stone
Written by Mia Tramz
Character Design by Bono & Steven Pierre Gordon
Animation by Steven Pierre Gordon
Sound Design by Erik Lohr
Motion Graphics by Alexandra Boden
Special Thanks to Kathy McKiernan, Travis Cook, & Matt Valerio

Outthink Hidden

New York Times T Brand Studio
December, 2017
   Launched around the same time as the *Hidden Figures* movie released (December 25, 2016), the *New York Times* T Brand Studio worked with production studio Fake Love, IBM, Oglivy & Mather (a PR company), and 20th Century Fox to create an augmented reality experience around

the idea of honoring hidden heroes in STEM fields. The idea, summarized by Fake Love, was to: "Create an extension to the movie *Hidden Figures* that educates the world on the Fox movie about African American women working at NASA in the 1960s."

The app for iOS and Android was the first augmented reality project for the NYT brand studio. After launching, the app received coverage in media and tech outlets such as Mashable, UploadVR, and Adweek. Many of the articles at the time compared the brand studio project to Pokémon Go, but the comparison ends at a basic level of virtual objects in physical space—*Outthink Hidden* is about accessing and consuming educational content, whereas Pokémon Go has game mechanics for scoring, levels, and interaction between multiple users.

The initial packaging of *Outthink Hidden* may feel gimmicky, but the substance and the stories it highlights make it a relevant and interesting use case of augmented reality and multimedia for education. Hidden within the strangely named app ("T Brand AR") are some great stories accessible in multiple formats.

Unlocking Hidden History

The *Outthink Hidden* app consists of four main sections: locate, view, learn more, and instructions. Locate takes the viewer to a map to see where the closest geographic location is that will allow the viewer to see the "hidden figures." Alternatively, for those not in proximity to a figure on the map, users can go to the IBM website (ibm.com/hiddenfigures) to unlock the stories. "View" pulls up another screen where the user, if in proximity to one of the locations, can place a 3D-modeled statue into

Figure 7.4 Outthink Hidden, courtesy of Fake Love.

their own environment and take a photo. "Learn more" brings up a mobile multimedia project with separate sections on each of the ten people featured in the app.

The first three are the leading women of the *Hidden Figures* movie—Katherine Johnson, Mary Jackson and Dorothy Vaughan. These are followed by seven more (mostly female) influential thinkers overlooked by history, who did everything from inventing braille to coming up with the idea for elevated railroads. Johnson, Jackson, and Vaughan each have a 2-minute video (with interviews with the women who played the characters in the movie), an audio piece (about 1:45) and a short text write-up. For each of the ten people featured, the user can choose to place a virtual statue in their physical environment and then trigger audio to hear more about who the person is, and what they accomplished.

"I loved the idea of being able to just give them [people] these huge almost surreal, larger than life sculptures and put them anywhere you wanted," creative director Layne Braunstein says. In some cities there were designated areas for those sculptures, and in others the user could place the sculpture anywhere. "There's something really powerful about it ... I'm going to put this massive sculpture here for this person who didn't get the recognition they deserve," Braunstein adds.

Learning through the Process

Ogilvy & Mather, in charge of PR for the *Hidden Figures* movie, approached Layne Braunstein and his production team at Fake Love. Initially, it wasn't conceived as an AR project, "We always start with the story first, and then bring technology later," says Braunstein, "The idea first was that we should look at these people in history and give them the recognition they deserve." Through discussions, they narrowed their ideas to the concept of being able to place statues all over the world, and AR was a way to do this.

Braunstein says the project was a learning process, in part because they were dealing with brands and clients who hadn't done AR before, but Fake Love didn't have extensive AR experience either.

Fake Love put together a series of pitches and Braunstein says it took about three weeks for everyone to agree on a concept. The preproduction process took another few weeks, and then Braunstein says it took about two months to build the app. They started with a small team of 2–3 people, but eventually expanded to include a front-end coder and more backend developers as well as 3D animators, for a team totaling eight people.

Some of the hacks or skills they learned—such as placing the statue, and scaling it—are now native; the APIs they work with now have simple ways to do things they had to build themselves the first time around. He says "this whole process has been streamlined."

Figure 7.5 Outthink Hidden, courtesy of Fake Love.

Interactivity and Accessibility

For Braunstein, audio is an essential part of an interactive experience. "You should always try to make an experience as multisensory as possible because that's how you view the world," he says. "If you don't have sound there's something missing because you're not using one of your senses." He adds that the reason they decided to also have text was to make sure the app would be accessible for all people.

One of Braunstein's biggest takeaways from this project was the importance of working with a cross-discipline team. "You need people that understand games," Braunstein says. "You really need 3D designers, you need people that understand graphics, art directors—people from different industries have to come together and work together in a new way to create a piece." Braunstein is working to build out a team around **WebAR**, which he believes will replace a lot of apps.

Braunstein and the team realized that some of the more complicated or high-tech ideas they had for the project (such as animating the sculptures to add movement), did not add much for the user. Braunstein says people didn't care about the movement at all, instead most users wanted to be able to place the statue, take a picture with it, and read the information, "I think people overcomplicate a lot of the things that they do. Especially in AR or VR," says Braunstein.

Pushing Stories

Fake Love has been experimenting in the storytelling space for the last five years, and Braunstein says they are always thinking about pushing the boundaries of storytelling. "When we do AR now, and we're doing stuff for clients we look at not just what's in the phone, but what's around you—making it a more holistic experience," he says. They have been experimenting with Google Tango and thinking about how to make a geo-located "soundwalk" in AR. "We're slowly opening up the door for each project in terms of what can be done after," he says.

Takeaways

Imagined worlds:
• AR can be a "larger than life" way to present a desired/alternative reality.

Story effect over special effects:
• Complex animation didn't appeal to most users of this app, who were most interested in its photo functionality.

Sound:
• Audio adds an extra layer of sensory experience, but text was also necessary for accessibility.

Accidental immersion:
• Users of *Outthink Hidden* AR sometimes walked into real objects while staring at virtual statues on their phones.

About This Project

Publication: *New York Times* T Brand Studio, 2017
URL:
App: https://itunes.apple.com/us/app/t-brand-studio-ar-augmented-reality/id1184006872?mt=8, https://play.google.com/store/apps/details?id=com.nytimes.tbrandar&hl=en
Interview Date: February, 2018
Interview Subject: Layne Braunstein, co-founder and chief creative officer of Fake Love

New Dimensions in Testimony

Take A Stand Center Holographic Theater

USC Shoah Foundation, Illinois Holocaust Museum
Fall, 2017

Roughly 60,000 students visit the Illinois Holocaust museum in Skokie, Illinois every year. Since the founding of the Holocaust Memorial Foundation of Illinois in the late 1970s—and the opening of the 65,000-square-foot museum in 2009—many of them have had the opportunity to interact face-to-face and ask questions of a Holocaust survivor. But with the number of living Holocaust survivors decreasing, this will only be possible for a few more years.

Now, visitors to the museum can interact with a holographic representation of one of 15 of these survivors, answering questions on stage in a 65-person theater. As audience members ask questions of the holocaust survivor via a moderator, the projection responds in the original, unedited words of the survivor.

"The only reason that people understand or have a sense of the Holocaust is really because these people, more than any other group of people that have experienced something like this, have been out in the public speaking about it," says Heather Maio, who spearheaded New Dimensions In Testimony, the historical preservation project on display in this theater. She says the project is about dialogue, "to replicate the experience of meeting and engaging with a Holocaust survivor."

The holographic theater is just a taste of what's possible with the content gathered through the *New Dimensions in Testimony* project, which—given the very present knowledge among those in the Holocaust education field that soon there will be no more living Holocaust survivors to tell their stories—aims to be as "future proof" as possible.

The experience in Skokie is not a true **hologram**, but rather a display style called "pepper's ghost" that projects an image onto a screen using the two-dimensional video produced for the first phase of the project—although the assets exist to create a fully three-dimensional hologram, once the display technology exists to make use of it. The interactive also works on a flat TV screen. Presented in the theater, it has an impressive feeling of depth, and gives a taste of what's possible with this content.

New Dimensions in Testimony is a partnership between the USC Shoah Foundation, the USC Institute For Creative Technologies (ICT), the Illinois Holocaust Museum and Conscience Display. So far, the ongoing project has documented the testimonies of 15 Holocaust survivors and one survivor of Nanjing Massacre, the 1937 episode of mass rape and murder by Japanese troops against residents of Nanjing.

While we recognize that this project in its current form has a different presentation than the headset-based content we typically refer to as augmented reality, but if we define AR or MR as virtual graphics in physical space, then this project is indeed a form of AR. In addition, we recognize the importance of looking at the intention of this piece—to exist in a future augmented reality format—and the power of its being presented in a way that more than one viewer can interact with it at once.

Keeping History Alive

The idea for *New Dimensions in Testimony* came from Heather Maio, who has a background in museum exhibition design for Holocaust education, with a focus on intergenerational storytelling. Maio says that, while the

Shoah Foundation has an immense archive containing 55,000 video testimonies of survivors and witnesses of the Holocaust and other genocides, she—like many others in her field—was feeling anxiety about what would happen to Holocaust education once the last survivors passed away. She pitched the idea for the project to the Shoah Foundation, and assembled partnerships to move the project forward—both in terms of technology and funding. Two years after Maio had first pitched to the project, production began in 2014.

Susan Abrams, who joined the Illinois Holocaust Museum as CEO in 2014, had also been considering ways to create holograms of Holocaust survivors. Her museum connected with the Shoah Foundation early on in the project and became partners.

Figure 7.6 New Dimensions in Testimony, courtesy of USC Shoah Foundation.

Extensive Production Process

Each of the survivor testimonies took around a year to produce. They began with two months of research to tailor the questions to the person's experience. Then, their testimonies were captured as they sat at the center of a stage built specifically for this project, surrounded by lighting and cameras arranged in a dome, recording enough angles to produce a high-fidelity 3D image of them. The survivors each spent a week answering questions, and their testimonies generated between 30 and 90 terabytes of data each (for reference, the entire hard drive on an off-the-shelf laptop in 2018 might store 2 terabytes of data).

From there, it took 6 to 10 months for **post production** on each of the testimonies—and that was only working with a single camera angle. Teams at ICT and the Shoah Foundation had to go through the footage by hand to remove the background, isolate the images of the survivor and edit each response as a clip—a process that took months, even with just one camera angle. "It was a really, really intense graphics project," Maio says. "It would have been a hell of a lot easier to make them an avatar," she says, but making a true-to-life representation was paramount to the vision of a project that would preserve these testimonies for posterity.

The responses of each of the 16 survivors in the *New Dimensions in Testimony* project are stored in a database of, on average, 1,250 questions. Some survivors answered as many as 2,000 questions.

In order for people to be able to ask questions directly to the survivors, the team had to develop a **natural language processing** system—a way for the system to understand users' questions—so the simulation could draw up appropriate answers to any questions asked. They did so by first coming up with a base of questions the system could be asked, by adding as many different ways as the team could think of to ask each of the questions the survivors had answered. Based on that, the system began making its best guesses as to which response to offer based on what audience members asked. The system is continually evolving,

Heather Maio says, as people interacting with it ask new questions and the simulation attempts to answer them. While the number of responses is fixed, they are continually adding new variations on questions to improve the relevance of the responses. After questions are answered, reviewers go through and tag whether the answer was appropriate to the question, and link that question to the response to help further train the system. Maio says there are about 45,000 alternate questions currently in the database.

Reception: A Shared Interactive Experience

Maio and Abrams both say it's been rewarding to see how the project is received.

"When we started this project we didn't know if it would actually work," Maio says. "We didn't know if people would feel a connection to that person and would do what we were hoping it would do." She says when people interact with a survivor on the video screen, it can feel like a video call. "They forget that they're a filmed version," she says, "So we've had people, you know, emotionally react to the survivor's stories or the answers that they're getting."

Abrams says she's seen a similar effect in the holographic theater. Despite the presence of a moderator, she says audience members often address the survivor directly with their questions.

One of the things Maio hoped to see was audiences feeling the freedom to ask questions they might not otherwise ask of a survivor, with the knowledge that they can't harm a recording by asking potentially hurtful or overly personal questions, or by forcing them to relive their trauma by re-telling it. While she says many viewers express this sentiment, the experience feels authentic enough that many still exercise a level of social caution and politeness with the simulation.

What's Next

From Abrams perspective, presenting *New Dimensions in Testimony* as a projected image on stage, and describing it as a hologram, was in part about ease of communication in attracting audiences to the experience. "If I tell you, oh, you can have an interactive experience with a recorded survivor, you're thinking how that sounds pretty interesting," she says,

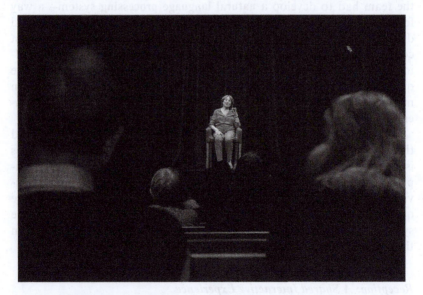

Figure 7.7 New Dimensions in Testimony, courtesy of Illinois Holocaust Museum & Education Center.

"But if I say you can talk to a hologram and have a conversation with a hologram, your eyes light up." The idea of speaking to a hologram in 2018 has an element of excitement and novelty.

What the experience offers, however, is a glimpse of what an interaction could be like with a proper interactive hologram—a 3D visual of a survivor that viewers can walk around, giving a sense of unmediated presence—of really being there in the room. While real hologram technology isn't anywhere near being able to offer this kind of experience, Maio says something close to it could be achieved with an augmented reality headset such as the *HoloLens* or *Magic Leap*. And *New Dimensions in Testimony* has gathered the data to make those experiences possible, as soon as the viewing technology catches up.

"It gives me the chills," Abrams says of the fact that *New Dimensions in Testimony* has been able to capture these survivor stories, "just in the nick of time."

Takeaways

Creating a feeling of presence:
- "Pepper's ghost"—projecting an image onto a screen using the two-dimensional video can give the audience a feeling of presence.
- The creators of *New Dimensions in Testimony* say the interactive experience is authentic enough that people often respond to the virtual survivors as if they are real.

An open dialogue:
- Interacting with a virtual survivor gives the audience the freedom to ask questions they may not otherwise ask, because they cannot harm a recording.

Future-proofing:
- The captured holograms are ready to be integrated into a **HoloLens** or **Magic Leap** experience when the technology catches up.
- As of 2018, recording assets for a high fidelity 3D interactive hologram is an enormous task: Creating these testimonies took two months of advance planning, a week of recording, and 30 to 90 terabytes of data per survivor.

About This Project

URL: www.ilholocaustmuseum.org/tas/
Interview Date: December 2017
Interview Subjects: Heather Maio, Susan Abrams
Taxonomy: Augmented Reality, hologram, interactive[5]
Team: Heather Maio, ICT, Shoah Foundation

Hello, We're from the Internet

Group show by MoMAR

March 2018

The first augmented reality exhibit at New York's Museum of Modern Art was not commissioned or coordinated by anyone affiliated with the museum. Instead, a group of independent artists, led by Damjanski and David Lobser decided to do a guerilla-style augmented reality art show—curating the work of seven artists using the MoMa's permanent collection of Jackson Pollock as the **trigger-point** for the art. To see these pieces, the viewer must first download the MoMAR app—available for both Android and iOS—and then go to the fifth floor of the MoMa. As the description for the AR exhibit states, "We chose the room for two significant reasons. Firstly, it is part of the permanent collection and remains unchanged within the walls of the museum. Secondly, it has a bench." When the user opens up the app and holding the camera up to any of eight different paintings, another layer of art emerges. Each piece is different in style, scope and intention—some with a game-like feel and others with movement, animation, or audio.

> *An unauthorized gallery concept aimed at democratizing physical exhibition spaces, museums, and the curation of art within them. MoMAR is non-profit, non-owned, and exists in the absence of any privatized structures. MoMAR uses Augmented Reality to overlay art onto existing artwork and frames housed in museums and gallery spaces around the world.—momar.gallery, about section*

Figure 7.8 MoMAR, courtesy of Aaron Venn.

Artistic Inspiration

Damjanski and Lobser said the concept for the exhibit came from a series of conversations, and the desire to bring their own art into the MoMA. "We wanted to bring our work to this institution, but we didn't want to have to go through the normal channels," says Damjanski. They're also following in the footsteps of the "exhibition of rejects," an 1863 exhibition of works rejected by the official Paris Salon. There were a number of artists from that show who became well known—such as Édouard Manet and Camille Pissarro. Lobser also notes the concept of "The aura of the art—the idea that the original painting is going to be more special." He argues linking art to the space and place of the original work gives it an additional layer of meaning.

Both artists say they love the MoMA, but they're also interested in critiquing the institution. "Who gets to be in the museum, and who stays out of the museum?" says Lobser, who is not a fan of Pollock's work. "There's also the issue of white males being overrepresented at the MoMa," Lobser adds.

In the explanation of the project, they also write about a private collection of natural history curiosities donated to the University of Oxford in 1683 and later opened to the public, marking this as the "first permanent public exhibition housed by a corporation." The act of "opening art to the public" closes its definition to the commons:

From a Conversation to Reality

Lobser and Damjanski began talking about the project in the summer of 2017, and began pulling the project together in January 2018. They started by recruiting artists—many of whom are friends of Lobser who went to Interactive Telecommunications Program, part of NYU's Tisch School of the Arts. "I wanted to work with people who are artistic but also technical enough to do their own work," says Lobser. "It was fairly simple and loose, the whole process." After sending an initial call-out they met with artists three weeks later and held a 24-hour hackathon at NYU, where they put everything together. They developed using **Unity** and at the hackathon they submitted to the app store (for both iOS and Android). The only minor hiccup was ensuring the whole app was under the required app size for Google Play.

> *Explicitly defining both space and art as exclusive and invulnerable ...*
> *If we are to understand that art is the great measure of our culture we must also acknowledge it is owned, valued and defined by 'the elite.' We must also recognize then that the term "open to the public" is not an invitation, but a declaration of values. Values that are not our own. And so it has remained for 335 years. Until now.*

Figure 7.9 MoMAR, courtesy of Aaron Venn.

Releasing MoMAR into the World

Initially, the team didn't do much to get news of the app out into the world. They shared the app with Hackernews and ProductHunt, and articles were later written by publications such as *Gizmodo,*[6] *VRScout* and *Wired*.

Damjanski and Lobser say sharing has been more word of mouth and organic. "On the opening night, so many people were taking pictures ... 50–80 people, you had other people wondering what the people were looking at and asking 'what is it?'" Damjanski says, adding that there was an extra layer of conversation in addition to the art. He also noticed an interesting interaction of people walking in-between the AR and the piece of art, a further element of visual art. As of April 2018 the app had about 100 downloads on Android and nearly 1000 for iOS.

Open to All

Lobser and Damjanksi say their audience is all people who enjoy museums and contemporary art. "Already the experience of seeing those works was worth it," Lobser says. "You release something like this into the wild and the audience is whoever it winds up being." He adds that he cares most about what the other people who worked on the project feel about it. They're taking a more relaxed, experimental approach to

Figure 7.10 MoMAR, courtesy of Martin Strutz.

promotion with the view that "ultimately, people have to decide if it works," Damjanski says.

Inside the Jackson Pollock exhibit in March 2018, many visitors held up their phones and took selfies. As the user looks at their own phone, the app lends a feeling of being part of a secret art club—one not everyone else knows about. The use of the physical gallery to display art that essentially appears on a small screen gives a feeling of a larger piece of artwork.

Both Damjanski and Lobser hope they're able to break through the novelty of AR and the technological "wow factor" and allow people to engage and interact with the art itself. "What we enjoy about it, is that it brings a certain amount of interactivity," says Lobser. "It brings the body into play more than screen-based stuff," giving the viewer a better sense of the art in relation to the other art in the room. Lobser, who took on much of the coordination of the exhibit, believes the art is much stronger as a collection. Damjanski says using AR "can add your body to the art." It can also animate and incorporate video to create more interactive objects from 2D images.

By creating an open source document, they are also allowing artists to emulate and copy what they have done—augmenting physical spaces. Already individuals in China, Buenos Aires, Belgrade, Los Angeles, and Munich have contacted them, letting the team know they are working on different AR projects.[7]

Takeaways

AR adds the user and interactivity:
- AR art is a way to bring the body into play, giving the viewer a better sense of the art in relation to the viewer.
- AR in this form also brings a form of interactivity.

Document and share:
- MoMAR's open source document allows others to learn and build upon their project.

About This Project

Publication Date: March 2–May 3 2018
URL: momar.gallery
Interview Date: April 7, 2018
Interview Subjects: Damjanski and David Lobser
Team: Sarah Rothberg, Gabriel Barcia-Colombo, Tara Sinn, Louise Foo, Harold Haraldsson, Scott Garner, Damjanski, and David Lobser

Four of the World's Best Olympians, as You've Never Seen Them Before

The New York Times
February 5, 2018
    The *New York Times* took a deep dive into augmented reality for the winter Olympics—using AR features to show four Olympians "as you've never seen them before." Opening the story in the *New York Times* app, users can place each athlete—in life-size form, into their living room (or wherever the viewer happens to be reading). The viewer can then walk around the 3D image, stepping closer and farther away. Continuing to scroll through the article, the user can skip placing the Olympians or go back and forth from placing the image to reading. In the desktop version, the user scrolls to reveal text and images and the presentation style is reminiscent of the award-winning multimedia piece known as Snowfall. It's hard to communicate the winter Olympic games in a visceral way through TV screens, but with AR, *The Times* uses "realistic scans to bring the athletes to you, in real scale, and talk about what they do, using interactivity to let you explore everything about this frozen moment-in-time in their performance," says Graham Roberts, director of immersive platforms storytelling.

The Beginnings of AR Explorations

The Times has been exploring what opportunities AR might bring since November, 2016. Initially they focused on Tango, a Google project formerly known as Project Tango which used computer vision for mobile phones to detect a position without using GPS—allowing for a more place-based visual mapping. *The Times* brand studio experimented briefly with target-based AR, which is promoted by a visual marker or image, like a QR code as used in *Hidden Figures* AR. *The Times* has since evolved to a more modern version of AR, "meaning not the target-based versions we'd seen for a number of years," says Roberts. The Google Tango audience was extremely small (only those with the latest Tango enabled phones), so they decided to "learn what we could and wait and see," says Roberts. With Apple announcing *ARKit* in the summer of 2017, they began taking AR more seriously, "This was really the tipping point," Roberts says. They used an internal week to experiment called "maker week"[8] to prototype and figure out what the best approach might be. From there they worked closely with the product, newsroom and design teams building the AR functionality directly into the core *New York Times* app.

The Olympics offered a clear news peg to experiment and plan ahead for. Roberts says they felt they could push the development for the news peg of the games. It's interesting to note that many media companies experimented with VR innovation during Brazil's summer 2016 Olympic games as well. "We have a long history of doing innovative visual journalism projects around the Olympics, such as The Modern Games VR, the Fine Line, All the Medalists, etc," says Roberts. The team had been experimenting with capturing 3D images of people for AR from the beginning, and Roberts says it was a great opportunity to use the medium to introduce readers to some of the names they would be seeing over the coming weeks, "I loved the idea of being able to pause Nathan Chen mid quad, walk out onto the ice, and explore his form, and learn about what makes him so great," says Roberts.

From Real-Life to Augmented Reality

Roberts says the project took a couple of months to complete. After securing time with each athlete through their agents, the team traveled to them to do the scans. The athletes were scanned using the structure sensor for iPad, a device that attaches to an iPad and can quickly 3D scan objects and people. They asked each athlete to demonstrate their form at key moments in their performances, says Roberts, and they asked how the form helps them compete. In **post production**, they put the scans into context, like putting Nathan Chen at 20 inches off of the ground. In some cases they did further posing of the scans using photo references to get them into extreme poses, notably, J. R. Celski's extreme lean as he turns while speed skating. Instead of having Celski pose extremely close to the ground, since that would be impossible given restrictions on gravity and balance, they took the scan, and then based on photos they placed him as he might have been turning a corner.

For post production they used Maya, Blender, Substance painter and SceneKit—all tools for 3D graphics to texture and improve the quality of the 3D assets.

Guiding the Viewer in AR: Walking Is the New Scrolling

Knowing what to do with new technology can be tricky. There's no innate guidance, Roberts compares AR to the mouse in 1983 or so. When the 1983 mouse came out with Microsoft Word it was complete with a musical tutorial which taught newcomers how to use it.[9] *The Times* clearly guides the reader—telling them what to do and how: The article auto locks as it reaches the AR window, a gif explains exactly how to move the phone to find a plane to place an object, and language feedback explains what to do next. They further orient users by telling the user to, "treat the object 'as if it were there,'" and they prompt interactivity by encouraging the viewers to walk around and view the image from different angles. "We are treating walking as the new scrolling," says Roberts. "It is the most natural way to discover new things ... we don't use visual hot-spots for interactivity, but simply give you new information as you walk around the object, and as you enter into different zones." Additional graphics around the athletes pop up to explain parts of the information as the viewer walks around.

What AR Adds to the Story

In a presentation at the NYC Media Lab, Roberts explained how a few unique elements of AR make it an important and useful storytelling tool. It's a way to regain perspective through scale, it can be a more human mode of interaction and can have potential impact on visual journalism he says. In regards to regaining resolution, Roberts refers to the way "visual journalism has been miniaturized with the mobile revolution," since mobile is the default way most readers come to the news. "Mobile is an amazing thing, but it is also a very small display," Roberts says, adding that "there is definitely something lost in comparison to the nice big 2-page print spreads visual journalists used to be able to design for," Roberts says. Journalists can get some of this scale back in AR.

AR can be considered a more human-mode because, it gets rid of much of the abstraction of interface, "we don't need pinch to zoom or swipe, or tap. We are 3-dimensional beings in a 3-dimensional world. If something is inherently 3D the best way to tell you about it is to put it in front of you," says Roberts. He believes it's more human, because the format treats digital information as if it were there with us, allowing us to interact in a more human way.

Finally, Roberts sees it as a way to lean in to the future of spatial computing—the thing he believes will comes next after the phone,

"Mobile phones are unlikely to be the final form factor for how we interact with digital information," Roberts says, "the tremendous investment and the amazing strides being made around virtual reality and augmented reality and all of the emerging devices that work in this way tells us that spatial computing—where our digital information is projected directly into the world around us, is on its way."

Designing for the Future of AR

In many cases, AR is designed for the phone, but Roberts sees the phone as a bridge. It's "an amazing way to try out AR now," but he believes people should design "with a more forward looking vision for what it will mean when there is no longer a device that we hold." Echoing his comments on the initial instructions needed for the 1983 mouse, Roberts says "People of course get very used to things working in a particular way. Once you give a little nudge though, the intuitiveness can really take over and that's when people … are really connecting."

For Roberts, this is just the beginning of a new form of storytelling, "not the arrival," he says. Roberts is not surprised by VR's evolution past the hype cycle being met with skepticism, "this is because people see the awkward hardware that currently exists as what this is all about. Immersive could be as big as the internet eventually. It will probably be as big of a disrupter as mobile," he says.

Takeaways

Teach your audience:
- Prompting your audience and showing them what and how to use a new medium is a useful tool to get them used to new mediums.

AR can be a great tool for:
- regaining resolution (as compared to scaled-down content for mobile screens);
- more natural, "human" modes of interacting with content;
- spatial storytelling;
- communicating perspective through scale.

Walking is the new scrolling:
- Allowing for additional information based on how close or far a user is creates a more interactive experience.

A news peg with broad appeal:
- By experimenting with projects around an event happening at regular intervals, companies are able to plan and anticipate experimental stories that might appeal to their audiences.

About This Project

URL: www.nytimes.com/interactive/2018/02/05/sports/olympics/ar-augm
ented-reality-olympic-athletes-ul.html

Interview Date: April, 2018

Interview Subject: Graham Roberts, Director of Immersive Platforms
Storytelling

Team: Production by Jon Huang, Blacki Migliozzi, David Stolarsky, Ben
Wilhelm and Tom Giratikanon. AR experience design and production
by Evan Grothjan, Graham Roberts, Miles Peyton, Yuliya Parshina-
Kottas, Karthik Patanjali, Bedel Saget and Joe Ward. Android development by Walter Dziemianczyk and Ramona Harrison. iOS development
by Cameron Pulsford and Krzysztof Zablocki. Design by Gray Beltran,
Lian Chang, Rebecca Lieberman and Rumsey Taylor. Additional production by Adam Pearce.

Terminal 3

Tribeca

2018

Bringing War to the Living Room

*Holograms for Syria (2017), Malik's first HoloLens project, brought
2D images into the viewer's surroundings.*

It was the disconnect Asad Malik felt traveling from Pakistan
to the U.S.—from a country where he felt the impact of war directly, to one where it's mostly out of sight—that prompted him to
experiment with augmented reality. "In everyday life here [in the
U.S.] you don't feel its effects or impact the same way as you do in
Pakistan or Libya," he says.

But load up Holograms for Syria on a HoloLens, look around
and "you see images of war," Malik says. Holograms for Syria was
first shown as an installation at Bennington College in Vermont.
Viewers were able to see photographs of war that have appeared
in the news, blown up into lifesize images to look as if they are
placed in the viewer's physical space. "An image of a dead child
lying on the beach is now lying on your sofa," Malik says in reference to the image of 3-year-old Alan Kurdi, a Syrian boy who
drowned in September 2015 during his family's attempt to cross the
Mediterranean.

"it makes you look at your space very differently because these
images are actually engaging with your space," Malik says. Holograms for Syria forces the viewer to see the direct connections

---

between a living room and Syria, forcing the viewer to consider what relationship these two countries have as well as the shared humanity. "All these things are completely interconnected and in this case—they're visual," Malik argues. After the viewer emerges from the experience and takes off the HoloLens, Malik hopes the feeling of interconnectedness will stay with the viewer. His aim is to condense the gap between people—in this case it's between those in the U.S. and Syria.

Figure 7.11 Terminal 3, courtesy of Asad Malik.

Muslim Identity through Story

Asad Malik, creator of the *Terminal 3* augmented reality experience, derives his ideas from lived experience. "If I'm going to do underrepresented stories, my own is a good place to start," he says.

As an international student of Pakistani origin living in the U.S., he's been questioned by the FBI twice, and received second-screenings at airports around the world on multiple occasions. He doesn't identify as religious, but he is often perceived as Muslim.

Malik is slated to graduate from Bennington College in Vermont in 2019. *Terminal 3*, which premiered at Tribeca in 2018, is an augmented reality piece designed for **HoloLens** that takes Malik's experiences of racial profiling in airports as a foundation. As soon as the viewer sits down and puts on the HoloLens, questions appear. The experience is structured to feel like the viewer plays the role of interrogator—sitting across from someone of perceived Muslim origin, the user takes part in questioning a hologram sitting in a chair across from them.

Virtual Presence and Physical Presence

This interactive AR experience is inspired by Terminal 3 of the Abu Dhabi international airport, where the U.S. has a preclearance facility for those traveling from the Middle East and Asia to the U.S.— this allows all immigration, customs and agriculture inspections to happen in Abu Dhabi before departure.

At Tribeca, the project consisted of two rooms. The first room is the interrogation room. Here, viewers were given a HoloLens to see and interact with a hologram of a person. After the user enters the room, they hear walkie-talkie instructions that another person is coming in. The viewer will hear dialogue such as, "Hope you're ready. You know the drill." Across from where they sit is an image of a seated person, discernible as a set of curved blue lines around their shape.

Floating questions appearing alongside the volumetric capture of a person: "Can I see your passport?" When viewer repeats the question, the hologram responds. After a few initial questions, a **branching narrative** begins and the viewer chooses between two questions for each interaction. Throughout the 8–10 minute experience the hologram gets progressively more realistic, their skin tone flickering in and out and their features becoming visible as their responses get more personal and intimate. As Malik says, "you're the interrogator now, you get to choose either questions that are humanizing or dehumanizing." As the experience progresses, the walkie-talkie voice puts on increasing pressure: "Look, we don't have all day," it says. "Are we almost done here?"

At the end of the interrogation, the user is prompted to choose whether they think the person they've spoken with should be allowed to enter the country. At the Tribeca installation, once this decision was made the user took off the HoloLens and walked into the second room. Here, they saw the person they'd just spoken with in the flesh.

Working to bridge the gap between media and reality to create a more human connection is a theme of Malik's work, "I think it's really that juxtaposition between virtual presence and physical presence," he says, "that makes it a very interesting kind of art piece." He adds that the piece could also be read as a commentary on how decisions are made in public institutions—"you make a decision that affects real people but you make it on the basis of some abstraction."

It's notable that while many immersive experiences try to put the viewer in the shoes of someone who is struggling—a refugee, for example—in order to tap into a sense of empathy through shared experience, this project puts the viewer firmly in the position of power relative to the people it features. But in this, it's able to shine light on the complexity of the interaction taking place and the power structures that inform it. The user can experience the contrast between the cold efficiency of an interrogation and the effort it takes to set aside one's sense of another person's humanity. Rather than building empathy through first-hand experience, it simulates a social interaction that fosters understanding. In this way, it bears some similarity to Scatter's Blackout—a VR experience also featured in this book and created with **DepthKit**, in which viewers can hear the inner monologues of people in a subway car.

Eliciting Real Stories

Viewers of *Terminal 3* experience an encounter with one person, whose dialogue and imagery are built by recording an extensive interview using DepthKit. At the time of writing, the team had conducted ten extensive interviews with people who have a Muslim background or are perceived

Figure 7.12 Asad Malik in the studio.

as Muslim. From each of those interviews, they assembled a branching set of questions and responses that progress based on how the user interacts with the characters.

Malik says the whole interview process takes three or four hours. Each person comes into a green screen studio with a DepthKit to capture the 3D features. The individuals are interviewed by two people—one who plays a "good cop" and the other playing a "bad cop." Interviews start off with a one-on-one "interrogation" or play-acting, in which the interviewee imagines they're coming from their homeland or a country they have traveled to and the bad cop asks them questions for about ten minutes. After this, they do the same thing with the good cop asking questions for a 10-minute session. Then they do a 1–2 hour session of general questions and getting to know the person. Finally, the team conducts a final session in which a third person re-interviews with targeted questions about some of the things that were mentioned in the longer interview.

The final interview allows the producers and interviewers to plan out the questions and target interesting stories or anecdotes. Malik says most of the content comes from this final interview. The topics are wide ranging, but touch on ideas of identity and family.

Malik says he is interested in the contradictions within each person, "Everyone has ideas, views and ideologies that don't fit with their persona or their image or something they've said contradicts something else that they believe in," he says.

After conducting the interviews, the team brought the footage into the **Unity** game-engine software to clean it up, build interactivity, and prepare it for the HoloLens.

Making the Technology Work for the Art

Working at the edge of what's possible with off-the-shelf technology comes with challenges. For Malik, one of the toughest aspects has been programming for the HoloLens and working within the limitations of the hardware. "It's really in its infancy; it's hard to work," he says. The HoloLens has a limited **field of view** and his project is running up against the limits of its processing power.

There are also limitations to the kind of story that can be told while retaining interactivity. The branching narrative is conceptually difficult, as it's a challenge to give the user agency while still telling a coherent story

The team used DepthKit to create the volumetric captures, which some people refer to as holograms. For the creators, DepthKit served as a low-cost way to create volumetric video (developed by Scatter in 2016). At the time of production it was one of the only off-the-shelf technologies available for volumetric video capture. While other technology may have resulted in a more realistic image, those options were out of the budget for this project. Malik has an artistic rationale for the lower resolution of the volumetric video scanned with DepthKit: He says the form is part of the statement, as the visual image is a reference to being scanned or being surveyed. This format keeps what is needed—mainly a sense of presence through body language and voice. "We feel those are the crucial elements to get the message across," Malik says.

From Theory to Practice

Malik considers himself an artist. His work intersects with the journalism and documentary fields and one of his goals is what he calls "cultural augmentation," the idea of accelerated globalization by bringing things, people and ideas from all over the world together. Malik imagines a hologram of a Neonazi in a liberal arts college, a hologram of a refugee in the White House, and a homeless person in the Uber CEO's office.

Malik believes augmented reality allows people to talk and communicate thoughts, ideas and stories in a new and different manner. He refers to *Terminal 3* as an AR documentary stemming from a desire to build more understanding. "It's very easy to put someone in a basket and say that this person is a Muslim so they believe in this, this and this," Malik says. The shorter story vignettes within the branching narrative in *Terminal 3* go deep into the characters' personal lives, talking about how each person grew up, what their beliefs are, and showing the complexities of each person's identity.

Publishing for Festivals and Everyday Access

Malik says he has a strong aversion to phone-based mobile AR because he believes it should be hands free, at the same time he's excited at the prospect of bringing the experience to more people through an app version—especially since the HoloLens is inaccessible for most people. Malik and the team hope to eventually publish a mobile version allowing the holograms to come into the viewer's space, so the viewer can ask questions or choose questions the characters will answer.

Takeaways

Realism, not photorealism:
- Body language and sound are critical elements for establishing a sense of presence. Lower resolution imagery can be forgiven if these elements are strong.

Auditory interaction:
- By using auditory prompts, the user is able to interact and advance the story without interruption to figure out which button to press or how to move to the next part.

Branching narrative:
- Creating a branching narrative is one way to give the user agency in the story while still retaining a story arc.

Compressing distance:
- By bringing content into a viewer's own space, augmented reality can remove some of the emotional distance between the viewer and the story.

Simulating social interaction:
- Rather than building empathy through first-hand experience, T3 simulates a social interaction that may foster a greater understanding for both the person playing the role of interviewer as well as interviewee.

About this project:

Interview Date: January, 2018
Interview Subject: Asad J. Malik
URL: https://1ric.com/project/holograms-from-syria
Team:
Creator & Director: Asad J. Malik
Key Collaborators: RYOT, 1RIC, Kaleidoscope, Unity
Executive Producers: René Pinnell, Bryn Mooser, Anita Gou, Hayley Pappas, Matt Ippolito
Producers: Jill Klekas, Jake Sally, Nigel Tierney, Zeda Stone
Co-Producers: R.D. Delgado & Paul Gerrard
Associate Producers: Jacqueline Westfall & Everett Hendler
Story Editor: Viva Wittman
Sound By: Jack Daniel Gerrard
Director of Depth: Musa Ghaznavi
Creative Director: Philipp Schaeffer
Cast: Zubair Siddiqui

Notes

1 "A new app called fARTjacker uses augmented reality to put a slightly new spin on a very old category of app: farts. The app, which uses your iPhone's camera, lets you add fart effects on top of your camera and record videos. Think Snapchat's rainbow puke, but for farts." https://mashable. com/2017/12/20/fart-app-augmented-reality/#k8E0PbcIUkqn.
2 Allum, Cynthia; Goldberg, Elyssa; Weinberg, Matthew; Bhagwat, Rashmi; Shanbhag, Siddharth. RYOT Studio, NYC Media Lab and Columbia Business School. February 2018. "The State of Augmented Reality: How current industry success stories can inform future use cases." www.ryotstudio.com/ whitepaper/RYOTStudio-CBS-AR-WhitePaper.pdf.

3 Carmody, Tim. "Why print legacies like time are betting big on augmented reality" January 8, 2018. www.adweek.com/digital/why-print-legacies-like-time-are-betting-big-on-augmented-reality.
4 Gibbs, Nancy. "Bill Gates: What gives me hope about the world's future." January 4, 2018. http://time.com/5086907/bill-gates-nancy-gibbs-interview/.
5 The authors recognize that this project in its current form has a different presentation than the headset-based content we typically refer to as augmented reality. However, if we define AR or MR as virtual graphics in physical space, then this project is indeed a form of AR. In addition, we recognize the importance of looking at the intention of this piece and the potential for it to exist in a future augmented reality format.
6 Ehrenkranz, Melanie. "Artists protest elite art world with unauthorized AR Gallery at the MoMA" March 5, 2018. https://gizmodo.com/artists-protest-elite-art-world-with-unauthorized-ar-ga-1823518003.
7 "Welcome to the open source section of MoMAR!" Instructions 1.0 beta. Accessed April 2018. http://momar.gallery/img/opensource-v1-beta.pdf.
8 Lichterman, Joseph. "With its Maker Week, The New York Times is trying to foster teamwork and, possibly, new products." September 7, 2016. http://www.niemanlab.org/2016/09/with-its-maker-week-the-new-york-times-is-trying-to-foster-teamwork-and-possibly-new-products/.
9 Chen, Jason. "The original 1983 Microsoft Mouse," February 2, 2007. https://gizmodo.com/233684/the-original-1983-microsoft-mouse.

8   Immersive Audio

It's harder to make real audio than special effects audio.
(Alejandro González Iñárritu)

Hallelujah VR, Within, Ecco VR
Reeps One: Does Not Exist, Aurelia Soundworks and The Mill
Designing for Video Games, Nick LaMartina
  Many filmmakers begin with an audio track, editing together the audio
onto a timeline followed by the visuals serving to complement the audio.
In some ways, and in some cases, immersive media and VR specifically
have over-emphasized the visual, forgetting the importance and power
of sound and a rich immersive auditory experience. This chapter looks
at how one audio designer approaches designing video game audio and
delves deeper into two case studies on sound-centric projects by focusing
on the immersive audio components rather than the visual elements.
  Hallelujah VR brings the viewer into the center of a beautifully arranged acapella performance of Leonard Cohen's famous and widely
covered song by the same name. *Reeps One: Does Not Exist* is a fast-paced
music video pushing the boundaries of sound, fast cuts and movement.
  Immersive audio is worth a series of books in its own right.[1]

Hallelujah VR

Within
April 2017
  Hallelujah VR is a music-focused virtual reality experience featuring
an acapella version of Leonard Cohen's "Hallelujah," arranged and performed by singer and composer Bobby Halvorson singing five different
acapella parts, recorded separately, and placed in the round. It's a powerful, intimate, almost overwhelming sound experience.
  The piece opens with Halvorson standing in darkness. He begins to
sing the first verse, and a few seconds later, another version of him appears, singing harmonies. As additional harmonies are layered on, additional copies of him appear until the viewer is surrounded by five singers.

As the song approaches its crescendo, the scene opens up to Halvorson standing in front of a full choir in a spectacular cathedral.

The experience was created by the VR company Within, directed by Zach Richter, produced by Eames Kolar and composed and performed by Bobby Halvorson. Ecco VR, led by Joel Douek and Benedict Green, did **spatial sound**.

The project was first shown at the Tribeca film festival in 2017. At that festival, it was possible to view it on the proprietary player made by camera manufacturer Lytro (which went out of business in early 2018). That experience offered six degrees of freedom from a seated position. Users could lean forward and look around, to see the depth in the image and hear the audio adjust as they moved, though they couldn't walk around.

Joel Douek of Ecco VR estimates the uncompressed version of the 4-minute sequence for the Lytro player was about 22 terabytes of data (for reference, the entire hard drive on an off-the-shelf laptop in 2018 might store 2 terabytes). For other platforms—including Gear VR, YouTube, and Facebook—they produced a 3-degrees-of-freedom version that has the full quality sound.

On Set

Ecco VR joined the production team at the storyboard level, so they could work with Halvorson closely to understand the venue and work with the limitations of the Lytro camera.

They realized early on that they were going to need a lot of microphones.

They already had a relationship with the audio equipment company Sennheiser, which lent them $80,000 worth of microphones (we'll discuss how all these mics were used in the next section) and came on set to help them run everything and set it up.

They had a crew of four on that shoot. Benedict Green of Ecco VR says in general virtual reality productions tend to trigger the need for

Figure 8.1 The spatial audio mix for Hallelujah. Courtesy of Ecco VR.

additional audio crew a lot faster than traditional media. He says that's in part because the camera normally films in all directions simultaneously. In order to hide the sound production equipment you have to place multiple microphones attached to multiple recorders, rather than having a person moving around with a single boom mic, as is often the case on film sets. "It's just a little messier from a sound point of view," Green says, "and needs a little more thought and organization."

During **post production** they worked with a small UK-based company called Two Big Ears, which was later acquired and provided the technology for Facebook's Spatial Workstation, to add the translational change in the sound—that is, to place the sound sources in space so that the viewer could move toward them and hear them get closer.

They figured out what gear they should use, and researched what Halvorson would need during recording in order to get the performance right. In order for him to be able to sing on time and in tune with himself, he needed to hear tracks for harmony and timing while singing. During the recording, he wore a tiny in-ear speaker that is invisible in the video.

Many Microphones

For the main part of the song they used two lavalier mics on Halvorson. An additional shotgun mic picked up audio at a greater distance, and another ambisonic mic picked up the entire sound field.

"That's usually our strategy going into any shoot, to have a lot of coverage," Douek says. "Most of these projects have never been done before."

Douek notes that, while they tend to bring an **ambisonic** mic on set, they don't always use the audio from that mic in the final project, and even if they do it's only for ambient sound. The sound field it provides is most useful to them as a reference for placing audio sources in a scene, because it has spatial information. Douek says it's a mistake to think that even a high quality ambisonic mic can pick up audio that will sound great, because it's placed with the camera, far away from the audio source and usually closer to fan noise from the camera or other gear.

The choir that comes in toward the end of the song was recorded with lavalier microphones on the first row of singers. In addition to the front lavalier mics to pick up the first row's voices, they also attached microphones to their backs to pick up the second row of singers. There were several other hidden microphones among the choir at a greater distance to pick up the sound of the space. A stereo mic pointed backwards into the cathedral space picked up the sound of reverberations coming back, and that comes into the mix as the choir and the cathedral come into view.

"We really wanted to transition into this very different acoustic space," Douek says, "both smoothly but definitively so that when you're in there you feel that you're in a giant cathedral."

Figure 8.2 The many tracks in a "massive Pro Tools session" for spatial audio.
Courtesy of Ecco VR.

Arranging in Post Production

All these separate recordings allowed them to arrange the positioning of
the singers' voices in the experience in the way that sounded best. They
also did this with Halvorson's voice. Because he had been recorded in
"wedges,"—that is, they recorded only a section of the sphere at once—
they were able to move those different recordings around and decide
which voice would go where for the best balance. They also thought of
the call-and-response singing Bobby did as directional cues that would
motivate the viewer to look around and hear where each voice was coming from.

Douek and Green are both composers, so they're accustomed to thinking about how to create a good harmonic balance and mix. "And the rule
with orchestral music and choir music in any setting, not just VR, is that
if you arrange it right both physically and musically then it mixes itself,"
Douek says.

Green notes that they also monitor the immersive mix live as they're
working in their audio software, rather than having to export to hear the
fully **spatialized** sound.

A Giant Pro Tools Session

Once Ecco VR had all the assets from filming, they brought it all into the
audio editing software Pro Tools, in combination with the Two Big Ears
(now Facebook Spatial Workstation) plugin for spatializing the sound.

They looked at the visuals to figure out what they needed it to sound like, and began spatializing. After cleaning up interferences from all the different microphones, they began building the sound that they wanted. Douek describes this as working toward "a healthy balance between a sense of presence and a sense of the space and the more distant mics." The term "presence" has its own history in the audio world that differs from the way it's used among VR creators. Douek is referring to audio that sounds as if it is close to the listener's ear; the opposite of presence is distance.

As they were assembling the sound, they went back and forth with the project producers, making changes to the positioning of the visuals as needed to improve the musical experience.

When they finished mixing, they output it as second-order ambisonics for Lytro's player. They later created different exports for other platforms, paring some down as needed based on the limitations of the players.

Filtering for the Viewer

Douek says through the whole production process they think about what kind of experience they want the viewer to have, and make sure they record what they need to be able to produce that. Distant mics will give the viewer a sense of the space, and close mics will give a sense of closeness.

Creating an immersive soundscape, he says, is about filtering what the viewer hears, directing their attention to simulate the way the ear filters sound in the real world. And that means making deliberate choices about what to include and what to leave out.

"If you have 25 different things that you're going to spatialize, it all adds up to nothing," Douek says. "Whereas if you have five or six, to draw your attention here and there, the brain can compute that and it adds to the sense of immersion. Beyond that, it's just a mess."

He says that's partly due the way viewers consume media versus the way they perceive the real world:

> In a real experience our brains are filtering out the air conditioner and this and that sound and the car going by, and helping us focus and listen. So that's what we do in our concept and in our post production, is we're going to try to give people not a hundred percent realistic version of the sound in reality. We're going to give them, as far as possible, a realistic sense of how they would perceive the situation.

Publication and Reception

Leonard Cohen had given the sign-off to use the song, and he died shortly before the experience was filmed. "And so in a sense it shifted from something that was, you know, a version of one of his songs to something that was much more of a tribute to him and his music," Douek says. "What we want most of all is the people to feel no disconnect between themselves and the musical experience."

Douek says people who watched the experience at Tribeca came out in tears, not thinking at all about the technology that went into the piece. "That's where we operate and we exist—we think at this subliminal level where sound and music happen," Douek says, "and so creating something that works really well and stays out of the way of distracting you from that kind of immersion."

Takeaways

Filter what the viewer hears:
- Creating an immersive soundscape is all about filtering what the viewer hears and directing attention to simulate the way the ear filters sound in the real world.
- To do so, make deliberate choices about what to include and what to leave out.
- Attempting to spatialize 25 different things may be useless, but drawing attention to five or six things is more doable.

Multiple audio sources and balance:
- Recording multiple sources will allow for more options in post production.
- Make sure to record what will be needed in post production. Distant mics will give the viewer a sense of the space, and close mics will give a sense of closeness.

About This Project

URL: www.with.in/watch/hallelujah
Interview Date: April, 2018
Interview Subject: Joel Douek, Benedict Green
Team:
Within: Zach Richter, Eames Kolar, Bobby Halvorson
EccoVR: Joel Douek, Benedict Green

Reeps One: Does Not Exist

Aurelia Soundworks and The Mill
June 2016

In an effort to continue experimenting in the immersive audio space, music producer and sound designer John Hendicott teamed up with production studio The Mill to experiment with an audio-first piece. Beatboxer Reeps One and Hendicott came together to produce a song designed for an immersive audio experience. The song is a 2-minute piece starting in the studio and moving to various locations in southern California, from Joshua Tree National Park to a warehouse in downtown LA and a date palm plantation and back and forth between locations. The cuts are quick, and it's a definite audio-first production, yet the visuals and physical locations add to the auditory effects, with the physical space and multiple locations directly impacting the design of the piece.

The experience was launched in June 2016 in collaboration with YouTube at Cannes Lions and went on to win "Best Sound Design Experience" at Raindance Film Festival, as well as nominations at the UKMVAs and the Proto Awards.

Creating an Immersive Song

The *Does Not Exist* experience begins in a studio environment, much like the recording of the audio began for the project. Many of Reeps One's other beatbox performance videos start in a similar setting.

Reeps One and Hendicott were in discussions for about a month before recording. Hendicott says the song that forms the basis for the piece—the song came together one day in his studio in London. "We want it to sound like we're in like ten different environments. So when we sat down, we just kind of worked out between ourselves," says Hendicott. The visuals were filmed over the course of 3–4 days shortly thereafter. In starting with the studio environment, Hendicott says, they wanted to trick the viewer into thinking they might be looking at one of the artist's normal videos, then the viewer might "kind of freak out when they realize that it's actually a 360 and then it gets to different environments."

Collaborating with a visual director from the Mill, they created a timeline of where each location would appear. For example, the first 15 would be in a studio and the next 5 seconds he'd be in a massive warehouse, then a bedroom, then a desert. "We kind of planned it out in some of the chronology of the shoot," says Hedicott, and then they also did some **blocking** to choreograph the piece. Thinking through the visual and auditory cues for each transition, Hendicott says, was "a push and pull" with the visuals.

They filmed for three days in Los Angeles and one day in Joshua Tree, at a total of 12 different locations. They filmed the video in sections of 90 degrees at once, using a DSLR camera with a wide angle lens. This allowed them to light the scene from behind the camera for each take and to use a boom mic just outside the frame. It also allowed for Reeps One to appear in multiple places at one time in the final video.

Figure 8.3 A large warehouse in LA was one filming location for the *Does Not Exist* piece. Courtesy of John Hendicott.

Audio within the Physical Space

Hendicott has worked with beatboxers before, but this time in the initial brief to Reeps One he wanted to focus the vocal effects on those that could be generated in reality and physical space, rather than in a studio with an engineer. "You can play with the idea of echo because we can find a location which will echo your voice," Hendicott said. On the music side, Hendicott says he had seen several VR experiences that were poorly adapted from a music video, with little to no reason for the production to be in 360.

Hendicott was also thinking through how sounds react in different spaces, and he knew that the sound needed to be fairly loud to create reverb. If they decided to have a certain part of the experience be really big and spacious, then they decided to shoot in a big desert or warehouse environment. He also thought through some of the guiding auditory elements he already knew: For example, that high-pitched sounds are easier to discern in terms of the direction than low frequency sounds.

For Hendicott, the most important thing was working with contrast: "going from a very small, tight space to a huge space." Contrasts helps to tell the story of 3D sound, he says.

They also moved Reeps One around in the scene and used the audio to cue the viewer where to look. "You need to be able to hear that he's behind you," says Hendicott. "Part of the playfulness of the experience is for people to hear that and then move their heads around."

Hendicott also says that at the time of creating it, it was one of the first pieces to use sound as a starting point. The sound and visual teams coordinated to allow the audio to lead.

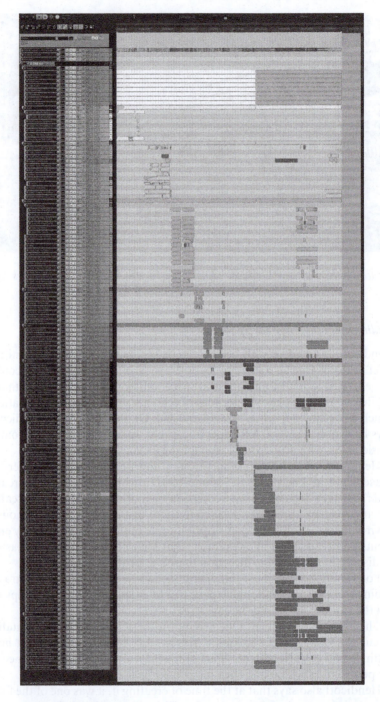

Figure 8.4 Many tracks went into the audio mix for *Does Not Exist*. Courtesy of John Hendicott.

Capturing All of the Assets

Hendicott used multiple recording setups to collect all the audio assets. He captured in-studio audio, live audio from the camera on-location and he also placed various mics on-location. Part of the experiment was to compare all the different audio elements, Hendicott says.

Throughout the post production, Hendicott says he was thinking about how much they wanted it to sound like it really would in real life. He felt it was important for viewers to have a sense of presence at all times. "What we ended up doing was a real mix of live recordings and studio recordings enhanced with spatial audio plug-ins, reverbs and delays and depression and stuff to make it like a hyperreal experience rather than a faithful reproduction of what happens in real life," Hendicott says.

Challenging Quick Cuts

As Hendicott was going back and forth with the visual team, one of the general rules they were experimenting with was the perceived wisdom in the VR world suggesting creators should avoid cutting between scenes too quickly. "The whole point of this was turning that on its head and saying, OK, how fast can we cut and still make sense?" Hendicott says.

He says some people who watch the video find the cuts too quick, but for most of the people who watch it, it works fine. "We were fully prepared to take it too far," Hendicott says. "We really wanted to find the limits."

One of the conclusions they reached was that, given a coherent soundtrack reflecting the environment, and done in a thoughtful and "rhythmic way," the viewer is okay with quick cuts. "If they enjoy it or not is a different matter," Hendicott says.

Audio and Publishing Platforms

During the production process they used LogicPro, Reaper and Blue Ripple's third-order ambisonic plugins.[2] In ambisonics, order refers to the number of audio channels used to make up the sphere—higher order means more resolution and greater precision in the sound field. First-order ambisonics has four channels; third-order has 16. YouTube had recently launched their 360 audio capabilities for first order sound, so they published it there. But they mixed it all in third order, which is much higher resolution. So when they dropped it to first order, Hendicott says "it's like a mush … It's very blocky and horrible." Despite the fact that they had a third order version ready, there were no platforms that supported this version at the time.

A year after the project initially published, Facebook released an update to make second-order ambisonics possible and it took Hendicott

Figure 8.5 An equirectangular still from the final Reeps One video. Courtesy of John Hendicott.

another two months to remix the whole piece again. "It was something I desperately wanted to do because, after all this hard work, I don't want the only example of this video to exist in this first order format on YouTube, which doesn't sound very good," he says. He adds that it was a big breakthrough because they finally got to a stage where he was happy with the sound.

By retaining the third order information, they captured a version of this piece that can be used when the playback technology catches up. Additional audio channels offer the ability to lock sounds to head, for example, playing mono or stereo sound to the viewer in addition to the rotation-responsive spatialized sound. Towards the end of *Does Not Exist*, there are sounds that do not come from the performer and don't come from the environment. Hendicott says this is where they got really creative using sounds such as an organ and a bass. "I made those all locked to your head position, which creates a far more punchy sound event," he say. All of the sounds of the space and Reeps were in the 360 environment.

Learning to Listen

Audio is tricky—unlike video you can't immediately see what is wrong with it. Hendicott says people don't understand how to describe it. But audio can serve as a useful guiding tool within a story or music video. Hendicott believes you can do certain things with 3D sound that are more effective than video, and use the imaginations as a storytelling tool.

Takeaways

Quick cuts:
* Quick cuts may be worthwhile—and easier to tolerate—with an audio-first production when guiding the viewer through with auditory cues.

Multiple audio sources:
* Recording multiple sources in the field, will give creatives more options in post production.

About This Project

Reeps One Project: www.facebook.com/reepsone/videos/1015532062383 6049/
Interview Date: April, 2018
Interview Subject: John Hendicott, sound designer and music producer, Aurelia Soundworks
Team: The Mill

Designing Audio for Games

Nick LaMartina

Nick LaMartina is an audio director for Entertainment Arts and mostly scores audio for games, but he also does audio field recordings in his free time. "Just like a photographer I'll bring it back home and edit," he says, describing one field recording from Jamaica where the beach had varied topography. Each different location had a unique sound, he says, describing the many scenes on the same beach.

When he captures recordings in the field, much like a photographer, he'll first quietly observe his environment. There has to be a good balance, he says. He tries to capture the entire environment. For the rocky beaches, he says there were several points when the waves were slamming against the rock. He searches for a place and moment to find the right balance within a scene, searching for a balance of details.

Scoring a Video Game

When LaMartina first sits down to design sound for a game he'll look at the art itself. He'll look to see if there are lots of warm versus cold colors. Then he'll often play an early prototype to get a sense of the pace of the game and the intensity, "Does this music need to be quick?" He notes that audio, whether music or sound effects, is a time-based art form, and when designing or creating a score or audio track the creator needs to have an understanding of the pace and a sense of the emotion in the experience.

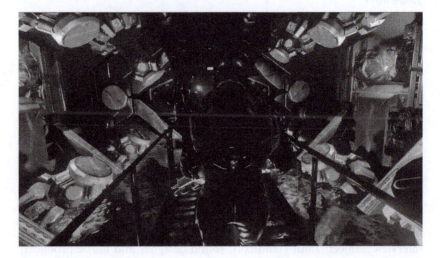

Figure 8.6 The art itself is a starting point in creating a musical score for a video game. Image courtesy of Nick LaMartina.

LaMartina has worked extensively for Entertainment Arts in the mobile game industry. "We have a very limited screen," says LaMartina. Audio will "confirm what we see, but we inform what we don't see," he says of the neurological link between the eyes and ears. In mobile gaming, the user interface and effects may be way off the screen—but they are very specific tones or music stingers. For example in *Dungeon Keeper*, a competitive city builder game, LaMartina says he would "play very specific tones and musical stingers, drum, key, gong" to emphasize user interface elements. He says doing sound design in the VR space is actually the exact same type of approach, "We want them to be able to look around and see the depth of the experience."

When designing for mobile, LaMartina says, creators should accentuate any messages they want to draw attention to, but overall he says it has to be subtle, "People won't really say something until they notice you are doing it wrong."

In his early experiments focusing on how to tell stories with spatial audio, LaMartina says, it was important to have sound come from a specific location and work to emulate directional sound using reverb as a way to create a sense of enclosure.

LaMartina's advice for creators is to make sure the audio performs its most important role. "Get in there, experience it," he says, and play it. If there's something the creator wants to make the viewer pay attention to, and the player or user is missing it, LaMartina will adjust and test it out. "Finding friends and family with a very low tolerance for BS is helpful," he says.

Figure 8.7 Binaural audio capture, courtesy of Nick LaMartina.

Takeaways

Matching audio to story:
- What part of a story or game is being enhanced through the audio? Decide how to locate and enhance to match the game or story.
- Consider what emotional impact is intended, and design audio with this in mind.

- Is the story or game fast-paced or slow-paced? Design the audio in a way that complements the pace.

Expanding an environment:
- In mobile game design, the audio suggests what's off screen. In immersive space, it locates sounds sources but also serves to a sense of depth.

When in doubt, test it out:
- Watching test users can tell the creator whether audio cues meant to guide the viewer are working or not.

Notes

1 Joel Douek and Benedict Green, who did the audio for Hallelujah VR, are working on a book on immersive audio as we complete this book.
2 Hendicott, John. "How to create a 3D music experience in VR." August 4, 2017. https://medium.com/@John_Hendicott/how-to-create-a-3d-music-experience-in-vr-reeps-one-does-not-exist-case-study-641df55d00c8.

Section III
Bringing It All Together

9 Storytelling without Close-Ups
The Big Picture

Storytelling grammar is a shared effort; viewers must understand the medium and its parameters and learn how to read the storyteller's cues.

Readers of novels have to learn that exposition and character development at the front of the book will reward them in later chapters. Movie watchers know to brace themselves when "foreboding" music foreshadows something scary. And great directors know how to play with these conventions to surprise their viewers.

We are in the midst of a collective process of discovery as we figure out how to engage in this creative conversation with immersive media. As we get comfortable in these new media, the level of nuance to this conversation is sure to shift.

This is an overview of some lessons we've learned that apply generally across immersive storytelling. Assembled, these components make up the basic framework for breaking out of the frame (or disregarding it entirely, if possible!) and thinking about stories in 360-degree space.

The Viewer Is the Camera (Agency)

In immersive experiences, the viewer controls where they are looking at any moment, creating their own framing of what they see and in a sense building their own sequence of each scene. This is something the creator must cede to the viewer.

"So there is a frame," Sarah Hill of StoryUp says, "it's just that it's rotating inside the sphere, and it's your job as a storyteller to ensure they're looking in the appropriate direction."

Creators interviewed for this book have offered some analogies to understand this relationship. Max Salomon of Black Dot Films says with the right guidance the viewer will create the "induced edit" a director intends. James George of Scatter describes the role of the interactive immersive media creator as "shamanistic"—giving the viewer clues along the way as they take their own journey through the content.

The Camera Is the Viewer (Interaction, Embodiment and Social Cues)

Because the viewer is acting as a camera within an immersive scene, looking directly at the camera (the actual camera in 360 video, or a virtual camera in a 3D modeled environment), gives the sense of looking directly at the viewer.

This can be used as a tool to give the viewer a sense of presence and embodiment, and it can also take the viewer out of the story if a character breaks social expectations by staring too long. Another concern is the characters looking "through" the viewer.

Nathalie Mathe of NativeVR says she likes to use 3-person scenes for this reason, so the characters can naturally look at the viewer and away from them. Cassandra Herrman asked her interviewee for After Solitary to look around the room, so his gaze wouldn't fall too long on any one area and create an uncanny distraction.

This also means that the creator has to decide what role the viewer is playing in the story. Are they acknowledged at all, or are they an invisible observer? If they are acknowledged in the scene, is it a first-person experience, or are they witness to another person's story? These choices will inform how the characters should interact with the camera.

A Space-Centric Art Form

Something that comes up over and over again in conversations with immersive creators is the notion of taking a viewer somewhere.

As Joel Douek of Ecco VR puts it, film and television are "time-dependent art forms … VR is not about time; it's about space." But he emphasizes that the space needn't be a physical one—though in many cases the first thing that comes to mind is access and taking people somewhere far away or exclusive, and that's been done to great effect in many examples in this book. "You can just be in a place," Douek says, "like under water in the Galapagos. There's no need to be a story, it's just a place. And yet it's so rich and replete with information and experience."

But this conceptual framework can also be used to think about taking people into a different point of view. Actually seeing the world "through someone else's eyes" has been something of a holy grail for some creators, although, as Sarah Hill points out, it may be more conducive to empathy to be alongside a person in an experience, rather than to try to experience something as that person.

Alexander Porter of Scatter emphasizes the power of transporting people to places that are radically close to home. Allowing viewers to experience things that might be totally familiar, but with a different context, creates the possibility of a new perspective.

Augmented reality is similarly about space, though the mechanism is flipped—bringing content to the viewer's own physical world and creating a personal connection to the material.

Think Twice about Strong-Arming the Viewer

A lot of newcomers to immersive storytelling are tempted to wrest control from the viewer and force them to look at a certain thing.

First, this isn't really possible because they can always look away. Second, it misses the point. If we want to take advantage of what immersive media has to offer, we have to let the viewers explore and experience the environments we put them in.

There are methods to guide the viewer toward a linear narrative, but if we're going to force them, why not just put the whole thing in a rectangular frame?

In a Medium post titled "How to Greet a Rebel: Unlocking the Storyteller in VR," VR creator Jessica Brillhart suggests that not only should VR filmmakers anticipate that some viewers will look away from an intended point of interest, but that creators should reward them for doing so.[1]

FOMO Awareness

While it is tempting to fill an environment with action in order to make use of 360-degree space, it's frustrating for viewers to have a constant fear of missing out on the action in another part of the scene.

Most creators of narrative experiences try to anticipate or guide where the viewer will look, and strategize to make sure major story points aren't missed.

Gentle versus Overt Cues

The creators interviewed for this book have used all sorts of techniques to guide viewers and make use of immersive space. And cues don't always have to be subtle. In the case of Euronews, having hosts to direct the viewer in 360-degree video was the best way to use the immersive canvas while delivering information quickly.

After Solitary, on the other hand, uses sound cues among its tools to draw viewers' attention to the important action. *Climbing Giants* employs a variety of subtle visual and audio cues to manage the viewer's attention without ever explicitly suggesting where to look. And *Blackout* and *Testimony* put viewers in an environment and let them explore on their own, driven by their interest to follow linear storylines or hop around among stories.

Truly Immersive Audio

Audio in immersive space opens up a world of possibilities for storytelling. As Joel Douek of Ecco VR points out, in traditional audio formats (think surround sound), rear-channel audio in a theater isn't rewarded. Immersive media creates an environment where sound can truly surround the user.

However the audio designer also cedes to the viewer some agency in what they hear. As the viewer moves around or turns their head, they're adjusting the sound mix with their attention and position relative to the sources.

Leave Time to Explore

Whether you're placing a viewer in a 360-video scene or placing a 3D animation on their tabletop, they are likely to need more time to acquaint themselves to every new scene and figure out how to follow the action. That means the pace of immersive storytelling—how quickly the scenery can change or the action can unfold—often needs to be more spacious than other media, in which the creator has much more power to directly control what the viewer is seeing.

That doesn't mean quick cuts and fast action can never happen, but they should be done thoughtfully and not just mimic a traditional film.

Cognitive Overload

Between audio and 360 degrees of scenery, immersive media demands a lot of the viewer. Creators have learned to exercise caution when incorporating information from multiple sources — for example, narrative audio in addition to a graphic in a 360-degree environment may be more than a viewer can take in.

It's useful to test out immersive pieces on viewers to make sure they're able to take everything in, and then tweak the pacing as needed or reduce the amount of sensory inputs and information being thrust upon the viewer at any moment.

Agency and Engagement

Narrative immersive media can fall into what feels like an awkward middle ground for user agency. In 360-degree video, viewers have control over where they look, but can't interact.

A number of creators we've spoken to in this book have found ways to give viewers a sense of agency in how they experience the story, based on the idea that embracing the need for agency allows viewers to better engage with the content.

For linear storytelling, a common theme among creators seeking to give viewers' more agency is by simply asking for inputs to continue the story. *Nasdaq* VR does this by pausing at several important points until the viewer opts to continue. *Hell and High Water* VR and *Capturing Everest* use a "relay race" method to string together different chapters, so the user gets to make the choice whether to continue through a linear story. *USA Today*'s *Border Wall*, which is much more of a free exploration of content, is still broken into chapters that suggest a semi linear experience.

Among the more open-ended experiences, *Testimony* and *Blackout* offer a variety of linear stories in a story space, and the viewer can choose whether to follow one from beginning to end, or whether to hop around.

Breaking an immersive experience into chapters can also help viewers by allowing them to leave and come back (*The Wall, Capturing Everest*). An episodic story works well for a narrative arc with clear stages, and gives viewers a chance to take a break. "Previously" and "Coming up" sections hold the story thread for viewers to leave the series and come back.

You Control the Environment

While much is made of the loss of control immersive creators grapple with in losing the ability to force perspective, in virtual reality they gain an immense amount of control over the viewer's environment.

A number of the creators we've spoken with have caught on to this and used it to their advantage. The maker of *Testimony* VR sought a "comfortable" listening environment to help the audience open up to challenging content. NPR's *Stand at the Edge of Geologic Time* aimed for a "feeling of contemplation" that would similarly make space for a fully engaged listener in an audio-centric story.

While most of the augmented reality content we've looked at is at the mercy of the viewer's physical environment, as the technology develops creators are likely to have more flexibility in how much of the physical environment they incorporate in the experience, versus how much they cover with graphics.

Storyboarding: Linear vs. Branching Narrative?

Storyboarding for immersive media varies depending on the level of user agency, and can look like a storyboard for a traditional film narrative.

For 360-degree filmmakers with a strongly linear approach, a storyboard can look like a traditional film storyboard, with an equirectangular projection of each scene and an anticipated path from one scene to the next.

But it's also up to the filmmaker to decide whether they want to plan for multiple possible visual paths through those scenes—so a storyboard for a 360-degree film might just as well fan out to multiple possible views in some places, then narrow back down as the filmmaker uses cues to guide the viewer back to an essential moment in the story.

With projects that offer more user agency, a storyboard will look more like a web of potential connections among nodes in a story, or like a user-interaction flow chart that's partially open-ended, with different storylines developing based on user inputs, and other possibilities narrowing as the viewer progresses through the experience.

Where Else Can We Glean Insights?

There is no prior medium whose grammar maps directly to immersive media, but creators often cite a few places they look to for guidance.

There is, of course, film—as much as we warn against overestimating the commonalities. For 360 video in particular, there is technical overlap in capture and editing methods. And as Max Salomon of Black Dot Films conceptualizes it, guiding a viewer through a 360-degree scene could be considered an "induced edit": The viewer looks around, but the director is giving them cues all along. Other creators have talked similarly about guiding attention.

Creators of interactive virtual reality experiences often refer to the world of video games to think about user interaction design. Journalist and web developer Armand Emamdjomeh spoke of **affordances** — letting the user know what interactions are possible in a virtual environment.

Many VR creators say they've learned that immersive media has more in common with theater than with film — and especially with immersive theater. They think of the viewer as being in the scene, with the actors moving around them, and borrow insights on blocking and how to direct attention.

Some suggest sprinkling in a bit of magic—that is, channeling the way a magician might think about directing attention without overtly guiding the audience. And in 2017, Katy Newton and Karin Soukup spoke with magicians to understand their strategies. Newton summarized some of the findings in a talk at IAB Engage 2017,[2] discussing the way magicians guide and direct their audiences with cues, including gaze.

Using the whole immersive canvas and having the user turn is one way to think about displaying information. An alternative is directing a user's attention in one direction and turning the carousel around them.

Notes

1 Brillhart, Jessica. "How to greet a rebel: Unlocking the storyteller in VR," December 7, 2015. https://medium.com/the-language-of-vr/how-to-greet-a-rebel-unlocking-the-storyteller-in-vr-d40b2cc05f55.
2 Newton, Katy. "Hocus Focus" Talk, IAB Engage 2017. https://medium.com/@ax.mediaexperiments/hocus-focus-what-magicians-can-teach-vr-328c8acea44c.

10 Viewing Mode, Form and Content
Best Practices

Not all immersive media is alike. In the last chapter, we looked at some big-picture lessons that apply to immersive storytelling in general. This chapter dives into what we've discovered about the specific forms discussed in this book, and tips and tricks that can help tell a better story.

The lessons below are broken down into sections that mirror the order of the case study chapters in Section 2.

Immersive Narratives and News

The first thing Jessica Lauretti, Global Head of RYOT Studio learned, which she tells everyone is: "You can't apply what you know about filmmaking to VR ... it's much more akin to UX [user-experience] design or immersive theatre—there's no other creative medium where you are thinking of the audience or viewer as one of the elements of the piece." Lauretti says that as a creator, you have to forget what you know, and open your brain like a magician might.

Looking at what we've learned through immersive narratives and news, there are a few major themes that come to the surface. The first is access, and the second series of lessons is related to shooting and editing. Third, there are a few ways of thinking about voice, subtitles and scripting, and finally, a few lessons on testing your content.

Ultimately, in immersive news stories "It is still journalism at its core," says Kevin Tsukii of Emblematic Group, "You still have to do a lot of reporting and if anything, you have to do even more."

Access: Take the Audience Somewhere

Immersive media appeals when it can take viewers somewhere they couldn't otherwise go.

Many of the immersive news narratives transport the viewer somewhere they wouldn't have access to and the best do so in a unique way, with a story to immerse the viewer into the experience. To make these immersive stories powerful, sensory cues—like the mention of the smell of baking bread, can give an additional suggestion of "being there."[1]

We Who Remain[2] takes viewers to a place where journalists are banned and Felix & Paul's tour of the White House[3] with then-president Barack Obama (not featured in this book, but available on YouTube) provides a unique view of something many people only see from the outside.

Shooting: Planning and Letting the Action Unfold

As with flat video, there are different ways to think about an immersive story on a practical and philosophical level. With *Clouds Over Sidra*,[4] we see long cuts that take inspiration from theater, rather than traditional film, and the fourth wall is broken through brief eye contact with the camera—placing the viewer in the scene.

Some shooters have the luxury of time to shoot over a long period of time and review—as was the case of *We Who Remain*—while others plan more strictly shot-by-shot yet still use the audio and visuals to tell the story and guide the viewer, such as *Climbing Giants*.[5]

As we see in a few different pieces, it can be hard to identify the main character in a 360 scene full of people. The solution in some cases has included "**standup**" scenes, in which the characters introduce themselves directly to the camera. Some pieces use graphics or lower thirds to identify people.

The use of scanned environments (like in *Limbo*) can be a useful tool for showing natural movement, which makes graphics feel more believable than if they were animated.[6]

Editing: Gently Guiding the Viewer

In *The Occupation of Alcatraz*, we see how visuals of the past are overlaid onto the present.[7] By embedding archival imagery in a 360-degree space, the filmmakers give a sense of connection to past events (or an added historical context to a place. Alcatraz and other 360 videos use guiding action at the edges of the viewer's **field of view** when looking to one **point of interest** to lead them to the next point.

Other tools for guiding the viewer may include:

- lighting, color and contrast: An area that is brighter than the rest of the scene, or a bold color that stands out, will draw the eye;
- quality of sounds: Viewers will look for the source of a sound, and some sounds suggest a certain region in 360 space, the sky if they hear an airplane, or the ground if they hear the sound of a stream;
- indirect verbal cues and descriptions: Viewers will look for something a character or narrator mentions;
- camera movement: Viewers will often follow the direction of camera movement to see where it is going;

- the character's **gaze**: Viewers will follow where a character is looking. More than one person looking in a certain direction provides an even more powerful cue.

Speed and pace arguably impact the experience more so in an immersive narrative piece than in a flat video. In some cases, giving context to set the stage can be useful to allow the story to unfold. An information-dense **explainer** section in *We Who Remain* takes place in a small area of a 360 scene with no action in other areas. One tool for narrowing focus and integrating flat videos is to project these on a wall. In this case it was done on a classroom wall. *Alcatraz* plays archival footage on the exterior wall of the famous prison.

Creators pushed back against received wisdom that quick cuts are disorienting—or even nauseating—when used in immersive space. And it should be acknowledged that, often, viewers need some time to orient themselves each time there is a cut to a new environment. But *VRtually There*,[8] and *Reeps One: Does Not Exist*[9] experimented with pacing and found it really depends on the story. Sometimes quick cuts give just the right effect. If there's any question, it helps to test-screen the piece to see how viewers respond.

Who Is the Viewer: First Person, Second Person or Third Person?

In *Limbo*,[10] the narrator addresses the viewer, narrating their experience to create a sense of personal connection. The viewer is meant to be experiencing the story first-hand. *UTURN*[11] is another first-person experience, in which the viewer can look down and see the body of the character they're meant to be inhabiting, and characters address them directly.

In other experiences, the main character addresses the viewer directly and looks them in the eye, setting them up as an observer who is present, but not necessarily a participant. In many pieces for Euronews,[12] the viewer is guided by the journalist who is usually visible throughout the story.

In other pieces, such as *Climbing Giants* or *The Occupation of Alcatraz*, characters serve as narrators in a more traditional voice-over style, speaking personally but not in a way that suggests they are aware of the viewer in the scene.

Where Is Your Audience Watching?

Understanding where the viewer will be watching the experience and tailoring for the platform is an important aspect of the creation process for 360-degree video, as different platforms offer different kinds of inputs for the viewer to look around.

For a desktop or **magic window** viewer, looking at the rear of the 360 space only takes a click or a swipe, but for a person wearing a headset it can be a challenge to turn fully around while seated. For viewers navigating with a mouse or trackpad (rather than in a headset), slower **guiding action** makes it easier to keep up.

Voice, Subtitles and Script

Immersive narratives and news pieces occasionally include a scripted voice-over, or captions. Arguably captions or subtitles can break presence, limiting the immersive effect by reminding viewers they are watching a screen. They also require attention, making it harder for viewers to take in.

For projects in which the characters speak a different language than the audience, some creators elect to use an actor for voice-over rather than overlay subtitles on the screen. Voice-over narration is additionally useful because subtle or direct cues to guide the viewer's gaze can be scripted in.

Using multiple voices to tell a story is another way to think about scripting. By mixing narration and interview audio, *Limbo* was able to directly guide the viewer but still include first-hand accounts of interviewees.

Walk-Around

Our chapter on **walk-around** VR features interactive pieces in which the viewer can walk around and change their point of view as they watch the events play out. We use the term walk-around to convey that these include fully navigable 3D environments, though the term "invisible visitor" also describes the particular kind of story we explore in our walk-around case studies.

Projects of this type are built with a variety of techniques including volumetric video, photogrammetry and 3D modeling. What they have in common is that the viewer is an unacknowledged observer, and a variety of storytelling techniques have emerged to work with this constraint.

Production: Know Your Tools

Volumetric video capture often requires filming in a specialized studio, limiting who can be recorded in this format.

Before recording volumetric capture to be placed in a virtual environment, it helps to plan, or block, the movement of the character and the placement of the viewer based on that environment. Thinking of the viewer as if they are part of an immersive theatre piece with the characters moving around them allows for a more interactive experience.

Cuts, Transitions and Teleporting

When a character appears in volumetric video in a virtual environment, it's jarring to see their image skip, so creators aim not to cut together the way they could in traditional documentary film, where jump cuts can be avoided by changing the camera angle. Fading a character out and back in is one way to create a smooth transition in place of a cut.

Teleporting the viewer from one area of an immersive environment to another can have the effect similar to a film cut in changing perspective and driving the narrative forward. But to travel from one location to the next by moving in VR can be tricky depending on the size of the physical space and VR hardware set-up.

In *Kiya*,[13] the viewer is teleported to the front yard of a house before gunshots go off. The violence is out of view, but the viewer still fills in the gaps with their imagination. This perspective also allows them to experience the reaction of the witnesses, which lends additional meaning to the event.

Audio: Place and Guide

Sound cues can serve to enhance a story and provide an additional element to bring the audience into a story or scene. When possible, repeating a sound cue gives viewers a second chance to follow the action.

Sound cues are also useful to ease the transition when teleporting the viewer. In addition, the kind of sound that can tell a viewer where to look, for example, the sound of birds can draw a viewers to look toward a window or the sound of an airplane or doors can guide the audience in a specific direction.

Managing the Characters' Gaze

Eye contact—or lack thereof—sends strong social signals. A volumetrically captured character, when placed in a walk-around environment, will look where they looked during the recording and not follow the viewer with their eyes. This means the viewer can step into and out of their gaze and they don't respond. In an effort to avoid the uncanny feeling of the character looking "through" the viewer, the directors of *After Solitary* instructed their interviewee to continuously look around the room, and not rest too long on any gaze.[14]

For a different solution to this question, it's worth checking out Life VR's *Buzz Aldrin: Cycling Pathways to Mars*.[15] In that experience, the recording of Aldrin rotates to always face the viewer as they move. This gives the feeling that he is speaking directly to the viewer, but can also feel overwhelming at times, as it's impossible to escape his attention.

Immersive Interactives

For storytellers building interactivity into their projects, there is always a tension between the level of user agency and the ability to get the story across.

This is a challenge that's not specific to immersive media, though in some senses immersive media demands user agency in a way that earlier media forms don't, because by definition it demands that the viewer be active in choosing what they see.

A common thread among creators of interactives is the idea that giving the viewer agency helps them engage with the story by turning them from an observer into a participant.

Here are some insights into ways storytellers can build rewarding interactions into immersive pieces.

A Space to Explore

Some projects work with the spatial nature of immersive media in their interactivity.

USA Today's *Border Wall*[16] (which we've grouped with mixed media projects for the purpose of this book, but contains many different elements of interactivity) sets the user on top of a map of the entire U.S.–Mexico border, allowing them to **teleport** from place to place to discover content. *Discovering Gale Crater* uses a similar mechanic to show the user different labeled points in the space.[17]

In *Blackout*, the user walks around a subway car and approaches its passengers to trigger different stories. In *Testimony*, the user is stationary but explores the space with their gaze. In the Gear VR version, the user can choosing whether to watch the loosely linear stories consecutively from beginning to end, or whether to hop around.

Driving the Story Forward

Finding a balance between a linear narrative arc and free exploration can give users agency but also keep them from getting lost.

Sometimes, interactivity can be as simple as prompting an action from the user for the story to unfold. This happens several times in the *Wall Street Journal*'s *Nasdaq* roller coaster,[18] as the experience pauses to highlight important moments and asks for user input to continue.

Hell and High Water VR,[19] which is a series of 360 videos in an app (and is discussed in the mixed media section of this book), relies on a similar principle by breaking up the content into shorter chapters, and letting the viewer choose at each juncture whether to watch the next experience.

In the *New York Times*' Olympics AR[20] experience, the user scrolls to reveal the content, then walks around to reveal information.

Signaling What's Possible

In interactive experiences, it's important to clearly signal to users which interactions are possible in the virtual world. The best games and interactives rarely put their audience in a situation in which they have no instructions for what to do next—but giving instructions that are intuitive and unobtrusive takes a lot of thought. *Gale Crater* does this by offering a tour of an interactive space that can help orient users and deliver important information.

Testimony's **gaze-based** interaction is designed to be intuitive and driven by the user's interest.[21] Once a user looks at something, they learn the mechanism for interacting. It also gives viewers the ability to take a break from a difficult story and come back to it, without having to take off the headset. *Blackout*[22] and *UTURN* are similarly gaze-based (though *Blackout* allows the viewer to move around the scene as well.)

Sound to Indicate Place

Sound can serve to enhance an interactive and guide the viewer.

Testimony is scored throughout, and added sound effects and visuals highlight details in the spoken narratives, and heighten the experiential quality of the piece. The shift in the sound bed signals a change in environment—from the main immersive space to watching a testimony, and back.

The creators of *USA Today*'s *Border Wall* project also used sound to help communicate to the viewer that they were in different environments. Using consistent sound in the map area of the experience serves as a navigational aid, helping users know where they are and avoid getting lost among the content.

Sound is also an area where storytellers working with factual content have to exercise caution. The makers of the *Discovering Gale Crater* interactive chose not to invent ambient sound for the surface of Mars because they couldn't verify its accuracy.

Sound itself can also be the central to the interactive nature of a story.

In *UTURN*, sound makes up an essential component of the interactivity. The experience dynamically mixes two entirely different sound environments, with separate scripts, for a user-driven interactive experience. The augmented-reality museum experience *Overheard*[23] is also sound-based, with different audio stories intersecting—at which point the user can choose to follow a different thread, or stay with the one they've been listening to.

WebVR for Accessibility

The problem with creating interactives for high end VR headsets is that— at least as of 2018—few people have access to these devices and distribution therefore has a fairly narrow reach. Some creators are solving this problem by developing their projects to be viewed on the open web.

Creating a project with **WebVR** for browsers means a wide audience can experience it without having to download an app or have a specific device. The disadvantage is that it takes longer to develop projects that work on many browsers and devices. What's more, while a lot is possible with WebVR, having to stream the data over the web, versus downloading it to an application for a mobile device or a computer, puts a limit on the complexity of the experience.

Three projects discussed in this book that are created with WebVR are the *Nasdaq* roller coaster, *Discovering Gale Crater* and *Testimony.*

Interacting with Data

Two of the projects featured in the Interactive section of this book are data visualizations. In the *L.A. Times' Discovering Gale Crater,* we see how giving the user agency to explore an environment can give a sense of its scale and topography.

The *Wall Street Journal's Nasdaq* project provides another example of how visualizing data in an immersive 3D environment can give viewers a new way to connect and understand. The experience pauses and prompts the user several times to move forward, in one case pausing before a dramatic drop so the user must choose to continue down it.

Mixed-Media Packages

To combine different types of media is an art form on its own.

Adding an immersive element can provide depth or add something no other medium is able to do. But it can also be difficult to transition between immersive and flat media.

When incorporating various media, it's important to be conscious of how often a user is being asked to jump in and out of a headset.

Know Why You Are Incorporating an Immersive Element

In a multimedia project, immersive media can be employed as a component to add a sense of place. It can be used to communicate scale and space, but the key is to know why it makes sense for a project to incorporate an immersive format.

NPR's *Stand at The Edge of Geologic Time* places viewers in 360-degree images of Rocky Mountain National Park with accompanying soundscapes.[24] In addition to several environments to experience, the project offers a narrated tour. On mobile and headset that tour is immersive and adds a sense of being there alongside the narrator, a geologist. But the makers realized that people accessing the piece from a desktop weren't clicking and dragging to look around. So, they adjusted it to pan around like a traditional video, because in that case, the 360 version was taking away from the experience rather than adding to it.

Splitting out the Context

One of the first lessons when experimenting with mixed-media storytelling is to use each medium for its strengths.

For *The Call Center*,[25] they didn't try to tell the whole story as an immersive piece; instead they used the immersive medium to give a sense of being at a call center and a war zone. In the text piece, the creators gave more background and context to the broader story. Establishing context for an immersive experience can leave more space and build the foundation for the immersive storytelling component to focus on the experience.

Immersive Media as the Platform

The other way to do mixed media with immersive storytelling is to embed other media, for example photos, flat video or data visualizations, within immersive space.

In *The Wall*, the sheer breadth and depth of the project allowed for bringing together a variety of media around a specific issue. Users can watch short videos, flip through photo slideshows, or walk around different locations for a multimedia experience without ever breaking out of the headset. In this way, immersive space serves as the platform for the other media, previewing what can be done when immersive is treated as the default, rather than a special add-on.

The Wall requires a high-end headset and tracking so that viewers can teleport and walk around to find the content. *Testimony*, which embeds flat video and animations in 360 space (and is in the interactives section of the book) does this as a stationary experience.[26] Zohar Kfir, who created the project and whose background is as an artist and filmmaker, sees VR space as an empty museum with infinite possibilities.

"AR in VR"

In VR, unlike in AR, the project creator controls the entire environment, and can build upon and enhance the viewer's surroundings, for example by adding additional information or graphics to a 360 video.

Robert Hernandez at USC says it can be useful to think of this style as AR within VR. For *Hell and High Water* VR, graphics, labels and data visualizations pop up throughout to add context and explanations for the story.[27] In *Discovering Gale Crater* (discussed in Chapter 5), labels pop up in a VR landscape, and users can navigate them to hear additional information. And both *The Occupation of Alcatraz* (in Chapter 3) and *We Who Remain* (Chapter 3) project informational graphics and images onto surfaces in the VR world.

Minimize Sensory Overload

With graphics, video and audio in VR can easily overwhelm a viewer with overlapping sensory inputs.

It helps to avoid including audio and visuals that compete for attention; if there's an informative graphic in the scene, a break in the narration can help viewers focus. Allowing a graphic to stay visible for a longer period of time.

Augmented Reality and Mixed Reality

Alina Mikhaleva recalls being at a Future of Storytelling event in 2017 in which she was attempting to check out an AR app. She stood there for 15 minutes trying to get it to work, to no avail.

Just a year or so later, the ease with which mobile technology allows for seamless integration of AR into a story (such as the *New York Times* piece on the 2018 Olympics) has, indeed, provided the potential to take storytelling to another level.

Now that it's reaching a turning point for accessibility, here are some lessons on when it might make sense to use AR and the best way to tell a story in this medium.

Add Layers of Information

AR can be a useful tool to add to what already exists. In this way, we see how the *Time* magazine Optimism cover and *Sports Illustrated* AR cover (for *Capturing Everest*) build upon the magazine brand.[28] The additional layers of information are not necessary to the story, yet they provide additional context for those interested in learning more. Thinking through augmented reality in physical space allows for another layer onto the space, as illustrated by *Overheard*.

AR has also been used to enhance or modify a museum space through visuals (e.g., *MoMAR*[29]) or with audio (e.g., *Overheard*).

Alternatively, it can serve to present an alternate reality in the way *Outthink Hidden*[30] adds to our historical understanding of heroes.

Know Your Audience

Priya Shakti used a comic book to tell a story, but it has AR elements to bring video and additional context to the audience.[31] But the creators of this project were careful—they know their target audience may not be able to access the elements through AR, so they don't rely on it to tell the full story.

In contrast, the *New York Times* includes the AR piece on the 2018 Olympics that might be difficult to understand without viewing the AR.[32]

Mind the Viewing Mode

For phone-based AR the current wisdom suggests keeping videos to no more than two minutes since the user will need to hold their phone or tablet in a certain position to view the piece.

For *Terminal 3*,[33] which uses **HoloLens**, the experience could be longer, since it does not rely on the user holding up their phone. With advancements in the ability for AR to be embedded into wearables this constraint could change rapidly.

Playing Scale

AR can be a "larger than life" way to present desired information. With the *New York Times* piece on Olympians, the audience is able to see the Olympians to scale for a better understanding of their skills and physical bodies.

Sound Can Add Weight and Emotion

Audio adds an extra layer of sensory experience.

Music and soundscape design in AR can also serve to set a tone or transport the user—as was done with certain scenes in *Overheard*.

Creating a Feeling of Presence and the Freedom to Interact

The creators of *New Dimensions In Testimony* say the interactive experience is authentic enough that people often respond to the virtual survivors as if they are real. There's also an element of freedom with the *New Dimensions In Testimony* project; it allows the audience to ask questions they may not otherwise ask, because they cannot harm a recording.

Future-Proofing

Capturing holograms and taking volumetric video can allow a media company or production studio to prepare a project to be integrated into a **HoloLens** or **Magic Leap** experience when the technology catches up. As of 2018, recording assets for a high fidelity 3D interactive hologram is an enormous task, but we expect this to get easier as technology advances.

Immersive Audio

Immersive media opens up new possibilities for audio, which is as essential as imagery in creating an immersive environment. Audio in an immersive piece can be anywhere from a single channel playing in both ears to a fully spatial experience that communicates depth and location, and responds to viewer movement.

While the importance of audio is a constant theme among creators, it often goes unnoticed until there is something wrong or until the pace, mood or tone pulls the listener out of a sense of presence.

In many of the projects we've studied, audio serves an essential role. In some cases it is used to guide the viewer and provide essential information, and in other cases it is used to create an added layer of depth with **spatialized** and **binaural** sound.

Use Audio to Set a Tone

Some of the lessons discussed in the audio case studies come back to the importance of determining what the role of spatial audio will be. What part of a story or game is being enhanced through the audio? Is this creating a sense of fear or emotion. The first step in ensuring the audio is doing what it's supposed to do, is to decide what the role of the audio is in a given experience. The audio may serve to enhance an emotional impact, or quicken or slow the story.

Hear What You Can't See

In traditional and immersive media, audio can add things to a scene that aren't visible to the viewer. For example footsteps might signal someone coming or going, or a police siren could be audible before the car is visible.

But in addition to telling an off-screen story, as might be done in a film, audio signals of this type can be useful tools for guiding the viewer in immersive space. If the source a sound isn't visible in the viewer's field of view, they can turn to look for it.

Who's Talking?

Some find the sound of a disembodied narrator unsettling in immersive media because there's no way for a person to be hidden "behind the camera," and viewers will therefore look around for the narrator. One solution to this is to use a character as the narrator, and have them on screen whenever you hear their voice-over.

That said, whether the off-camera narrator feels wrong also depends on the tone of the piece and the audience. Look at the *Occupation of Alcatraz* and *Climbing Giants* to get a feel for voice-over from on-camera characters. *Hell and High Water* VR (in Chapter 6) uses off-camera narration to guide the viewer and offer context. And Euronews (in Chapter 3) uses on-camera news hosts for their pieces.

Doing the Filtering for the Viewer

As in traditional film, the audio in an immersive experience is not a literal representation of real-world audio (though this is a common assumption among beginners). Sound designers are constantly making choices about what to include. And in a way, there's a lot more leeway to control the user's experience with audio than with visuals.

As immersive audio specialist Joel Douek (who did the audio for *Hallelujah* VR,[34] discussed in Chapter 8) puts it, in the physical world people's brains selectively filter sound based on what they're paying attention to—e.g., you might not notice an airplane in the distance or the constant hum of your air conditioner, but a microphone will pick it up. The user relies on the audio designer to tell them what to pay attention to. And this can be especially important in VR: "It's like putting someone in a brand-new city they've never been to," Douek says, "and expecting them to make sense of it, surrounded by lots of strangers. You have to help them."

Traditional film has its own best practices for introducing and balancing different audio components in a scene. How and when to apply this kind of filtering is sure to evolve as immersive media mature.

Head-Locked vs. Spatialized Audio

In immersive sound design, **head-locked** audio refers to sound that comes with the viewer (the kind of audio we're accustomed to in traditional media), while spatialized audio is pinned to the environment and dynamically mixed, so that the viewer hears something different when they move or turn their head.

For immersive experiences that use both head-locked and spatialized audio, a common way to decide which to use is whether the sound has a source in the immersive environment or whether it's narrative in nature. By this principle, voice-over narration and a musical score should be head-locked, and dialogue, ambient audio and foley should be spatialized. Head-locked audio can also feel personal to the viewer, approximating an internal experience relative the spatialized sound in the surrounding environment.

Rich, layered audio can give a sense of movement to a still image, whether the audio is responsive or not—as illustrated by the use of binaural audio in NPR's *Standing at the Edge of Geologic Time*. Using spatialized sound to give a sense of a place in addition to head-locked audio for narrative elements can help to create a potentially more convincing sense immersion in a space.

Respect the Space

Audio for immersive media opens up a world of possibilities in that sound can come from anywhere in a scene,whereas earlier formats were always tied to a finite number of speakers in a room. But by that same measure, it's also limiting in that spatialized audio will be confusing if it doesn't match the environment. Sound designers mixing for speaker-based audio get to use some creative license, playing with compression or fades, for example, to create a subjectively better mix. In an immersive environment, however, sound is also a tool for the viewer to understand the space around them and what's in it, and it must remain tied to that space or it loses its function.

If you change settings without consideration of the psychoacoustics, you're also changing the sense in which things are distant or not," Joel Douek of Ecco VR says. "so you're deconstructing all the spatialization work that you've done."

Collect Multiple Audio Sources

When filming 360-degree video, recording multiple sources will allow for more options in **post production** and is essential for high quality audio. Some creators have the misguided idea that a high-quality ambisonic microphone will pick up a good enough representation of the sound.

In reality, even the best ambisonic mic (which must sit next to the camera if the spatial sound is to be accurate) is limited by its distance from sound sources. Lavalier mics can be used to get clear dialogue, and additional mics placed at a distance from the camera will pick up other sounds in the scene that can be mixed or spatialized during post production.

Hiding the Mics

In live capture of 360-degree space for VR, sound equipment will be visible in the scene, making it all but impossible to incorporate a boom mic as would be done on a traditional film set. For this reason, many creators rely on lavalier mics for dialogue. Additional mics can be hidden within a scene to capture ambient audio.

In some cases, a VR experience can be recorded in more than one section. *Hallelujah* VR , for example, was filmed in five different sections that were added together in post production, so the creators were able to hide some of their sound gear behind the camera.

Test It Out

Much like many VR creators suggest, testing games and experiences on colleagues, friends and family, getting feedback on an immersive soundscape is an important part of audio creation for immersive experiences. This is particularly useful when testing whether particular sound cues consistently guide viewers' attention as desired.

Notes

1 *Clouds Over Sidra*, United Nations VR (UNVR). January, 2015. https://with. in/watch/clouds-over-sidra/.
2 *We Who Remain*, The Emblematic Group, AJ+ and NYT-VR. March 13, 2017. www.nytimes.com/video/magazine/100000004980989/we-who-remain.html,

www.ajplus.net/project/sudan-vr/, http://emblematicgroup.com/experiences/ we-who-remain/, www.ajplus.net/project/sudan-vr/.

3 *The People's House*—Inside the White House with Barack and Michelle Obama. Felix & Paul Studios. May 17, 2017. www.youtube.com/watch?v=bq W2qm02jwI.

4 *Clouds Over Sidra*, United Nations VR (UNVR). January, 2015. https://with. in/watch/clouds-over-sidra/.

5 *Climbing Giants*, Black Dot Films for National Geographic Partners, LLC. March 4, 2017. www.youtube.com/watch?v=f7wTolIlK_s.

6 *Limbo*, *Guardian* VR. July 5, 2017. www.theguardian.com/technology/ 2017/jul/05/limbo-a-virtual-experience-of-waiting-for-asylum-360-video?, also available through the Daydream Guardian VR app and YouTube.

7 *The Occupation of Alcatraz that Sparked an American Revolution.* Seeker VR, June 2017. www.youtube.com/watch?v=TBjuhFOeitE.

8 *VRtually There*, available on YouTube and the *USA Today* app. www. youtube.com/channel/UCSIgn1BzT9oD5E3pk9ceKvg.

9 *Reeps One: Does Not Exist* – VR Beatbox with 3D sound. John Hendicott (Aurelia Soundworks) and The Mill. June, 2017. Available on Youtube and Facebook. www.facebook.com/reepsone/videos/10155320623836049/, www. youtube.com/watch?v=OMLgliKYqaI.

10 *Limbo*, *Guardian* VR. July 5, 2017. www.theguardian.com/technology/2017/ jul/05/limbo-a-virtual-experience-of-waiting-for-asylum-360-video?, also available through the Daydream Guardian VR app and YouTube.

11 "Episode One: The Tech Startup," *UTURN*, NativeVR. 2016. Samsung GearVR and Oculus Go headsets, www.uturnvr.com/index.php/about./

12 Euronews, 360 videos. 2016-2017 (ongoing). www.euronews.com/tag/360-video.

13 *Kiya*, The Emblematic Group. Premiered at TED Women, 2015. http:// emblematicgroup.com/experiences/kiya/, www.youtube.com/watch?v=qYs AIukRqog.

14 *After Solitary.* PBS Frontline, The Emblematic Group. Premiered at SXSW March, 2017. http://emblematicgroup.com/experiences/solitary-confinement/, 360 version on YouTube: www.youtube.com/watch?v=G7_YvGDh9Uc, www. facebook.com/frontline/videos/10154080970816641/.

15 LIFEVR, "Buzz Aldrin: Cycling Pathways to Mars." March 2017, https://store. steampowered.com/app/608000/Buzz_Aldrin_Cycling_Pathways_to_Mars/.

16 *The Wall: Unknown stories. Unintended consequences.* The Arizona Republic and Gannett . November, 2017. www.usatoday.com/border-wall/, www. viveport.com/apps/3f16c881-0be2-475b-be59-7da4b1d0093f, www.azcentral. com/story/news/politics/border-issues/2017/09/22/trump-border-wall-project-9-months-on-us-mexico-border/691732001/.

17 *Discovering Gale Crater*, Gale Crater. *L.A. Times*, October 2015. http:// graphics.latimes.com/mars-gale-crater-vr/.

18 *Is the Nasdaq in Another Bubble?* A virtual reality guided tour of 21 years of the NASDAQ. *Wall Street Journal.* April 23, 2015. http://graphics.wsj. com/3d-nasdaq/.

19 *Hell and High Water* VR is a collaboration between Jovrnalism and *ProPublica/The Texas Tribune*. The experience was produced by Jovrnalism (based at USC Annenberg and led by Professor Robert Hernandez) is aimed at using VR to help illustrate the investigative story. *ProPublica/The Texas Tribune*. November, 2016. www.propublica.org/series/hell-and-high-water, www.youtube.com/watch?v=D0rASFoaoog.

20 Branch, John. Four of the Best Olympians, as You've Never Seen Them. The *New York Times*. February 5, 2018. https://www.nytimes.com/interactive/2018/02/05/sports/olympics/ar-augmented-reality-olympic-athletes-ul.html.
21 *Testimony*. Zohar Kfir, Selena Pinnell, Kaleidoscope VR, Evolving Technologies Corp. World Premiere Tribeca Film Festival 2017. http://testimony.site/, https://www.oculus.com/experiences/gear-vr/1454065214635967/.
22 *Blackout*. Storyscapes, Tribeca. World Premiere, 2017. Scatter. www.tribecafilm.com/filmguide/blackout-2017.
23 *Overheard*. Minneapolis Institute of Art, Minnesota. 2016. https://new.artsmia.org/art-tech-award/overheard/, http://overheard.luxloop.com/.
        2016. https://itunes.apple.com/us/app/overheard-mia/id1116319582?mt=8.
24 *Stand at The Edge of Geologic Time*. NPR. July 20, 2016. https://apps.npr.org/rockymountain-vr/.
25 Kaplan, Adam and Aaron Ohlmann. *The Call Center: Lives on the Line in Iraq, In the Line of Fire. GOOD Magazine*, April 9, 2017. www.good.is/features/trauma-in-an-iraqi-war-zone.
26 *The Wall: Unknown Stories. Unintended Consequences*. The Arizona Republic and Gannett. November, 2017. www.usatoday.com/border-wall/, https://www.viveport.com/apps/3f16c881-0be2-475b-be59-7da4b1d0093f, www.azcentral.com/story/news/politics/border-issues/2017/09/22/trump-border-wall-project-9-months-on-us-mexico-border/691732001/.
27 *Hell and High Water* VR is a collaboration between Jovrnalism and *ProPublica/The Texas Tribune*. November, 2016. https://www.propublica.org/series/hell-and-high-water, https://www.youtube.com/watch?v=D0rASFoaoog.
28 *Time* magazine. RYOT for *Time* magazine, Life VR. January 4, 2018
        http://time.com/5084021/optimism-ar/
29 Group show by MoMAR, March 2018. https://momar.gallery/.
30 *Outthink Hidden. New York Times* T Brand Studio. December, 2017. http://fakelove.tv/work/outthink-hidden, https://www.ibm.com/thought-leadership/hidden-figures/.
31 *Priya's Shakti* (Chapter 1), *Priya's Mirror* (Chapter 2). *Priya Shalti Comics*. 2014. www.priyashakti.com/#comics.
32 Branch, John. *Four of the Best Olympians, as You've Never Seen Them*. The *New York Times*. February 5, 2018. www.nytimes.com/interactive/2018/02/05/sports/olympics/ar-augmented-reality-olympic-athletes-ul.html.
33 *Terminal 3*. Asad Malik. Premiered at Tribeca, 2018. www.imdb.com/title/tt8111470/, https://venturebeat.com/2018/04/24/ar-experience-terminal-3-puts-you-in-the-boots-of-a-u-s-customs-officer/.
34 *Hallelujah* VR. Within and EccoVR. April 2017. www.with.in/watch/hallelujah.

11 Additional Features and Emerging Technology

Just when journalists and filmmakers are beginning to master certain tools, new ways of telling a story or creating content evolve.

This book has dealt primarily with immersive content at the edge of what's possible. In this chapter, we take a look at what's on the horizon. We look a bit deeper into some of the emerging technologies mentioned in the previous chapters, as well as a few things creators may want to pay attention to as the technology continues to develop.

Live Photogrammetry and Advances in Volumetric Capture

Live photogrammetry, also known as volumetric capture, scanning or holograms have been discussed in reference to *Limbo, Blackout, Terminal 3* and *After Solitary* but it's also necessary to understand the work that currently goes into creating a live scan of a person, and the range in both realistic rendering and cost. Many companies have been working on this technology—namely Scatter (through the creation of DepthKit), **8i**, Intel and Microsoft.

In an April 2018 article in Variety, Janko Roettgers describes how Microsoft has been working on hologram technology for close to eight years.[1] Microsoft's first capture studio was in Redmond, Washington and they opened a capture studio in San Francisco in 2018. Roettgers says the company has "ambitious plans to license its technology to a variety of operators—collaborations that could perhaps one day result in futuristic photo booths, capable of turning anyone into a hologram for a few bucks." The current studio has 106 cameras processing the raw video at a rate of 10 GB of data per second. "Ultimately, Microsoft wants to make 3D holograms look virtually indistinguishable from regular video," says Roettgers.

He also says there are plans for Microsoft to license its technology to third parties and allow them to open their own capture studios around the world.

Storytelling through a 180 Lens

Asier Rios, a program manager at Google and a producer with YouTube VR and Daydream is something of a "VR180 evangelist." But what exactly do we mean when we say VR180?

The VR180 played on a computer looks like a normal video, but when watching the same video in a headset it is **stereoscopic** with a wider (180) **field of view**. "Something that we learned from creators is that they want to create content for all audiences," says Rios.

It's also a question of cost—both for cameras and production. With VR180, content creators are able to spend less on buying a camera, less time and money for post-production and use less bandwidth to play the videos. "If we really want to scale, the production needs to be easier. Right now, creating content is really challenging for 360, without even doing stereo," he says.

In 2018, Google was working with a few different companies to launch a point-and-shoot camera with two fisheye lenses.

Rios says he prefers 3D videos because that's how humans see life. He sees VR180 as a step in the right direction, "in reality, this is the beginning of the beginning of the beginning—90 percent of the population hasn't experienced a good 360 video," he says.

WebVR: Volumetric on the Web

WebVR (or WebXR) is a specification that allows for publishing immersive media directly to the web for viewing in a browser, and across devices.

Emblematic Group is now working to make it easier to create volumetric web experiences with a platform and tool called Reach. The concept is to allow journalists, documentary filmmakers and storytellers to be able to drop green-screen captured footage of an interview into an immersive environment. These "photograms," as Eren Aksu at Emblematic calls them, could be used for stories from the U.S./Mexico border or the Supreme Court.

Several projects included in this book have used WebVR in order to make them accessible to a wide audience: *L.A. Times'* Gale Crater experience and *The Wall Street Journal's* Nasdaq roller coaster were built in WebVR because both news organizations seek to make their content available to a general audience. Zohar Kfir chose to move *Testimony* to a WebVR platform because she felt its content—personal accounts of sexual assault survivors—should be accessible for more people to see.

As of this writing, creators can publish their own work to the web, but it can be a somewhat complicated process for beginners. With Reach, the Emblematic team would like to simplify the process and get it closer to one click to publish on the web.

Artificial Intelligence and Voice Activation

Many immersive storytellers are eager to see how artificial intelligence (AI) could be used to help tell stories, as well as a more complete integration of voice-activation/commands. Jeremy Gilbert, Director of Strategic Initiatives at the *Washington Post*, believes smart speakers will be a critical technology of the future, as a tool for answering questions. "Just think about our stories as answers," Gordon says. In addition to giving context and background, he says, "news providers need to be the ones who are in position to say, here's the answer to that question."

Ori Inbar, founder of Super Ventures, believes AI will allow **XR** devices to learn user behaviors and populate virtual worlds, "In the near future, one will not be able to work without the other," he says.

AI startups have begun to get into storytelling, at the moment, many projects are still experimental. Jessica Lauretti, Global Head of RYOT studio, believes AR and AI will "literally change the course of history."

Powering a Story with Your Brain

Sarah Hill, a former journalist and immersive storyteller and current CEO of StoryUP has been experimenting with using what she calls an "emotion chip" using emotions to power a story.

Hill has a product called Helium—combining VR with a brain computer interface. The idea is to use a standalone headset and a tiny headband attached to an **EEG** strip. The headband contraption measures some of a user's brainwave patterns and the output can be inserted into a story, Hill explains. This value can be assigned to something in the game engine environment, "this could potentially make people more self-aware of their emotions and how emotions have power to move things in story, not only in the virtual world, but the real world as well," Hill says. Her current project is an app called Positivity which uses emotions to grow a butterfly.[2]

Positivity is available as a VR experience for Gear VR, but a user would need to have the $200 headband to make it work with their own emotions. The experience is meant to be repeated and help a user train their mind to be able to improve. "It really sounds weird, but you become aware of the thoughts that you need to invoke," she says. "It's like a thermometer for your brain, if you will, that tells you how you're feeling," she adds. The app is not meant for any kind of diagnostic treatment, and there are warnings clarifying its purpose.

Hill would like to see more projects experimenting in this realm. "For the future of immersive journalism, it would be fascinating to see more creators think about emotions and how this media can affect emotions both good and bad," says Hill.

The Arrival of Light Field Technology

Greg Downing specializes in image-based 3D technologies and computational photography and has a long history in the immersive interactive space beginning with interactive panoramas for the web. Photogramme-try has gone through a big revolution since many techniques have been automated. In the early days it might have taken few weeks to get 15 pho-tographs aligned (the first step in photogrammetry) and now with 1500 that step is measured in minutes. Downing says photogrammetry works well on specific types of scenes, if you don't have view-dependent tex-ture. In contrast to photogrammetry that builds 3d models from photo-graphs, light fields are "using the photographic samples of the real world to display all the reflections, refraction and other optical properties of the world around the viewer," says Downing.

Downing worked on a VR project for the Smithsonian museum with Intel (2017–2018), did some VR for Bjork (2015–2016), and a piece he worked on about the first female shaman in one Amazonian community—Awavena, with director Lynette Wallworth premiered at Sundance. This piece uses Lidar scans, aerial photos, point-cloud ren-ders and switches the viewer between **3DOF** and **6DOF**.

In photogrammetry the viewer is not able to see the reflective quality that can be seen with light field technology. For example, in Welcome to Light Fields, a demo Google released on Steam, in a mosaic scene, the viewer can see how the light bounces off each tile depending on what an-gle they are viewing it from. As Downing says, "the exciting thing about the way Google built that tool is that it is like a glimpse into the future." Hopefully this glimpse into the future will allow the rest of the VR world to start thinking about what kind of projects can be created in the future.

He emphasizes that we're leveraging both the modes of capture as well as the way material is being presented with newer headsets. "Hopefully in five years the audience is large enough that it can support original con-tent and it starts to become self-sustaining," Downing says.

A Wider Field of View

Hold up your finger and move it slowly from the center of your vision to your periphery, following it with your eyes. If your vision is not impaired, you can follow that finger until it is parallel to your ear—meaning hu-mans can see more than 180 degrees of the world around them without turning their heads. VR headsets, however, offer a **field of view** of around 110 degrees as of mid 2018. The field of view on the Microsoft HoloLens is even narrower. Immersive media as it currently stands is like looking through a diving mask onto an immersive world. Everything is there, but our visual faculties are constrained.

While storytellers make much of using the periphery to guide the viewer, this constrains the ability to use that area of our vision to its full potential. As the hardware gets better, storytelling is likely to adjust to take advantage of this added visual space.

Haptics and Touch

"A little touch goes a long way," says VR filmmaker Nathalie Mathe of haptic inputs—something as simple as holding a hand during an experience can give useful feedback and can also hugely enhance the viewer's sense of **presence** and **embodiment**.

At film festivals or galleries, creators are able to create a **haptic** experience using physical objects in the space where people experience their work. The makers of *Blackout* re-created a subway car at Tribeca in 2017 so that people could sit on the seats or hold a pole during the experience. They also noticed that people watching the experience next to others would sit side by side, touching, and not break contact.

Director Alejandro González Iñárritu's virtual border-crossing experience *Carne y Arena*, originally offered as a major installation at the Los Angeles County Museum of Art, put the viewer barefoot into a room full of sand, used fans to create wind and a vibrating backpack to approximate the rumble of a helicopter.[3]

These installations prove the power of haptic feedback in building a realistic immersive experience, but they don't work for wider distribution. The sci-fi version of haptic technology is a full haptic suit, giving users feedback about their surroundings with simulated touch all over the body. There's a long way to go to make that a practical reality, but any new addition to haptic feedback at users' disposal will expand storytelling possibilities with an additional sensory communication channel.

Tracking the Viewer's Body (Better, Responsive Embodiment)

At the time of writing, most VR experiences rely on head and hand tracking to locate the user in space and track their movements. That makes for limited possibilities in giving the viewer a body in virtual space that follows their movements in a convincing way. Facebook spaces offer avatars with built-in animations driven by hand controller motions to communicate users' movements to others. Research projects that rely on embodiment use motion-tracking suits to follow users motion more closely, creating a more convincing virtual self. As hardware becomes available that makes more granular motion tracking feasible, greater possibilities for embodiment will open up more possibilities for creators to allow users to relate to their immersive stories.

Notes

1 Roettgers, Janko. "106 Cameras, Holograms and Sticky Tape: Inside Microsoft's Mixed Reality Capture Studios." April 24, 2018. http://variety.com/2018/digital/features/microsoft-mixed-reality-capture-behind-the-scenes-1202784950/.

2 Hill, Sarah. "Your Brainwaves as a VR Input." October 5, 2017. https://medium.com/storyup-studios/your-brainwaves-as-a-story-steering-wheel-be099d33135e.

3 Miranda, Carolina A. "Inside Alejandro Iñárritu's VR border drama at LACMA: What you will see and why you might cry." June 29, 2017. www.latimes.com/entertainment/arts/miranda/la-et-cam-alejandro-inarritu-carne-arena-lacma-20170629-htmlstory.html.

12 Immersive Storytelling and the News Media

I think there is a world market for maybe five computers.
(Thomas Watson, chairman of IBM, 1943)

The advent of immersive storytelling has come at the same time as the so-called clickbait economy, when content consumption is driven by curiosity rather than story. As Jessica Lauretti, global head of RYOT studio, says, we're in an era of peak content.

The constant swiping and scrolling through disposable content also means people are searching for meaning. On the opposite side of the peak content bubble is VR, Alina Mikhaleva says, where the user is fully present. "You have to be dedicated to experience something," she says.

VR is both more demanding but also more engaging. Instead of seeing the pace of news and VR in contrast to one another, Mikhaleva sees them as complementary. "Short-form content creates a lot of noise," she says, and hopefully breaking out from this noise is experiencing something true. "VR is much closer to real life," she says.

Immersive Media Signals Its Arrival

How do we know when a new media format has arrived to stay for good? There was skepticism with the arrival of the internet and confusion over what to put online—and similar critiques of who it is for, if only certain people have access.

What we've found by speaking to media companies such as the *New York Times, USA Today* and *Washington Post* is that no one wants to be left behind, but no one can say definitively where we're going. What comes after 5G and Augmented Reality is integrated into our physical space all around us? No one knows.

With a fragmented publishing landscape (see State of Platforms and Publishing) the role of creators and news media professionals doing immersive projects occasionally becomes not only creator, but also a guide to the user—how to understand a broad topic such as *The Wall* through multiple ways of understanding, such as how to place an object in Augmented Reality or how to watch a 360 video. In this chapter we'll look at some of the models for experimentation and innovation and how different publications are thinking about immersive storytelling within the broader news media context.

There is a fear, among major media companies that failing to experiment in immersive and experimental stories will mean losing a race, "If you wait too long, you run the risk of seeding those story forms to other types of media," Gilbert says.

With a competitive race in mind, some organizations are diving in with an immersive team—such as the *New York Times*, while others such as *Euro News* have a few dedicated people teaching the rest. Still others are experimenting to see what, if anything, works on the local, national and global scale.

Immersive Breaking News

One of the most-watched *Time* magazine videos was the live 360 video of *The Eclipse* in August 2017. Many will recall 2016 as the year of the livestream, when Facebook reportedly spent $50 million on 140 contracts to encourage the use of live video. For the 24-hour news cycle, it becomes increasingly important to broadcast breaking news in real-time or at least as close to real-time as possible.

The *New York Times* took on an impressive project in 2016 and 2017 (sponsored by Samsung), creating The Daily 360 aimed to tell a 360 story each day. "When we started The Daily 360, we didn't know if covering breaking news in this format would be viable," Co-Director of Virtual Reality Marcelle Hopkins says. Their first test came when the Cubs played in the World Series final in November of 2016. "We wanted to find out how fast we could produce and publish a 360 video," Hopkins says. They filmed the final moments of the game outside Wrigley field—the pure joy on fans faces and the chaos of the Cubs winning the World Series for the first time in 108 years is powerful. They published the 360 video just four hours later. Hopkins says this opened up other possibilities for covering breaking news. Since November 2016, they've done it several times since. As Hopkins says, "It's hard. It requires planning and organization, simplified storytelling, a fast internet connection, and sometimes an all-nighter."

Long-Term Experimentation

Many news media outlets see value in experimentation. As Jenna Pirog, senior director of immersive experiences at National Geographic says, "It's important for a media company to invest in innovation and technology—if one of these things does take off, you want to have the ideas and storytelling to match the technology." Jeremy Gilbert, director of strategic initiatives at the *Washington Post* says he see tremendous value for the post being a place where reporters, editors and designers are excited about the work they do because it can sometimes energize the staff and allow them to think differently.

Gilbert says the *Washington Post* newsroom first started thinking about immersive storytelling in the summer of 2014, just after Oculus demoed the DK 2. "We're still tantalizingly close, but not there on that," Gilbert says of the true potential for immersive storytelling. He says *The Post* spends a lot of time trying to figure out what kind of stories they can tell and why they would tell a particular story in 360 video instead of traditional linear video. "We as a newsroom are focused on producing stories," Gilbert says, not necessarily in the format on which those stories take shape. "We don't know yet which of those stories will resonate with the audience in the future," Gilbert says.

Who Produces What: In-House, Versus External Creatives

For the *New York Times*, most of the immersive journalism is produced by a core team straddling video and graphics departments, Hopkins says. They collaborate with journalists throughout the newsroom and have trained over 130 writers, editors, photographers, videographers and designers in immersive storytelling tools and techniques. "Immersive journalism has seeped into the fabric of our core," Hopkins says. "We're also keenly aware that the immersive platform is still very young," she adds. Hopkins says there's still more to learn about what they can do, and how they can use it. "Experimentation is essential to learning and growing, and we'll likely be doing that for a long while," Hopkins says.

Collaborative Approach

The Post takes a more collaborate inter-newsroom approach. "We're not afraid to reach out and grab different people from different parts of the organization," Gilbert says about how *The Post* approaches immersive storytelling. In the case of Augmented Reality, they have mobile app developers, an engineer and a couple of people on the graphics team. Gilbert says they tend to pull in reporters and editors who are subject matter experts. For example, they worked with Phil Kennecott, an art critic to create an AR element for an architecture story about Hamburg's Elbphilharmonie. They don't want the technique used to tell the story to overwhelm the need for expertise in the types of stories they aim to tell, says Gilbert.

Usability Testing

Both formal and informal testing was a consistent theme in discussions with various producers and news media. Gilbert says they are doing usability testing and spending time looking at the existing research.

"We still need to give a lot more guidance," he says in terms of telling people what behavior is expected of them. For AR, as of April 2018, "most news consumers still need to be told, here's how to place it." In addition, Gilbert says user experience cues are not unified to create a general understanding of what is expected. "You shouldn't need too much in the way of instructions," he says, but for users new to consuming AR and VR, many encountering the mediums for the first time are still in need of some instructions, "we owe it to them to help them understand what they're seeing," Gilbert says.

When looking at whether or not an immersive story is successful, *The Post* is evaluating how much time people spend, how many people saw the experience and how likely those people are to share it socially, or recommend it to other people. They're also looking at how much effort and time is spent to create immersive stories. "When you're doing experimental storytelling, you should, over time see a decrease in the effort needed to produce those types of stories," Gilbert says.

Lab Model

Many media companies are hedging their bets with a "lab" of sorts. The lab concept ranges in many factors including seriousness, financial commitment and time. The now defunct Buzzfeed Innovation lab (2016–2018) is no longer, nor is Fusion media's. There's still the Dow Jones Innovation Lab, Gannett Innovation Lab, and more recently McClatchy's Video Lab West and Google's VR Creator Lab. Many of these labs are taking on the immersive storytelling experimentation for a larger media company.

Other labs and innovators have chosen to wait until the so-called VR hype subsides. David Cohn, journalist and innovator isn't sure whether VR is a practical investment for a media company. "I can imagine a world in 5–10 years where VR makes sense. But I don't think it's a guarantee the way others do," he says. "There is still an element of VR that just feels like the Segway (it was going to revolutionize walking!) or when the iPad was going to save journalism and replace computers," he says. Cohn admits the Segway is still cool for certain purposes and the iPad is particularly good for plane journeys with children, "But it doesn't become this encompassing digital device with a huge audience that then has a demand for serious content.[1]

The Long Game

Gannett's (and *USA Today*) have taken a long-term approach. Using the innovation lab to make big projects happen (like *Harvest of Change* and *The Wall*) as well as working with several different markets.[2]

As Ray Soto, director of emerging technologies at Gannett says, it might be a 360 story or it might be an immersive interactive story. "We are looking at this as a long-term commitment," he says. They're constantly learning from the different projects and simultaneously working to see how much they can push the storytelling format. "I think the border was a really good example when you think about leveraging photogrammetry," says Soto. Strategically, Gannett and *USA Today* look for engaging stories that leverage technologies before they become mainstream. For VR specifically, while they understand there isn't a large user base, they want to create compelling experiences and get ahead of the technology.

Ethical Challenge of New Formats

For the purpose of the immersive news media context, many larger media organizations are guided by standard ethics handbooks. As Wes Lindamood of NPR says, overall "I don't think you can apply blanket ethics to VR," noting the various use-cases, he says "it depends on the context of use."

The ethics of Cinematic VR and documentary work such as *Clouds Over Sidra* may vary in comparison to the use-case of Euromaidan by Alexey Furman. "If the VR scene is being used for evidence that an event occurred, I think that is different than a VR scene that is used abstractly," says Lindamood. He adds that when used in a journalistic context, it is important for VR creators to follow the same standards as other visual journalists, such as the accuracy guidelines in the NPR *Ethics Handbook*[3] or the NPPA *Code of Ethics*.[4] Al Tompkins, a senior faculty member at Poynter, recommends newsrooms establish non-negotiable standards before seeking technology partners.

Another angle of the ethical conundrum is how to explain to potential interviewees or subjects who have never experienced 360 video or VR what the creator is planning to do with visual or audio being captured. "It got easier after we shot a few videos," says Dan Archer speaking on a project in Colombia. "I was able to transfer them locally to my smart phone and just show people examples," he says. This saved him from attempting to explain the process in Spanish.

For news media, the most salient question is one of access not just for creating a project, but does the consumer have the internet connection, device/headset, connectivity and ability to view an immersive story? If not, how do we create something for the audience meeting them where they are?

Notes

1 Cohn, David. "The Ethics of Virtual Reality Storytelling." November, 2015. http://blog.digidave.org/2015/11/the-ethics-of-virtual-reality-storytelling.
2 Moses, Lucia. "Inside Gannett's editorial innovation lab," October 14, 2014. https://digiday.com/media/inside-gannetts-digital-editorial-product-arm/.
3 NPR Code of Ethics. http://ethics.npr.org/category/a1-accuracy/.
4 Code of Ethics, NPPA. https://nppa.org/code_of_ethics.

13 The State of Platforms and Publishing

The horse is here to stay but the automobile is only a novelty—a fad.
(President of the Michigan Savings Bank
advising Henry Ford's lawyer not to
invest in the Ford Motor Co. 1903)

Platforms are intricately linked to their audiences. The last few years have seen a number of new VR platforms emerge, and some of those have already gone under. We've also seen existing platforms—such as Facebook, YouTube and Steam—add immersive media capabilities. Each platform has its own set of written and unwritten rules, as well as style that evolves. The ongoing development of the immersive publishing landscape will greatly influence the way these stories are told in the future.

One question that has perhaps not received as much attention as it should is the question of success—"What would be considered a success for VR?" Alina Mikhaleva of Spherica asks.

Looking at Netflix as a model, a successful VR platform might mean that a viewer comes every day, but in the current landscape, there is not enough content and very little is episodic. "If there is no compelling content promise on a regular basis. Then why did we expect people to use headsets on a daily basis?" Mikhaleva says.

And another question to ponder: What does immersive media look like when it is inherent to the platform itself—when the use of **head-mounted displays** is the main mode of accessing flat video? Or what does immersive storytelling look like when it can be projected onto the walls, and overlay the physical space all around us? How do stories change?

The State of Immersive Journalism (at this moment May 2018)

At present, distribution for immersive stories is a challenge. Browser-based immersive content is limited by existing technology, as are social-media distribution methods. Apps for viewing immersive content create a barrier to adoption, and high-end **headsets** are expensive and unwieldy.

On top of that, content for each of these viewing modes must meet a different set of technical specs.

And, as anyone who has searched for a project or published a piece knows, the distribution landscape is fragmented, with additional challenges for both the user and the creator all along the way. "What is the intended viewing form?" and "what works on this platform?" are two of the main questions when assessing distribution strategy in the current immersive media landscape.

However, we would be remiss not to note the potential for a shifting landscape with the addition of even newer platforms and ways of storytelling through Oculus Go, Magic Leap, BoseAR and the standalone headsets coming to the market as this book goes to print.

This chapter includes a look at existing platforms, and a few condensed case studies focused on the challenges that arise in publishing content.

The Platforms

YouTube: Continuing Investment in 360 and 180

On March 13, 2015 YouTube announced it would be able to support 360 degree video. For some, YouTube is the platform of choice because it is accessible to a large audience, easily embeddable and familiar.

In June, 2017 the platform announced **heat maps** for 360 videos with more than 1,000 views, as well as some stats on viewing patterns: people spent 75% of their time within the front 90 degrees of a video.[1] This viewing behavior is likely one of the reasons YouTube decided to put effort into VR 180 in 2018 (more on this in the Emerging Technology chapter). Alas, attempting to describe the scope of 360 videos on YouTube is nearly as difficult as trying to discern why YouTube has developed a niche for unboxing videos.

Facebook: Making It Social

With publishers flocking to Facebook to reach a broader audience, many of the creators and media we spoke with chose to publish their 360 videos there. In April 2018, Facebook made some big announcements at the annual F8 conference, namely regarding Facebook Spaces and Oculus Go (their latest standalone **headset**). On Facebook Spaces they said it would initially only be available for interaction with people a user knows.

Regarding the announcement of Oculus Go, Robert Hernandez, professor at USC (interviewed on *Hell and High Water*) says "This device changes the game on many level, including the practical travel/demo side. It works great … From how it fits/feels on your head, controller in your hand, audio in the straps and it is the best **HMD** I have used." Hernandez added that Oculus Rift and Oculus Touch unlock more possibilities, but the cost comes with a tradeoff (as of 2018 the Rift was around $600 and the Touch was $400 in addition to a gaming PC). An early review from Geekwire says: "this is a virtual reality experience that many of us would actually use." Facebook is also working to get 3D photos in the Facebook timeline.[2]

Vimeo: Catering to Creators

In early 2017, Vimeo began publishing 360 videos, saying: "We're insanely thrilled to announce that Vimeo 360 is here." The Vimeo announcement pointed potential 360 publishers to a series of 360 video school lessons as well as a curated 360 channel.

Vimeo aimed to set itself apart from others by highlighting their video quality, video school, a community of creators and fans and the marketplace to sell 360 video. Vimeo is known for catering to the needs of filmmakers and professionals—and has the added ability for 360 creators to rent or sell their films. Creators can set their price and distribution region giving the power of monetization back to creators.

SteamVR

Steam, a digital platform originally created for game distribution, launched its VR portal in 2016, shortly after the release of the HTC Vive headset.

SteamVR offers fully interactive, room-scale, walk-around VR experiences for Vive and Rift and also supports viewing of stationary content. There are a number of VR games available on this platform, as well as walk-around immersive stories, interactives, collections of 360-degree videos.

While the culture among media consumers is sure to shift, one complaint of immersive media creators with Steam is that the audience there is expecting games. As of 2018, the audience for non-game VR experiences is small.

Oculus and Gear VR: Awaiting the Next Evolution

The Gear VR (first released in November, 2015) was Samsung's HMD collaboration with Oculus. The first release of the Gear VR required a Samsung phone to plug in to the headset—and the headset also had an external touchpad, and back button on the side. The Gear VR was first announced in September, 2014[3] in hopes that developers would create content for the device when it released a year later.

Compared to other devices at the time, the Gear VR provided an affordable option (for those with a Samsung phone) and served an audience a few steps beyond Google cardboard. Still the initial version was prone to overheating and wore out the phone battery quickly. Because Gear VR was created in partnership with Oculus, some Oculus games have Gear VR versions and games such as Minecraft also work on Gear VR's platform.

Narrative content on Gear VR can be tricky to find, but with a familiarity with the brands, news media and creators examples become easier to locate and experience. At Facebook's F8 conference in 2018, Isabel Tewes—who works in Developer Strategy for Oculus—announced 40% of users never opened a VR game app, 99% of all users consumed video, and 83% of time spent was in media and entertainment apps.[4]

The Most Accessible: WebVR/WebXR

Creating a project with **WebVR**[5] (or WebXR as it has begun to be called, now that augmented reality support is being added) means a wide audience can experience it without having to download an app or have a specific device. But there are some disadvantages, too.

First, it takes longer to develop projects that work on many browsers and devices. What's more, while a lot is possible with WebVR, having to stream the data over the web—versus downloading it to an application for a mobile device or a computer—puts a limit on the complexity of the experience.

As more people lay the groundwork by creating projects in WebVR, and open-source tools become more refined and readily available, more creators are likely to break away from proprietary platforms and publish their projects directly to the web.

App-Based Consumption

Many large-scale media companies have their own app—and some have gone to the next level with an AR or VR specific app in addition to the traditional news app. Notably, the NYTVR, LifeVR, and The GuardianVR—plus myriad one-off apps for specific projects. CivilisationsAR, MoMAR, RYOT AR and the 321 Launch apps focus solely on the augmented reality side.

While having a proprietary app gives the creator more control over how their work is presented, asking viewers to download an app just to see a single piece is a pretty large barrier to reaching a wide audience.

VeeR, which touts itself as a "global VR content community" is available on all major VR platforms—HTC Vive, Samsung Gear VR, Oculus Rift and Microsoft on both PC and HoloLens and downloadable as an app on iOS and Android.

As of this writing, it's one of the fastest ways to edit a quick moment (in the VeeR editing app) and post immediately to social media or the VeeR platform without taking footage to a computer and editing with additional software. Initially a China-based company, VeeR now has an office in Palo Alto, California as well. Their vision is to be the "natural platform for everyone to express their creativity, promote their works, and engage in community," a Facebook for VR, if you will.

Case Studies: Publishing in a Fragmented Landscape

After Solitary

Target mode of viewing: HTC Vive
    To reach a wider audience Emblematic Group created a 360 video version.
    After Solitary is viewable on Vive, but the walk-around version is only available on the film festival circuit. Although it could be published on Steam, one of the challenges is that the Steam platform is rooted in gaming, and doesn't currently lend itself well to narrative experiences (or the audience isn't there).
    Viewers outside of film festivals can only see the 360-degree video version, and the project wasn't designed for that. Similarly, many people watch Kiya as a 360 video, even though it's available on Steam now.

The Room of Never Again

Designed to be watched as an HTC Vive project
    Versions of 360 video in addition
    Dan Archer's *The Room of Never Again* is an immersive interactive about Granada, Antioquia, in Colombia. The experience is based on scanning of a "memory house," a community space for collective mourning for those who died during the five decades of the conflict there. Archer said his target audience was predominantly young Colombians who see the conflict as part of history and perhaps not something relevant to them.
    Archer wanted to engage people beyond news consumers and bring the project to a broader audience. He did about nine stops in different rural areas as well as some cities. At each location he showed the Vive experience to 30–50 people. Archer took his own HTC Vive, a projector and his laptop and set up a simple hub. In some places, he says, young people treated the experience like a fairground ride, while in other locations just a few people wanted to try it. He says big ideas about empathy and new media don't add up to much if the hardware is alienating or inaccessible.

Contrast VR

Publishing on various platforms
    As of April 2018, all Contrast VR stories will also be available on Oculus Go

Zahra Rasool, editorial lead at Contrast VR, initially set up an immersive studio for Al Jazeera at-large as part of the Al Jazeera Innovation team. The studio officially launched in April 2017, but Rasool says there's still a question of figuring out the best way to use the medium since immersive storytelling doesn't currently have the same reach as traditional video.

From a newsroom perspective, she says, spending $150,000 on a project that will only live in festivals is difficult. As of this writing they've been working to build an Oculus Go app where all their content will live.

Combat VR

Publishing on various platforms
  Created their own app to monetize the content
Alina Mikhaleva, co-founder of Spherica, has been creating original content since 2014. In April, 2018 she and her team were about to launch six original films—a big content push from an independent studio. Mikhaleva says one of the biggest problems was figuring out monetization, since none of the big platforms could offer a clear form of monetization. Instead, they worked with programmers to build their own application.

With a free app including trailers and promo videos there's the option for an in-app purchase of $2.99 for over 30 minutes of content. Mikhaleva says their main focus is on mobile platforms, but they're also distributing as widely as possible—on HTC Vive and GearVR as well as Oculus Go, and aiming to release on the HTC Focus for a Chinese audience with unique language, titles and voiceover. Part of the goal is to show the potential of cinematic VR to the entertainment world.

Mikhaleva says a major challenge in distribution is discoverability. But since many platforms need good quality content, they're working with platforms to see whether the app can be promoted in new release sections. "I think they [platforms] understand that their main problem is volume," Mikhaleva says.

Direct to the Web: **The Nasdaq Roller Coaster** *(WSJ),* **Mars'** **Gale Crater** *(L.A.Times),* **and the** **Rocky Mountains** *in VR* *(NPR); and* **Olympians** *in AR (NYT)*

Publishing VR and AR directly to the web with WebXR
A number of projects in this book incorporate immersive media and are viewable directly in a browser on a mobile device, desktop or headset. In all of the cases listed above, the projects are put out by journalistic outlets with a wide national and/or international reach. And the projects' creators echo the this sentiment: Reaching the broadest audience possible is a top priority, and it's worth the extra work and debugging.

What these creators give up by publishing to the open web is a level of control in how the projects are being rendered and consumed. That stands in contrast, for example, to a project published on the SteamVR platform to be exclusively viewed on a Vive headset.

They also give up certain technical capabilities (though the technology is sure to catch up soon)—for example NPR's immersive *Stand at the Edge of Geologic Time* project might have included **spatialized** audio, but it was too hard to implement at the time the project was created. But as we wrap up work on this book, the ease with which creators can publish directly to the web is rapidly increasing. Many creators we interviewed who were unable to create WebVR versions of their work on the first iterations are hoping to get their own projects on the open web soon, too.

Notes

1 YouTube. "Hot and Cold: Heatmaps in VR," June 16, 2017. https://youtube-creators.googleblog.com/2017/06/hot-and-cold-heatmaps-in-vr.html.
2 Hernandez, Robert. Via Twitter. https://twitter.com/webjournalist/status/991455840900079616.
3 Samsung Explores the World of Mobile Virtual Reality with Gear VR. Sep 03, 2014. www.samsung.com/hk_en/news/product/gear-vr/.
4 Hernandez, Robert. Via Twitter. https://twitter.com/webjournalist/status/991416652121096193.
5 Repository for the WebXR Device API Specification, Github, https://immersive-web.github.io/webxr/.

14 Looking Forward

This 'telephone' has too many shortcomings to be seriously considered as a means of communication. The device is inherently of no value to us.
(Western Union internal memo, 1876)

In the near future, many creators expect to see more volumetric experiences and mixed reality projects, as well as interactive forms of choose-your-own-adventure and potentially adaptive storytelling. Or, as Kevin Tsukii of Emblematic Group puts it, "it won't be as isolating as 360 video on your face."

Here are some words from the wise on the kinds of stories that might be around the corner.

Personalization and Adaptive Storytelling

Nigel Tierney, at RYOT, believes there will be more personalization as well as adaptive storytelling. "How will I watch sports? Maybe I can control my own replays and viewpoints," he says. "Ultimately if we're looking at how the road map is laid out right now, forgetting about AR and VR for a minute, people are most concerned about personalization." Personalization may start with a choose-your-own adventure or branching narrative, but "I don't think we fully understand what it will be," Tierney says. Another example for where we might be headed is towards heatmap-driven stories or adaptive storytelling based on where the viewer looks.

Another way to think about adaptive storytelling is to break it down into the choices an editor or director must make. Max Salomon of Black Dot Films point at David Attenborough TV series Planet Earth as an example, suggesting the majority of time spent on that project consisted of executives arguing about what order the scenes should be in: "Should the tarantula come before or after the snake?" In the future, these choices may be for the audience to decide. "They'll decide how they want to explore the jungle," he says. "That's where we're headed next with a lot of this storytelling—we expect the story to be watching us back."

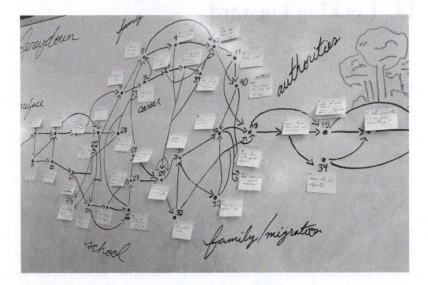

Figure 14.1 A sketch of a branching narrative (for *Terminal 3*).

Salomon believes it is not just changing the story based on the specific audience, but also adapting the story, in real time, to the interests of the audience. "We're not very far away technologically from the software knowing that you looked at the orangutan and the orangutan doing something as a result," he says. He believes we can start to build complex narratives, and the film that one person sees may be different than the next person.

Jenna Pirog at National Geographic echoes these sentiments: "The idea of a fully interactive character with smart responses—will create a new level of engagement," she says.

Merging Worlds

Ray Soto at *USA Today* would like to see more interactive stories, moving away from passive experience and towards branching narratives that also leverage immersive audio. "The six degrees of freedom you have to move around—there needs something that is a bit more compelling than just a seated position," Soto says. Kevin Tsukii agrees, "it will be in our world more—something you are able to walk around and move in."

Marcelle Hopkins at the *New York Times* says "it's hard to predict what will be a game changer," but for now she's focused on mixed reality, though it may not see mass adoption for several more years. "All of the work we're doing in these early days of VR and AR is preparing us for a screenless future in which interactive digital information is integrated into the real world around us," Hopkins says. She's keeping her eye on light field technology (discussed in the Emerging Technology chapter) for both capture and display as well as quantum computing, which could increase the processing power of immersive hardware and software exponentially. "Of course some technology that hasn't been invented yet could come along and radically transform what we're doing," Hopkins says.

Barry Pousman, director of photography for *Clouds Over Sidra*, who now works with the Institute for the Future, says he thinks the immersive landscape will change fast. He's got an eye on Apple's next moves, and their AR glasses patent: "When that happens it will change everything," Pousman says.

Experiencing Stories Together

One of the major complaints about virtual reality is how isolating it is. While AR is less physically isolating, consuming it alone still brings an element of social isolation.

How will the way we engage with immersive content change, and how will we tell stories differently, when we're able to consume alongside—or in cooperation with—other people?

Alt Space VR and Facebook Spaces offer a taste of what it feels like to be in immersive space with friends. Social AR will add another dimension to our sense of being present with the content.

Heather Maio, who created New Dimensions in Testimony (NDT), suggests that the ability to watch AR experiences as a group will add a heightened sense of being there—in the case of NDT, for example, in a classroom alongside other students, asking questions of a Holocaust survivor.

The Standalone Headset Struggle

On January 1, 2018, San Francisco-based technology journalist Daniel Terdiman wrote in Fast Company of the coming VR 2.0—"an evolution that could help the technology fulfill some analysts' predictions of it becoming a $38 billion industry by 2026,"[1]—with the addition of Oculus Go (a standalone **headset** not requiring a PC to function). Marcelle Hopkins, Co-Director of Virtual Reality at the *New York Times*, says fashion is one of the main hindrances to mass adoption, "There is a high bar for style when something that sits on your face," she says. "We will only see mass adoption when immersive wearables look more like the glasses we wear every day."

The trend seems to be towards the creation of a more mobile (untethered) and potentially social experience. Many cooks in the kitchen are working to figure out the best recipe combining **6 DOF**, **spatial audio** and portability—and perhaps something that doesn't look like the user is about to go skiing or get their hair dried at a salon. By the time this book prints, we're betting there will be a standalone headset (or a few).

Who Is Investing in This Stuff?

As of 2018, there is a significant growth projected for both AR and VR. International Data Corporation (IDC) predicts the VR/AR market will grow between 2017 and 2021 by around 100% annually and total spending on VR/AR products and services is expected to grow from $17.8 billion in 2018 to $215 billion by 2021.[2]

The number of U.S. citizens who engaged with AR in some form in 2017 is 40 million (12.4% of the entire population) according to eMarketer, and a study by Ericsson predicts 30% of consumers will use VR for TV and video watching in five years. The Ericsson study claims that 10% of consumers are already using a VR device, and 25% are planning to get one. According to their projections, one in three consumers would be using VR by 2020.[3] Despite large projected investments, newsrooms and media face the challenge and uncertain costs of equipment, production and distribution—and monetization is still hard.

According to Kaleidoscope's internal research, over $1 billion was invested in immersive art and entertainment in 2017.[4] The report notes that much of this went to large-scale production agencies rather than independent creators. Arnaud Colinart, Executive Producer at Atlas V., compares the U.S. model of investing with the French: "In France, unlike the United States, money is invested in VR projects without consideration of revenue," he says, "This allows for independent VR creators to push the medium forward in important ways. We need to create an ecosystem that supports the next Ridley Scott or Tarantino of virtual reality." The report suggests that foundations and governmental institutions will fund VR projects at a slightly higher rate in 2018 compared to 2017. The Kaleidoscope report also looked at location-based entertainment, Noting examples such as VOID, Dreamscape, and Nomadic which solve the hardware problems by providing a physical location to view a project. Kaleidoscope recommends artists to produce both an at-home version as well as a location-based optimized version of their project.

Funding Creativity

In many ways the media giants—namely Facebook and Google (YouTube) seem to have been so preoccupied by advancing the technology they forgot to consider content creation and the audience. As Alina Mikhaleva of Spherica says, no one signed up for Hulu as a concept; rather the audience wants to be able to watch the shows they like. There's content, audience and a desire for the medium. The immersive media world is beginning to develop the language, the people and the skill to be able to tell stories in new ways, but it's still a challenge to fund projects without clear monetization and a dedicated audience. On the other side, the technology will only be able to advance by allowing a diverse set of creators to experiment and test projects on different audiences.

This chicken or egg moment has some platforms—namely Oculus, YouTube and Vimeo—funding different kinds of programs to support creators. In 2016, Oculus began the first of an ongoing training and grant program called The Oculus Launch Pad, aimed at reaching out to underrepresented folks in the tech world such as women, gender non-conforming people and people of color.[5] Oculus has also funded "VR for Good," partnering creatives with non-profits around the world to show-case the use of the medium for positive change.

YouTube has worked to train creators in 360 filmmaking through the YouTube Spaces—training creators and giving access to cameras, as well as post-production support. The 2017 YouTube Space VR creators lab in Los Angeles brought together a cohort of creators for a series of train-ings, collaboration and mentorship. As of April 2018, the next Creator Lab will focus on 180 video.[6]

The Power to Do Harm

In 2017, reports came out that the young Oculus co-founder, Palmer Luckey had plans to take VR technology to the next level with the purpose of "helping to build a virtual wall that would keep people from crossing the US–Mexico border with the aid of sensors and drones," as Gizmodo reported.[7] Jennings Brown reported Luckey's company Anduril was com-posed of former Oculus and Palantir Technologies engineers.

Just a few months prior, TechCrunch had reported that a source who spoke with Luckey told the outlet that Luckey wanted to find ways to use AR for defense. "There's no telling what other creepy, sci-fi technology Luckey is looking to introduce to the battlefields," Brown says.

The Recreation of Memories Antisocial Immersion

Immersive storytelling—and VR specifically may be used as a form of escape, but there are also potential abuses to the medium and format. In an April 2018 article by Brian Resnick titled: We're underestimating the mind-warping potential of fake video,[8] he argues exactly that—focusing, of course, on flat video. But what happens when 360 video and immersive stories are re-created for propaganda, hate, or just plain deception? The implications are overwhelmingly dark and creepy.

In Monica Kim's 2015 article, "The Good and the Bad of Escaping to Virtual Reality," she says "with VR, it is possible that instead of simply escaping reality by focusing on a TV show ... people may choose to re-place an unhappy reality with a better, virtual one."[9]

New York Times journalist and media critic David Carr explored how virtual reality might make the problems of the world more pronounced, positing: "What matters more, the experience or the media representation of it?" Talking about the HoloLens he said in an article titled "Unease for What Microsoft's HoloLens Will Mean for Our Screen-Obsessed Lives," "Something about Microsoft's new technology creeps me out," he says, going on to say that "the amount of actual, unencumbered reality we experience seems endangered."

On most days, the skeptics are all but drowned out by positive visions for the future. "One day, we believe this kind of immersive, augmented reality will become a part of daily life for billions of people,"[10] Mark Zuckerberg said in a 2014 Facebook post. Is it just a new platform or is it also a minefield, full of potential explosions in regards to privacy, data and potential for misuse?

Privacy in VR

In the post-truth, post Snowden, Cambridge Analytica world, the awareness of personal data and how it may, or may not be used is at the back of many minds looking critically at immersive media. What data is being captured as a user is immersed in different platforms and game engines, who controls it and what does it mean?

In 2018, Looxid Labs won an innovation award for an emotion recognition system optimized for VR, including an eye-tracking system paired with EEG data. The company is working to understand preferences by showing images and having users rate what they prefer. It's a form of mind reading, if you will—that may be used for marketing and could also be harnessed for storytelling.

The Challenges

The challenges of telling a story within an immersive environment are still being worked out—some of which we've covered in previous chapters some of which include data size and speed of computing power. There are improvements and advances to be made from creation and production to accessing the final product. Ed Catmull, Pixar's co-founder, has been a skeptic of VR's use for narrative: "It's not storytelling," he says. "People have been trying to do [virtual reality] storytelling for 40 years. They haven't succeeded."[11]

Representation and Access

As Zahra Rasool of Contrast VR says, Immersive experiences are easier to be exploitative when it comes to representation, one way the Contrast VR team is working to stop this cycle is to collaborate with people from communities they are covering, bringing them on as co-producers to minimize exotification.

Trevor Snapp, co-director of *We Who Remain*, says VR's inability to compete with social videos on Facebook pushes makers to "avoid risks and just do what works. Like the wonderful Wild West of the internet was tamed by the convenience of what works, and not what could be."

Snapp sees VR, which thus far has been a largely corporate-funded enterprise, falling into the same trap: "it will be a lost opportunity if we don't embrace diversity in storytelling technique and storytellers quickly and rapidly."

Asad J. Malik, creator of *Terminal 3*, says he'd like to build an app or platform on which a variety of voices and stories can be shared through holograms—like bringing a CNN broadcast or TED talk into a viewer's living room. "This is the first step in terms of the greater goal of getting a hologram of every human on the planet." Whether or not these holograms serve as avatars in an oasis within future virtual reality alt-spaces is another question entirely.

Researching the Impact of Technological Advancements

One of the critiques, even from well-known investors in the field such as Chris Sacca, is on the lack of investment in research. As Sacca said in an interview with Tim Ferris in 2016,

> We approach a lot of this stuff with this universal embrace of progress with a really engineering-centric focus on what the measures of progress are ... Each year at CES [the Consumer Electronics Show] they show a display with more and more resolution and they show a virtual reality headset with less and less latency.

While Sacca is impressed he also says he "doesn't think we're making the same investment in the biological and psychological ramifications of some of these things."[12]

A Diverse, Inclusive Future

In *Making a New Reality*—Kamal Sinclair's six-part series on equity and diversity in emerging media, she discusses everything from AI and machine learning to the innovator stereotype and ideas for inclusive innovation.[13] In the final segment she focuses on the concerns of mitigating "our vulnerability to bad actors—people and entities that seek to exploit the disruption of new media and emerging technology for unethical or illegal objectives." This project is very different from the academic research referenced in the summaries above, yet an important body of work in considering the importance of bringing diverse perspectives into the creator and curatorial future space. Sinclair's examinations and research on Ethical Design Practices, Lack of Safe Spaces, and issues related to being Minorities in Majority Spaces provide insight into, as she says, a "positive direction in our process of making a new reality." *Making a New Reality* is published on Medium as part of Immerse, an initiative of Tribeca Film Institute, MIT Open DocLab and The Fledgling Fund.

The Horizon: Barely Touching the Possibilities for Immersive Storytelling

What can be gained by putting the viewer inside of a story? As Ray Soto at *USA Today* network says, "the art of storytelling provides an opportunity to deal with the present." The industry has come a long way over the past few years, but he also believes "we're just barely touching the opportunities of what's possible within immersive storytelling." Soto says one of the biggest challenges is to apply the lessons learned thus far to future storytelling projects. "How do we create a compelling user experience?" he says, rather than a gimmick for the sake of using new technology.

Futurists such as Amy Webb see the use of blockchain, AI and AR on the horizon. In an address to the Online News Association in 2017, she asked news creators to think ahead and begin to prepare for new and emerging formats.

Ultimately, we don't know what the future holds. As Nigel Tierney pointed out, predicting how we engage with YouTube, pre-YouTube: "No one would have said that it was going to be filled with reaction videos of opening boxes."

"The power of immersive journalism is in creating experiential pieces," says Marcelle Hopkins. "What we traditionally call a story becomes an experience in which our audience can witness, explore, discover and feel. It's a compellingly vivid and visceral way to learn about the world."

Notes

1 Terdiman, Daniel. "Why 2018 will be the year of VR 2.0," January 1, 2018. https://www.fastcompany.com/40503648/why-2018-will-be-the-year-of-vr-2-0.
2 IDC. "Worldwide spending on augmented and virtual reality forecast to reach $17.8 Billion in 2018," November 29, 2017. www.idc.com/getdoc.jsp?containerId=prUS42959717.
3 Ericsson Consumer Media Lab. TV & Media 2017. October 2017. www.ericsson.com/assets/local/networked- society/consumerlab/reports/ericsson_consumerlab_tv_media_report.pdf.
4 Kaleidoscope. "Emerging Trends Report by the Leadership Council for Immersive Art & Entertainment" September 2017. http://kaleidoscope.fund/update/emerging-trends.
5 Full disclosure: The authors were both involved in the inaugural two classes (2016, 2017).

6 Full disclosure: The authors were involved in the YouTube VR creators lab through working with Fusion media in 2017.

7 Hatmaker, Taylor. "Border wall bill draws on Palmer Luckey's new defense company," July 31, 2017. https://techcrunch.com/2017/07/31/anduril-palmer-luckey-smart-bill-hurd-border/.

8 Resnick, Brian. "We're underestimating the mind-warping potential of fake video," April 20, 2018. https://www.vox.com/science-and-health/2018/4/20/17109764/deepfake-ai-false-memory-psychology.

9 Kim, Monica. "The Good and the Bad of Escaping to Virtual Reality," February 18, 2018, The Atlantic. www.theatlantic.com/health/archive/2015/02/the-good-and-the-bad-of-escaping-to-virtual-reality/385134/.

10 Zuckerberg, Mark. March 25, 2014. www.facebook.com/zuck/posts/10101319050523971.

11 Dredge, Stuart. "Pixar co-founder warns virtual-reality moviemakers: 'It's not storytelling,'" December 3, 2015. www.theguardian.com/technology/2015/dec/03/pixar-virtual-reality-storytelling-ed-catmull.

12 Jebb, Louis. "Why we love what Chris Sacca has to say about the virtual reality industry." April 24, 2016. http://immersivly.com/tech/why-we-love-what-chris-sacca-has-to-say-about-the-virtual-reality-industry/.

13 Sinclair, Kamal. "The high stakes of limited inclusion." Immerse. https://immerse.news/the-high-stakes-of-limited-inclusion-908e8f6deda0.

Glossary

3DOF, 6DOF: See degrees of freedom.

Adobe Premiere: A popular video editing application made by Adobe.

A-Frame: A web framework that helps programmers develop interactive immersive experiences for a variety of web browsers and devices.

affordance: A term borrowed from video game design, relating to what interactions users perceive they are able to have.

ambisonics: A method for recording, mixing and playing back a three-dimensional 360-degree audio sound field.

audio transition: Using a sound cue to mark a changing scene or move from one part of a story or experience to another.

binaural: Describes recordings that are optimized for headphones and can recreate the human ear's perception of distance—making the audio feel more immersive.[1] This term should not to be confused with ambisonics or spatialized audio.

blocking: The physical arrangement and movement of actors or characters in a scene.

branching narrative: A story with different possible outcomes or paths depending on a set of choices made by the user (also commonly referred to as "choose-your-own-adventure").

call to action: A call to action asks or encourages a user to perform a task or interaction—e.g., click on a link, watch the next video in a series.

cardboard: A low-cost HMD made of cardboard, used to encourage interest and development in VR applications.

cut: In film, a transition from one shot or camera angle to another; also used for 360 video, and sometimes to refer to transitions that move the viewer or compress time in volumetric immersive experiences.

degrees of freedom: Degrees of freedom refer to possible movements of the user. Three degrees of freedom (3DOF) refers to the ability to look around a full 360 degrees: pan left and right, tilt up and down, and tilt to the left and right. Six degrees of freedom (6DOF) adds movement on three axes: vertical, side-to-side, and forward/backward. These two categories of movement are also referred to as rotational and translational, respectively.

DepthKit: A volumetric filmmaking tool to do volumetric capture.

directional sound: See spatial audio.

EEG: Electroencephalogram (EEG) detects electrical activity in the brain. This activity shows up as wavy lines on an EEG recording.

embodiment: In immersive media this refers to the viewer's sense of having a body in a virtual world.

equirectangular projection: A rectangular representation of the area of a sphere, used in editing 360-degree video. The area is distorted such that latitude lines are horizontal and evenly spaced, and longitude lines are horizontal and evenly spaced. Distortion is greatest at the top and bottom of the image.

explainer: A journalistic term describing content that explains a concept or gives context on an issue. It can be graphical or live action, and can be a section of a project (the graphical intro in *We Who Remain*), or an entire piece.

field of view: The height and width (in degrees) of the area a user can see at any given moment in an immersive experience.

gaze, gaze-based: The direction (horizontal, vertical) a user is facing in immersive space while wearing a headset. It can refer to inferred gaze based on the orientation of the head, or to actual eye-tracking (the former is more common as of 2018). In gaze-based interactivity or navigation the viewer gazes at a particular place in an immersive environment (e.g., a navigation menu or an image that activates a video), to trigger action.

guiding action: Movement or other cues that help direct the viewer's gaze from one area in immersive space to another.

haptics: Haptic technology simulates the sense of touch through the sensation of pressure, using devices such as a haptic glove or a vibrating backpack or controller. The term is also used for low-tech touch feedback, such as sitting on a chair that's represented in virtual space.

head-locked: Text or graphics in an immersive experience that move along with the user's gaze as they turn their head.

headset, head-mounted display (HMD): A head-mounted virtual reality or augmented reality device. Headsets can support different levels of interactivity depending on their ability to track the user's movement and gestures. Some come with hand controllers. All immersive headsets allow viewers to look around in 360-degree space. Headsets include Samsung GearVR, Oculus Rift, HTC Vive, Google Daydream and Microsoft HoloLens.

heat map: A visual representation of where users of an experience are looking.

hologram: A fully three-dimensional photorealistic representation of a person or object; in immersive media, this term is often used to describe volumetric video.

HoloLens: An augmented-reality headset sold by Microsoft.

immersive theater: In immersive theater or participatory theater the audience is part of the story, or immersed in the story in some way.

library (programming): Pre-written code that programmers use to make some tasks easier (for example, displaying 3D graphics in a browser).

Lidar: Lidar stands for "light detection and ranging": A scanner sends an infrared laser, waits for its reflection, then measures this distance. Each of these measurements is collected as a point to create a point cloud—a depth map of a place or object.

live-action photogrammetry: A form of photogrammetry capturing movement (see photogrammetry, volumetric).

Magic Leap: A company developing a highly publicized augmented reality headset, not yet commercially available as of early 2018.

magic window: Magic window viewing allows users to view 360° content without a VR headset. The viewing app renders a single (often full screen) monoscopic view of an immersive scene that is updated based on the device's orientation sensor.

Matterport: A 3D camera designed to scan the interior of homes, it has also been used for stories. Once an image or location is scanned the viewer can look up and down, left and right, move forward and backward.

monoscopic: Imagery from a single viewpoint for both eyes; 2D (see stereoscopic).

motion capture: Recording the actions of human actors for the purpose of animating a 3D-modeled character.

natural language processing: Natural language processing (NLP) is the ability of a computer program to understand human language as it is spoken. NLP is a component of artificial intelligence (AI).[2]

open-source: Denoting software for which the original source code is made freely available and may be redistributed and modified.

parallax (in VR): The difference in appearance of an object seen from two cameras filming from different positions.

photogrammetry: In immersive media this refers to the technique of processing still images taken at different angles to produce a high resolution 3D mesh; it is usually brought together through software to create a 3D model of a place or object.

picture-lock: The point in film editing when the visual sequence of shots is fixed (sound editing and visual effects work usually continue after picture lock).

point of interest: A point in immersive space where a creator hopes or expects the viewer will be looking at a given time in the experience.

post production: Typically used in reference to video production; may refer to any production process after the initial assets for a film or immersive experience have been captured.

presence: The feeling of being in and of the virtual world (often used interchangeably with immersion).

quad binaural audio: Binaural audio is recorded for each quadrant in a sphere (often referred to as North, West, South, East). The player software then crossfades between them as the (headset) viewer's head turns, for a dynamic spatial audio environment.

Reaper: REAPER (an acronym for Rapid Environment for Audio Production, Engineering, and Recording) is a multitrack recording and a digital audio workstation created by Cockos.

room-scale volumetric: Fully 3D graphics that allow the viewer to move around a scene by walking in a tracked room or by teleporting with a controller; also referred to as walk-around.

spatial audio: (also called spatialized, directional, positional, and 3D) This term refers generally to sound that is played back as if the it has a source in virtual space. There are many ways to achieve this effect, depending on equipment used for sound capture, editing techniques and platform.

standup: From broadcast journalism—a shot in which a person presents scripted or rehearsed information by speaking into the camera.

stereoscopic: Imagery showing a different viewpoint for each eye, providing a sense of depth; 3D.

stitch line: The place in a panoramic image or video where footage from two cameras meets. In 360 degree video, this is where parallax errors are visible.

stitching: In 360 video creation, combining footage from multiple cameras into 360-degree panorama.

teleport: To jump or be instantly transported from one place to another in a virtual reality environment.

trigger: (in reference to "trigger-based" augmented reality) An object or image in the physical world that, when scanned by an AR-enabled device using image recognition, unlocks or activates an AR experience.

Unity: A cross-platform game engine developed by Unity Technologies, used to develop video games as well as many interactive or room-scale VR and AR experiences.

voice-over audio: Audio recorded separately from a video and overlaid on the imagery. "Voice of God" or voice-over narration is a subset of this type of audio, and is scripted.

volumetric capture: The process of recording volumetric video, see volumetric.

volumetric, volumetric video, volumetric filmmaking: Relating to 3-dimensional moving imagery of a space or person recorded using scanning technology or multiple cameras filming simultaneously from different angles.

walk-around: See room-scale volumetric.

WebVR (WebAR, WebXR): Open specifications that make it possible to build for and experience AR and VR in a browser, across any number of devices.[3]

zero point: The vertical and horizontal center of the opening shot of an immersive experience; or 0,0 if the 360 space were thought of as having an X, Y axis. If the viewer returns to their original orientation when wearing a headset, they'll be looking at this point.

8i: A virtual reality software company focusing on volumetric human capture, or volumetric capture tools.

Notes

1 Feret, Quentin. "Binaural Audio: How 3D audio hacks your brain" October 20, 2017. https://arvrjourney.com/binaural-audio-how-3d-audio-hacks-your-brain-a3de0ceb4196.

2 Genzel, Dmitriy. "What Are The Differences Between AI, Machine Learning, NLP, And Deep Learning?" September 23, 2016. https://www.forbes.com/sites/quora/2016/09/23/what-are-the-differences-between-ai-machine-learning-nlp-and-deep-learning/#54d2af60274f.

3 "Bringing Virtual Reality to the Web," https://webvr.info/.

Index

3D 16, 18, 24, 42, 49, 60–2, 69–71, 75, 78–80, 82, 86, 90, 96, 101, 130–3, 139–40, 156–7, 161, 163, 168–70, 176, 187, 190, 194, 198, 200, 206, 210, 213, 219–21, 232, 249–51; models 16, 24, 60–2, 70–1, 79, 101, 132–3, 139–40, 155, 198, 206, 222, 249; volumetric 60
3DOF 23, 181, 222, 247
6DOF 59, 181, 222, 247
8i 62, 65–6, 219, 251

Adobe Premiere 26, 247
affordances 79, 202, 249
A-Frame 90, 247
After Solitary 64–6, 198–9, 207, 219, 234
algorithms 89, 100
ambient audio 38, 80–1, 97, 102, 117, 120, 132, 135–6, 139, 182, 209, 215–16
ambisonics 184, 189, 247
audience 1, 7, 12, 25–6, 28–9, 31, 38, 42, 48–9, 51–3, 55–7, 68, 79–81, 84, 86–7, 90–3, 98, 102, 106, 109–11, 124, 126–7, 130, 143, 149–50, 153, 159, 161–3, 166, 169, 171, 201–3, 205–9, 212–14, 220, 222, 227–38, 240–1, 244, 249
audio transition 67–8, 89, 186
augmented reality 1, 8–9, 15, 17, 85, 119, 126–7, 129, 135, 146, 148–55, 159, 163–4, 168–9, 171–3, 177–8, 198, 201, 209, 212, 225–7, 233, 242, 248–50

binaural audio 102, 106–8, 111–12, 193, 214–15, 247; quad 97–9, 250
Black Dot Films 28–31, 197, 202, 237
Blackout 99–103, 175, 199, 201, 208–9, 219, 223

blocking 66–8, 96, 186, 202, 206, 247
brainstorming 38, 108, 131, 134, 140
branching narrative 24, 49, 133–4, 174, 201, 237–8, 247

Call Centre, The 120–3, 211
call to action 131, 247
Capturing Everest 124–9, 152, 200–1, 212
cardboard 2, 14, 24, 82–4, 90, 106, 109–10, 136, 232, 247
cinematic VR 16, 23, 109, 116, 229, 235
clicks 48–9, 71, 78, 83, 90, 106–7, 110–11, 127, 139, 151, 206, 210, 220, 225, 247
Climbing Giants 23–33, 199, 204–5, 214
Clouds Over Sidra 24–7, 204, 229, 239
cognitive advantage 86
cognitive overload 200
color 29–30, 32, 61, 100, 108, 122, 125, 149, 152, 191, 204, 241
computer graphics 1, 62–3, 73
"cone of focus" 47–8
context 16–17, 34, 37–8, 44–6, 49, 69, 72, 76, 79, 84, 100, 105, 107, 110, 121–4, 128, 130–2, 135, 137, 140, 146, 148, 151, 169, 198, 204–5, 211–12, 214, 221, 226, 229, 248
cuts 30, 38–9, 48, 55, 63, 68, 89, 94, 107, 120, 127–8, 206–7, 247; long 27, 204; quick 26, 57, 66, 180, 186, 189, 191, 200, 205

data 1, 9, 42, 75, 77–9, 81–2, 84–6, 90, 104, 133, 138, 140, 161, 163, 181, 210–11, 219, 233, 240, 242
data visualization 9, 77–9, 81–2, 104, 133, 210–11
degrees of freedom 23, 59, 181, 238, 247. *See also* 3DOF; 6DOF

depth 18, 35, 42, 45, 55, 60, 69, 71, 96, 98, 101, 104, 107–8, 112, 123, 144, 159, 181, 192, 194, 210–11, 213–14, 249–50
DepthKit 60, 99, 101, 103, 175–7, 219, 248
desktop 34, 38, 48–9, 56–7, 69, 78–9, 83–4, 107, 109–11, 136, 168, 206, 210, 235
DevLab 87
dialogue 66, 93, 103, 114, 116–18, 128, 159, 163, 174–5, 215–16
directional sound. *See* spatial audio
Discovering Gale Crater 77, 208–11
disorientation 41–2, 44
Displaced Witness 72–5
distribution 14, 98, 126, 137, 209, 223, 230–2, 235, 240
dynamic 18, 29, 48, 90, 93–4, 96, 126, 209, 215, 250

editing 24, 26, 28–9, 33, 35, 43, 51, 65, 89, 118, 180, 183, 202–4, 233, 247–50; induced 28–9, 32, 197, 202
education 1, 7, 14, 74, 91–2, 109, 115, 145, 155, 159–60
EEG 221, 242, 248
Emblematic Group 33, 39, 60, 62–5, 68, 203, 220, 234, 237
embodiment 9–12, 93, 95–6, 198, 223, 248
empathy 8–10, 12, 25, 63, 98, 103, 123–4, 148, 174–5, 178, 198, 234
equipment 29, 38, 47, 126, 181–2, 216, 240, 250
equirectangular projection 35, 190, 201, 248
ethics 10, 24, 60, 63, 79, 81, 229, 243–4
Euronews 49–53, 199, 205, 214
experimenting 13–14, 26, 28, 30, 44, 50–3, 69, 71, 73, 82–6, 95, 100, 102, 106, 108, 110–11, 117–19, 131, 140, 143, 145–6, 157–8, 166, 169, 171–2, 185, 189, 205, 211, 221, 226–8, 241
explainer 37, 39, 109, 151–2, 205, 248
eye contact 9, 25, 27, 31–2, 68, 95, 99, 204, 207
eye line 67

Facebook 14, 24, 32, 38, 41, 48–9, 52, 64, 81, 111, 127, 181–3, 189, 223, 226, 230–4, 239–40, 242–3

field of view 17, 37, 48–9, 77, 88, 139, 141, 176, 204, 214, 220, 222, 248
first person 8, 11, 65, 72, 93, 95–6, 98, 198, 205
focus 2, 37, 39, 47–8, 52, 66, 74, 106, 137, 141, 205, 212
Four of the World's Best Olympians, as You've Never Seen Them Before 168–72

game engine 12, 60, 69, 77, 89, 128, 176, 221, 242, 250
games 3, 12, 16, 24–5, 42, 45, 60, 62, 65, 69, 77, 79, 81, 89, 101, 128, 134, 140, 144, 155, 157, 164, 168–9, 176, 180, 191–3, 202, 208, 214, 216, 221, 226, 228, 231–3, 238, 242, 247, 250
gaze 37, 68, 78, 88, 92, 101, 104, 110, 128, 198, 202, 205–9, 248
gear. *See* equipment
GearVR 110, 235, 248
Google 11, 14, 50, 145, 165, 168–9, 219–20, 222, 228, 240; Cardboard 14, 24, 82, 232; Daydream 40–1, 43, 56, 248; Tango 158, 168
GoPro 29, 33, 38, 55, 126
graphics 1, 16, 24, 34, 37, 44, 46–9, 60–3, 77–83, 85–6, 104, 131–3, 135, 137, 157, 159, 161, 170, 201, 204, 211–12, 227, 248–50; computer 1, 62–3, 73
guiding action 49, 204, 206, 248

Hallelujah VR 180–5, 215–16
haptics 223, 248
head-locked audio 141, 144, 215
head-locked text 122, 248
head-mounted displays 12, 17, 24, 95, 230–2, 248. *See also* headsets; cardboard. *See* cardboard
headsets 2, 11, 14–15, 17, 24–5, 32–3, 36, 38, 41, 43, 48–9, 56–7, 59, 64, 69, 78, 80, 82, 84, 87–8, 90, 92, 96, 100, 103, 105–6, 109–12, 128, 130, 136, 139, 141–3, 145, 159, 163, 206, 209–11, 220–2, 229–32, 235, 239–40, 243, 248–9
heat maps 231, 248
Hell and High Water 130–6, 200, 208, 211, 214, 231
Hello, We're from the Internet 164–8
Holocaust 9, 158–60, 162, 239

holograms 66–7, 159–60, 162–3, 173–4, 176–8, 213, 219, 243, 248
HoloLens 163, 172–4, 176–7, 213, 222, 233, 242, 248–9
HTC Vive 64, 103, 138–9, 142–3, 232–6, 248

imagery 18, 42, 49, 63, 77, 89, 92, 175, 177, 204, 213, 249–50
immersive audio 17–18, 111, 180–94, 199, 213–15, 238
immersive experiences 2–3, 13–14, 28, 71, 81–3, 106, 109, 124, 139, 142, 144, 174, 197, 201, 211, 214–16, 223, 226, 242, 247–9, 251
immersive interactives 76–104, 207–8, 221–2, 228, 234
immersive media 1–3, 7–10, 13–18, 24, 32, 69, 77, 81, 93, 95, 103, 105–6, 109, 124, 133, 135, 142, 180, 197, 199–203, 208, 210–11, 213–15, 220, 222, 225–6, 230–2, 235, 240, 242
immersive news 136, 203, 229
immersive theater 114, 119, 202–3, 206, 249
impact 10–12, 27, 46, 60, 90, 103, 130, 138, 148, 150, 170, 172, 186, 193, 205, 214, 243
improvisational theater 95
induced editing 28–9, 32, 197, 202
industry 2–3, 23, 55, 69, 131–2, 136, 146, 192, 239, 244
innovative 14–15, 63, 105, 138, 169
installation 72–3, 75, 172, 174, 223
interaction 76, 81, 90, 92, 99, 102, 140–1, 155, 162–3, 170, 174–5, 177–8, 198, 201–2, 208–9, 231, 247
interactivity 10, 15–16, 18, 38, 76–7, 88, 93–4, 103, 130, 136, 141–2, 157, 167–8, 170, 176, 207–9, 248
intimacy 9, 31–2, 35, 87, 103, 128–9
Is the Nasdaq in Another Bubble? 81–2

Javascript 77–8, 82

KeyMission 55, 126
Kiya 60–5, 207, 234

libraries 60, 80, 82
library programming 249
Lidar 42, 73–5, 140, 148, 222, 249
Limbo 40–4, 204–6, 219

live action 42, 44, 66, 248–9
live photogrammetry 219, 249
long cuts 27, 204

Magic Leap 163, 213, 231, 249
magic window 43, 48–9, 56–7, 106, 109–10, 206, 249
Matterport 69–72, 249
memory 47, 55, 234
Microsoft 170, 219, 222, 233, 242, 248–9. *See also* HoloLens
mixed media packages 16–17, 105–44, 208, 210–11
mixed reality 2, 14–15, 17, 149–85, 212, 237–8
monoscopic media 18, 24, 96, 98, 249
motion capture 62, 249
multimedia 64, 72, 87, 105, 121–2, 124, 127, 130, 133, 135, 138–9, 141–2, 155–6, 168, 210–11

narration 25, 40, 44, 46, 106–7, 110, 112, 121, 132–3, 135–42, 206, 212, 214–15, 250
narrative 3, 13, 16, 18, 23–6, 29, 35–7, 46, 49, 61, 63, 65–6, 76–7, 89–90, 92, 100, 103, 105, 107–9, 112, 117–18, 121–2, 126, 129, 132–4, 140–2, 144, 174, 176–8, 199–201, 203, 205–9, 215, 233–4, 238, 242. *See also* branching narrative
natural language processing 161, 249
New Dimensions in Testimony 158–63, 239
New York Times 14, 24, 34, 36, 45, 154, 158, 168–9, 208, 212–13, 225–7, 238–9, 242
Nokio Ozo 55

Occupation of Alcatraz that Sparked an American Revolution, The 44–6, 205, 211, 214
Oculus Rift 231, 233, 248
Olympics 9, 45, 168–9, 208, 212
open-source code 77, 80, 101–2, 167–8, 233
Optimism 151–3, 212
Outthink Hidden 154–8, 212
Overheard 105, 112–19, 209, 212–13

parallax 96, 249–50
PBS Frontline 14, 59, 64–6, 68
periphery 48–9, 222

photogrammetry 41, 60, 66, 139–40, 206, 222, 229, 249; live-action 219, 249
photorealism 63, 177, 248
picture-lock 35, 249
Pixar 242
platforms 24, 34, 38–9, 48–9, 52, 56, 69–70, 72, 80–1, 87, 89–90, 98, 101, 103, 105, 109–10, 126, 139, 142, 168, 172, 181, 184, 189, 205, 211, 220, 225, 227, 230–6, 241–3, 250
point of interest 48–9, 199, 204, 249
post production 75, 96–7, 126, 161, 169–70, 182–5, 189, 191, 216, 220, 241, 249
prisoners 65
Priya's Shakti 146–50
prototype 25, 43, 82, 100–1, 110, 140, 169, 191
PTSD 92

quad binaural audio 97–9, 250
quick cuts 26, 57, 66, 180, 186, 189, 191, 200, 205
reach 7, 27, 84, 90, 98, 103, 126–7, 148–50, 209, 231, 233–5

Reach 220
real estate 69, 71–2
Reaper 43, 189, 250
Reeps One: Does Not Exist 185–91, 205
roller coaster metaphor 56, 76, 81–6, 208, 210, 220, 235
room-scale volumetric 10–11, 59, 232, 250

Samsung Gear VR 51, 69, 87, 90, 93, 98, 110, 181, 208, 221, 232–3, 235, 248
ScanLAB 41–2, 44, 72–5
scanning 41–2, 44, 60, 66, 70–1, 73–5, 101, 109, 140, 149, 168–9, 177, 204, 219, 222, 234, 249–50
scores 34, 89–90, 92, 141, 191–2, 209, 215
Seeker VR 44–8
site-specific 75, 114, 119
software 26, 35, 42, 60, 71, 73, 80, 101, 176, 183, 234, 238–9, 249–51
sound cues 67–8, 110, 199, 207, 216, 247
soundscape 43, 81, 97, 106–7, 110, 116, 119, 184–5, 210, 213, 216

spatial audio 25, 97–8, 108–9, 111, 136, 144, 181, 183, 189, 192, 214, 239, 250
Stand at the Edge of Geologic Time 106–11, 201, 210, 236
standup 37, 39, 204, 250
static 42, 72–4, 89, 101
stereoscopic media 18, 24, 96, 129, 220, 250
stitch lines 35, 250
stitching 24, 26, 35, 40, 250
storyboards 43–4, 181, 201
storyliving 11
storytelling 2, 7, 9, 14–20, 24, 28, 31, 50, 53, 57, 59–60, 71–2, 76, 79, 85–6, 91, 98, 102–3, 106, 108, 112, 114, 118, 121–2, 124, 129–30, 135, 157–8, 168, 170–2, 190, 197–203, 206, 211–12, 219–23, 225–31, 235, 237, 241–4
structure 24, 43, 66, 77, 95, 102, 106, 126, 129, 134, 140–2, 164, 169, 173–4
Suite Life 69–72

tactile 75
teleporting 8, 59, 61, 63, 67–8, 72, 139, 206–8, 211, 250
Terminal 3 172–7, 213, 219, 238, 243
Testimony 86–92, 199, 201, 208–11, 213, 220
theater 2–3, 27, 68, 95, 114, 119, 145, 158–9, 162, 199, 202–4; immersive 114, 119, 202–3, 206, 249; improvisational 95
training 50–1, 54, 86, 111, 129, 137, 145, 241
transition 61, 68, 89, 106, 110, 128, 186, 206–7; audio 67–8, 186, 207
Tribeca 86–7, 99–100, 150, 172–4, 181, 185, 223, 244
trigger 127, 141, 151–4, 164, 208, 250

Unity 12, 42, 62, 66, 74, 89, 92, 101, 165, 176, 178, 250
UTURN 11, 93–9, 205, 209

violence 9, 60, 63, 87, 120–1, 148, 207
virtual reality 1–2, 8–9, 14–16, 18, 23, 28, 41, 53, 60–1, 77, 79, 81, 84, 90, 93, 109, 125, 131, 138, 171, 180–1, 201–2, 226, 229, 239–44, 248
virtual world 1–2, 81, 208, 221, 248, 250
Vive 64, 103, 138–9, 142–3, 232–6, 248

"Voice of God" 31, 250
voice-over audio 26–7, 30–1, 34, 40,
    121, 132–3, 135–7, 139, 205–6,
    214–15, 250
volumetric capture 24, 63–6, 68–9, 101,
    174, 176, 206–7, 219, 248, 250–1
volumetric video/filmmaking 60, 62,
    64–8, 99, 101, 176–7, 206–7, 213,
    220, 237, 248, 250
VRtually There 53–7, 205

walk-around. *See* room-scale
    volumetric
Wall, The 105, 130, 138–43, 201, 211,
    225, 228
wardrobe 66

We Who Remain 33–9, 204–5, 211,
    243, 248
WebAR 157, 251
WebVR 38, 77, 80–1, 86–7, 90, 96,
    104, 106, 108–10, 209–10, 220, 233,
    236, 251
WebXR 220, 233, 235, 251
woozy 72
workflow 50–1, 53, 111, 126

YouTube 14, 23–4, 32–4, 38, 41, 44,
    48–9, 53–4, 56–7, 64, 68, 81, 127,
    131, 150, 181, 186, 189, 204, 219,
    230–1, 241, 244

zero point view 48, 251